*Mogollon Culture
Prior to A.D. 1000*

# AMERICAN ANTHROPOLOGIST

## *Mogollon Culture Prior to A.D. 1000*

*By*

JOE BEN WHEAT

AMERICAN ANTHROPOLOGICAL ASSOCIATION

VOL. 57 · NO. 2 · PART 3 · MEMOIR NO. 82 · APRIL 1955

The *American Anthropologist* is published six times a year in the months of February, April, June, August, October, and December. Subscription by membership in the American Anthropological Association includes the issues of the *American Anthropologist* and the *Memoirs of the American Anthropological Association* as published. Entered as second-class matter in the post office in Menasha, Wisconsin. Accorded the special rate of postage provided for in paragraph 4, section 538, P.L. & R., authorized August 22, 1922.

PREFACE AND ACKNOWLEDGMENTS

It has frequently been contended that the archeological
Southwest was, in many ways, a single functioning unit. On a
broad general plane there was much the same development; each
people had an agricultural base, ceramic industry, and architectural development which shared certain generalized traits.
This idea was early manifest by considering the whole area as
"Puebloan" with all the cultural and temporal implications of
that term. Recently, and to some extent recognizing the more
complex structure of Southwestern culture history, such syn-
thetic schemes as Martin and Rinaldo's Southwestern Co-tradition (1951) and Daifuku's New Conceptual Scheme (1952) have
been proposed. That some broad general relationship existed
is not to be doubted. Nevertheless, this evident interfunc-
tioning should not obscure the fact that each of several areas
had its own history apart from that which it shared with the
others. This history and development is manifest in the consistently differing details of agricultural, architectural,
and ceramic complexes, and in other phases of culture. By
examining these we may come to understand the ultimate historical relationships of the several units. It is my purpose
here to examine in detail the culture development of the
people in the region which has come to be known as the
Mogollon area, and the relationships between these people
and other peoples of the Southwest.

In the years just preceding World War II, and increasingly
since that time, a considerable amount of archeological field

v

work has been directed toward the investigation of various aspects of the Mogollon Culture. Reports on numerous sites have appeared; some have included syntheses of greater or lesser scope. However, to the present time there has been no concerted attempt to bring together all the scattered data on the Mogollon, nor to analyze these data within a consistent frame of reference. That such a synthesis was needed has been obvious for some time. The present study is an attempt to fill that need. It does not purport to be a final "answer to the Mogollon problem." Rather, I have sought primarily to assemble the information now at our disposal; and secondarily, using these data as a base, to assess the role of the Mogollon in Southwestern prehistory.

This study is, then, an effort to bring together what is known today about the Mogollon Indians. It has grown out of the attempt to place Crooked Ridge Village, an early Mogollon site in east-central Arizona, in its proper chronological and cultural context in the Southwest. The discussion will be limited, for the present, to sites specifically called Mogollon by those who excavated them, and to sites within the same area dug prior to 1933 when the Mogollon concept was being formulated. Furthermore, this study will be confined to the pithouse horizon, for it has long been recognized that with the introduction of masonry pueblos and certain other elements, the Mogollon cultural pattern was submerged, or perhaps better, blended into something quite different. The history of this blending and the resultant culture patterns form another problem which lies beyond the scope of this study.

On behalf of the University of Arizona Archeological Field School, as well as myself, I wish to thank the Wenner-

Gren Foundation for its financial support of archeological research in the Point of Pines area, which includes Crooked Ridge Village.

I should like to acknowledge, with appreciation, the inspiration growing out of arguments, counsel, and aid given by Drs. Paul S. Martin, John B. Rinaldo, E. B. Danson, Charles C. Di Peso, Erik K. Reed, Earl H. Morris; Messrs. Terah L. Smiley, Bryant Bannister, E. B. Sayles; and all the faculty of the Department of Anthropology, University of Arizona. My indebtedness to Southwestern archeologists is evident in the bibliography for this study.

Most of all, I am grateful to Dr. Emil W. Haury, without whose advice and guidance this study could not have attained whatever value it may have. His generosity in time, in communicating his great knowledge of Southwestern archeology, and in other helpful means, can only be acknowledged, not repaid.

Finally, but by no means least, I am grateful to Pat, my wife, whose work, as much as mine, is embodied in this paper.

This study, in its original form, comprised part of a thesis presented to the Graduate Faculty of the University of Arizona, in partial fulfillment of the requirements for the Ph. D. degree. Another part of this thesis is published by the University of Arizona under the title, Crooked Ridge Village, Vol. XXV, No. 3, Social Science Bulletin No. 24, July 1954.

J. B. W.

University of Colorado
January 15, 1955

I / GEOGRAPHY OF THE MOGOLLON AREA

In cultural terms, the Southwest has never been satis-
factorily defined.  This is particularly true of the southern
boundaries.  Archeologists usually include the territory
occupied by the groups we term Anasazi, Hohokam, Mogollon,
and Patayan; it is this area that will be considered here.

Physiographically (Atwood 1940; Darton 1925; Fenneman
1931), the northern and eastern parts of this area belong
primarily to the Colorado Plateaus Province; the southern and
western parts comprise a portion of the Basin and Range Province.  Physiographers subdivide these major provinces into
lesser units having more significance for the archeologist.
The Colorado Plateaus Province is marked primarily by high
mesas and plateaus underlain by nearly horizontal strata of
strong, cliff-producing rocks locally covered by volcanic
features or domed by igneous intrusions.  This extensive area
is drained largely by the Colorado River and its tributaries.
Among the distinguishing features are the hundreds of deeply
entrenched canyons and great retreating cliffs or escarpments.

The Basin and Range Province is typified by more or less
isolated, roughly parallel mountain ranges, separated by basins filled, often to considerable depth, with unconsolidated
detritus eroded from the surrounding mountains.  Many ranges
are simple block fault mountains, but others are structurally
complex, frequently complicated by igneous activity.  Poor

drainage is characteristic of this area. Many basins drain into lower ones only during high water, while others have no exterior drainage at all and form playas or bolsons.

South of the Colorado Plateaus Province is the Mexican Highlands section of the Basin and Range Province. In north-western Arizona a bold escarpment marks the common border. The change from mesa and canyon to basin and range country is often sharp and dramatic. Farther southeast, the situation becomes increasingly complex, and it is difficult to define the precise transition. The southern edge of the plateau is deeply dissected. Furthermore, volcanic activity has raised mountains of considerable magnitude. To the west the Mexican Highlands merge with the Sonoran Desert. In the northeast the Mexican Highlands extend to Santa Fe and the mountain ranges which form the divide between the Rio Grande and Pecos rivers. The southernmost extension of the area lies beyond the scope of this paper.

The central portion of this mountainous belt seems to have been the Mogollon homeland (Fig. 1). On the southern edge of the Colorado Plateaus rises the great White Mountain Volcanic Belt which, to the northwest, blends into the Mogol-lon Rim. North of the Rim, drainage is generally toward the Little Colorado. White River rises on the north slope of the White Mountains, flows west and then southwest to its junc-tion with Black River to form the Salt. One of the important northern tributaries to Salt River is the Carrizo Creek sys-tem which includes Forestdale Creek, center of one of the northernmost Mogollon developments. This system heads along the Mogollon Rim and flows generally southward to join the main stream. The East Fork of White River rises on the

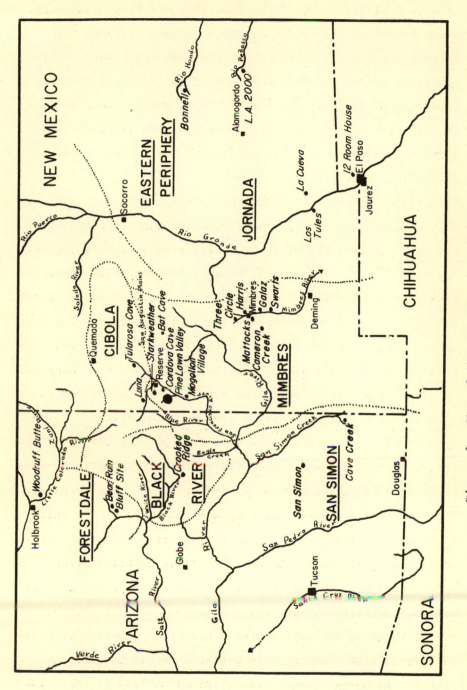

Figure 1. Map of the Mogollon Culture Area

southwest slopes of the White Mountains and flows southwest.
Black River has its source on the northeast slope of the
White Mountains and flows around the southern flank of these
mountains to join White River. The most important northern
tributary of the Black is Bonita Creek, which offers an easy
pathway from the parkland along the southern slopes of the
White Mountains to the Plateau country to the northeast, as
does Black River itself.

Rising a few miles south of Black River is Eagle Creek,
which flows south to join the Gila River west of Clifton,
Arizona. This is the first of a series of streams which, at
least in their upper courses, constitute north-south arteries
between the Mogollon and Anasazi areas. East of Eagle Creek,
and forming the divide between it and Blue River, is the Blue
range. Blue River rises east of the White Mountains and
flows generally southward, often through precipitous canyons,
to join the San Francisco River some 20 miles above its junc-
tion with the Gila, the master stream of the area.

Forming the watershed between the Blue and San Francisco
rivers is the high and rugged San Francisco range, which
seems also to have served as a barrier to cultural movements.
The San Francisco River heads in Arizona, east of the White
Mountains and just south of the divide, from which the northward flowing waters empty into the Little Colorado River.
From its source, the San Francisco flows east past Luna, New
Mexico, southeast to Reserve, New Mexico, where it is joined
by the Tularosa drainage system. From this junction it flows
southwest, south, and finally westward across the Arizona
line to the mouth of Blue River, then southwest to empty into
the Gila south of Clifton, Arizona.

The San Francisco River has two important western tributaries, Pueblo Creek and Leggett Creek. Both rise on the east slopes of the San Francisco range and flow generally southward to their confluence with the main river. Leggett Creek drains the lush Pine Lawn Valley, which is separated from the San Francisco Valley on the east by the Saliz range.

The upper courses of the San Francisco and Tularosa are separated by the Dillon Mountains, and the east-west trending Gallo Mountains form a last mountainous bulwark against the plateau lands to the north. Still farther east are the Datil and Gallinas mountains. South of these, and west of the Magdalena Mountains, is an area of internal drainage, the San Augustin Plains (variously St. Augustin, Saint Augustine), whose western boundary is the Tularosa range, its southern boundary formed by the Mogollon, Mimbres, and San Mateo mountain groups.

The upper Gila is divided from the upper San Francisco by the extensive and rugged Mogollon mountain mass, which gives rise to northern and western tributaries of the Gila. Eastern and southern tributaries rise in the Black, Pinos Altos, Burro, and Mimbres ranges which form a part of the Continental Divide. From its sources, the Gila flows around the southern slopes of the mountains, southwestward to the vicinity of the Arizona border, then northwestward to its junction with the San Francisco. South and east of the Continental Divide, drainage is to a series of inland basins or playas, mostly in northern Mexico, through such streams as the Mimbres River, or into the Rio Grande, which now drains into the Gulf of Mexico but formerly also drained into an inland basin in northwest Chihuahua.

Such is the terrain of the Mogollon homeland, the most maturely dissected area in the Southwest. It is also the best watered. Because of the height of the many mountain masses, rainfall often nears or exceeds 20 inches per year, and even today many streams flow all or part of the year.

Climate and vegetation vary according to range in elevation and precipitation (Nichol 1943). In the southern basins rainfall is proportionately less, and the lower reaches of the valleys are covered with desert grasses, mesquite, and many varieties of cactus, while along the stream bottoms the creosote bush and salt brush of the Lower Sonoran Desert extend into the area. On higher elevations grasslands pass into chaparral and oak woodland, and on the highest mountains are forests of pinyon, juniper, and pine. To the north the elevation increases; so does the rainfall, and with it, vegetation becomes successively Upper Sonoran with characteristic pinyon-juniper association, then Transitional, with magnificent forests of Western Yellow Pine. Higher, still, are Douglas-fir and stands of quaking aspen. On a few of the highest mountain areas the Canadian Zone is reached, with its characteristic cover of small plants, lichens, and many wild flowers.

Despite the advantage of an adequate water supply, much of the area is not suitable for agriculture because of the narrowness of the valleys. Some of these open out into broad alluvial flats, and in such places villages were concentrated. In the drier southern parts of the area more land was available and water became the dominant factor in selecting village sites.

## II / TAXONOMY OF THE MOGOLLON CULTURE

Before 1933, a number of sites had been dug in the area
including the drainage of the upper Gila, the San Francisco,
and the Mimbres rivers. Most of these were late Pueblo sites.
Customarily they were thought to represent a regional variant
of the culture now called Anasazi. A few investigators, however, suspected that these remains might have had a separate
origin. In 1933, Haury excavated Mogollon Village for Gila
Pueblo, and the following summer, Harris Village. These were
published in 1936 (Haury 1936a and 1936b). For the first
time there appeared a clear statement of sequent phases in
the area. But equally important was the resultant hypothesis
that these cultural remains were not a regional variation of
Anasazi but, instead, represented a hitherto unrecognized
group.

As more excavation was carried out, it became evident
that various subcultural patterns could be recognized. In
part, these have geographic bases. Boundaries between some
subareas are sharp, marked by definite topographic features.
Other subareas pass imperceptibly, so far as present knowledge
goes, one into the other, so that only climax patterns show
much difference. Such boundaries as existed were not always
stable, but fluctuated from time to time, due to movement of
cultural impulses into and out of various centers. To a
considerable extent, these subareas followed the same general
lines of development, but it is doubtful that the recognizable
stages in the various areas were entirely contemporaneous;

7

in some cases it seems clearly evident that cultural lags occurred.

Six branches or regional variants of the Mogollon culture pattern have been proposed. These are (1) San Simon (Sayles 1945), (2) Mimbres (Haury 1936a-b), (3) Black River (Wheat 1954), (4) Forestdale (Haury 1941; Haury and Sayles 1947), (5) Cibola (Gladwin 1934; Danson 1952), and (6) Jornada (Lehmer 1948). (See Fig. 1.) Two branches are known from only one site each, two from two sites each, and the other two from several sites each. On a geographical-cultural basis, it appears that the Mimbres Branch may be further divided into two subareas. Furthermore, it appears certain that when Lister publishes his data on Chihuahua and eastern Sonora, another branch containing an early Mogollon sequence will be established. When we know more of the other branches we may be able to further refine our divisions.

In order to trace the development of the various traits of any cultural manifestation it is necessary to establish some frame of reference. Many ways have been used to control data, to make them comprehensible, and to relate them to the central problem of the particular investigator. In archeology the framework is usually some sort of chronological scheme. Southwesternists have devised several such schemes. Those in common use today for describing individual culture patterns are the Pecos system, the Hohokam period system, and the phase (or focus) system, each having variations. In reality, these schemes represent different sorts of abstractions. Phase systems describe small arbitrary units somewhat limited in time and space. A phase tends to be narrowly defined. As a cultural manifestation it has quite specific attributes of architecture, ceramics, and other minor traits. The Pecos system and its Hohokam period equivalent, by contrast, are general, describing levels of attainment which might well be called technological stages. It should be remarked in passing, that technological stages, by their very nature, have little necessary or inherent correlation with chronological periods (as workers in the Anasazi field can attest). The systems are complementary rather than mutually exclusive.

No equivalent framework of technological stages has come into general use for Mogollon culture, although Gladwin (1948) proposed such a system. This scheme, based on pottery, consisted of the following periods: the stage of polished red ware, the stage of broad-line red-on-brown, the stage of narrow-line red-on-brown, and the stage of red-on-white pottery. Some such device would seem to serve a useful purpose, whether Gladwin's scheme or some modification of it be adopted, or whether some differently based plan is ultimately achieved. In the succeeding pages I shall follow a modification of this system.

There is considerable difficulty in selecting appropriate designations for various periods. Gladwin's terminology is cumbersome and is not entirely correct. The period termed "stage of polished red ware" is not everywhere characterized by an indigenous red ware, nor do all sites included in the stages of red-on-brown and red-on-white pottery have local varieties of these types. The system is also incomplete, for there is no designation for the period following the stage of red-on-white. Furthermore, it is based entirely on ceramics even though architectural components are suggested, often mistakenly, for each ceramic stage.

Perhaps what is needed is a set of terms descriptive of each of the periods in the same sense that Roberts' (1935) modified terms of the Pecos system are descriptive, or those of the Hohokam period system. Still, such terms are not satisfactory, because a term adequate for one subarea does not necessarily hold for other subareas. Numerical designations are not altogether satisfactory, but they do have the advantage of being culturally noncommittal, and once the main sequential outline is known, are not likely to be outmoded as we refine our chronological techniques. Such a system like-wise obviates the necessity of considering a phase with only a plain ware ceramic complex as being typologically equivalent to another plain ware phase when the majority of other traits would place it in a more advanced stage. Furthermore, the cultural catalog for numerically designated stages can be revised as this becomes necessary, without the concomitant necessity of changing a period name because it no longer fits the data. Therefore, for the purpose of this study, I shall adopt a numerical system of technological stages to serve as a frame of reference in which the various named phases may be analyzed. These stages will be fully characterized after the Mogollon sites have been analyzed; for the present, they will be listed together with the phases assigned to them by branch and sub-branch (Table 1).

It will be noted that some branches had more than one phase per period. In other cases a phase may extend from one period into the next. This is, of course, to be expected. Phases, being artificial units, are established on the basis of trait isolation by time or area or both. Conditions of excavation may enable one investigator to define smaller units

Table 1

| PERIOD BRANCH | 1 | 2 | 3 | 4 | 5 |
|---|---|---|---|---|---|
| Mimbres | Pine Lawn Georgetown | San Lorenzo (Postulated) | San Francisco | Three Circle | Mangus Mimbres |
| San Simon | Penasco | Dos Cabezas | Pinaleno Galiuro | Cerros | Encinas |
| Black River | Circle Prairie (early) | Circle Prairie (late) | San Francisco | Three Circle | Reserve Tularosa |
| Forestdale | Hilltop | Cottonwood | Forestdale | Corduroy | |
| Cibola | | | | Three Circle | |
| Eastern Periphery (Jornada) | | | San Marcial | Mesilla Capitan | Dona Ana Three Rivers El Paso San Andres |

Table 1. Phase chart by Period and Branch. No chronology implied. Blank spaces indicate that no phase has been defined.

than have been possible elsewhere. Thus, what is of necessity
considered a single phase in one site may be broken into less
inclusive phases in other sites. Such appears to be the case
with Pinaleno and Galiuro phases of the San Simon Branch when
compared to their typological equivalent in Mimbres Branch,
San Francisco Phase. Furthermore, there is a general and
understandable tendency for each investigator to interpret
defined phases so as to fit his data. This suggests that
phase assignment is an art, not a science. This has led to
misunderstanding and to various interpretations, some of which
I shall point out in the pages that follow. Such variation
in interpretation is, in numerous ways, all to the good of
archeology, but it is necessary to understand the nature of
the various assessments in order to describe the general
evolution of the Mogollon culture pattern.

# III / SUMMARY OF MOGOLLON BRANCHES AND SITES

The first Mogollon branch defined was the Mimbres. Here, sites have been excavated in the southern part of the Mimbres drainage and in the adjacent part of the Gila drainage.

Harris Village (Haury 1936b) is located about a quarter of a mile east of the Mimbres, New Mexico post office, on a large, flat terrace which rises abruptly some 20 m. above the east bank of the Mimbres River. It is about 1,850 m. above sea level. The village occupied several acres, part of which was not explored. Easily approached from all sides, defense does not seem to have been a factor in selecting the village site. The surrounding countryside is rugged and hilly, but agricultural land is available in small fields along the stream. The area is in the lower part of the pinyon-juniper belt, and a few trees occur on the site. Cottonwood, poplar, and walnut grow along the valley.

Thirty-four houses were wholly or partly excavated, but inasmuch as only about one-quarter of the site was explored, the total number of houses must have approached a hundred. There appeared no particular order in village layout, houses being scattered at random. Four ceremonial houses were excavated, at least one for each period represented at the site. Trash was deposited sheetwise between houses and in abandoned pits. Excavated houses represent three phases: Georgetown, San Francisco, and Three Circle.

Cameron Creek Site (Bradfield 1931), about 10 miles west of Harris Village, occupies the crest of a short ridge that projects into the eastern side of Cameron Creek Valley, about two miles northwest of Hurley, New Mexico. The site is about 800 feet from, and 125 feet above, the creek, which is a western tributary of the Mimbres River. Like Harris Village, it lies in the pinyon-juniper (Upper Sonoran) zone, but is close to both Lower Sonoran and Transitional zones.

Most of the 138 rooms excavated belonged to a Mimbres Phase pueblo, but some 40 pithouses or shallow unit houses preceded the pueblo. Although a few of the later pit rooms were possibly arranged about a small plaza, most of them were scattered. One large ceremonial pithouse was found, and five pit rooms had been converted for ceremonial use by rebuilding, but most of these had been used by the people of the surface pueblo. There was a trash heap, as well as sheet rubbish, but it is not clear to what extent the one is late and the other early. Bradfield did not name the phases represented by his earlier horizons, but it seems clear that Three Circle Phase is present. San Francisco Phase is probably represented by a few houses and vessels. The earliest houses may be Georgetown or possibly earlier, but they might equally well be early San Francisco Phase.

Bradfield also excavated Three Circle Ruin, on a tributary of the upper Mimbres. Since this site remains unpublished, it is impossible to include it in the analysis that follows.

Three other sites in the Mimbres drainage had brief pithouse occupations marking the transition from subterranean to surface architecture. Some 15 miles south of the Mimbres post office, Swarts Ruin (Cosgrove 1932) lies in the valley bottom of the Mimbres River, in contrast to the general pattern of placing villages on high ground. Of 172 rooms excavated here, 47 were scattered pithouses. One of these was a large rectangular ceremonial pit room. Although recognized as the earliest occupation of the village, these pithouses were not assigned to a separate phase, as such. Today they would be placed in very late Three Circle Phase or in Mangus Phase.

Galaz Ruin (Bryan 1931) lies upstream from Swarts Ruin about five miles south of the Mimbres post office and one-quarter of a mile southeast of the town of San Lorenzo, on the opposite bank of the river. It occupies a terrace above the ravine cut by the Mimbres River. Rolling hills rise on both sides of the river and are covered with scrub trees, brush, cacti, and yucca. Two connected tiers of pueblo rooms were superimposed on a lower row of partly subterranean, masonry-lined rooms. Four pithouses were also excavated. These are described as roughly circular pits with plastered and baked (sic) walls. Entrances are described as small, clearly defined tunnel-like holes. Since the pottery complex of these pithouses is not given, their taxonomic position cannot be determined. Hence, they will not be considered further here.

A mile south of Harris Village and the Mimbres post office lies Mattocks Ruin (Nesbitt 1931), situated on a terrace 100 feet above the west bank of the Mimbres River. Sixty-six rooms were excavated, including five pit rooms. It is not clear whether the pithouse horizon contained a ceremonial house. The earliest period here, as at Swarts and Galaz ruins, is late Three Circle.

In addition to the open sites listed above, several caves and shelters in the Mimbres and adjacent areas have

been described recently by Cosgrove (1947). Many of these
contain material which would now be assigned to the Mogollon
pithouse horizons. Since stratigraphic data are lacking,
however, these sites will not be discussed here, although
certain comparisons of material culture items have been made
by Martin and his associates (1952) and thus fitted into the
typological picture.

The northern part of Mimbres Branch occupied valleys of
the lower and middle San Francisco and the lower Blue rivers
and their tributaries. In general, this area is higher,
cooler, and better watered than the area just considered.
Agricultural land is perhaps more limited because of the
precipitous character of the river valleys. More sites have
been excavated in this section than in any other Mogollon
area. Further, most of them have been dug since the theory
of a separate Mogollon culture pattern was proposed. Hence,
excavation, and interpretation of data, have followed modern
systematics and are thus more usable than older data from
surrounding sections.

Mogollon Village (Haury 1936b) occupies the top of a
small mesa overlooking the east bank of the San Francisco
River about 10 miles north of Glenwood, New Mexico. The
mesa, about 1,700 m. above sea level, is accessible only from
the northeast where it merges with hilly country bounding the
valley. Pinyon and juniper are abundant in the hills, cottonwood fringes the river where agricultural land is available.

Eleven houses were excavated; at least eight more were
located. These were not situated according to any definite
plan. Two ceremonial houses were excavated. A number of
storage pits may represent a preceramic occupation. Trash in

the form of sheet rubbish was scattered about the village.
Two phases, Georgetown and San Francisco, were represented,
although one house could be called Three Circle by virtue of
the pottery in floor contact.

Starkweather Ruin (Nesbitt 1938) is located some three
miles west of Reserve, New Mexico, on the western section of
a small mesa about 1,850 m. above sea level. The mesa rises
40 m. above the north bank of Starkweather Creek, a western
tributary of San Francisco River. The mesa is easily accessible from the east, north, and west. Juniper, pinyon, and a
few pines grow on the mesa, and the creek bottom provided
land for agriculture.

Thirty-two structures were excavated, 12 surface rooms
of the Reserve (and Tularosa?) Phase and 20 pithouses scattered at random. One pithouse was a large, circular ceremonial room. Trash was in sheet form and in the fill of
abandoned pithouses. Three phases were recognized in the
pithouse horizon: Georgetown, San Francisco, and Three Circle.

Nesbitt also excavated a site named Wheatley Ridge but
did not publish a report. The few brief data available on
this site may be summarized here. Fourteen pithouses were
excavated, including a large ceremonial house 31 by 28 feet
in diameter, with a stepped lateral entry 10 by 30 feet
(Anonymous 1940). Houses were circular or rectangular, with
circular fire pits and lateral entries (Anonymous 1939).
Intrusive pottery included Gila Butte Red-on-buff, Lino Gray,
Kana-a Gray, and Red Mesa Black-on-white (ibid.). Burials
without mortuary offerings were also found (Anonymous 1940).
The houses were first considered to be Georgetown and San
Francisco (Anonymous 1939) and later Three Circle (Anonymous

1940). In 1949 Martin and Rinaldo (p. 192), considering an unpublished manuscript by Chandler Rowe, judged two houses to be San Francisco, apparently on the absence of Mimbres Bold Face Black-on-white pottery, and seven to be Three Circle. The remaining five houses are not placed temporally.

SU Site (Martin et al. 1940, 1943, 1947) is located about seven miles west of Reserve, New Mexico, along the crest of a low, flat-topped ridge 6,440 feet above sea level, extending from the San Francisco Mountains into Pine Lawn Valley. The top may be reached from any side, although the east end is quite steep. Nearby Leggett Creek, which flows southward to San Francisco River, probably furnished water, while cultivable land was available alongside the stream. The countryside, and the ridge itself, are thickly forested with pine, pinyon, juniper, and live oak.

Twenty-eight houses were excavated, and perhaps four or six remain undug. These were scattered at random in two groups, each clustered around one of the two large, early ceremonial houses. One small, late "kiva" was excavated also. Trash was of the sheet variety. Twenty-four houses were assigned to Pine Lawn Phase, four to Three Circle Phase.

Promontory Site (Martin et al. 1949), near SU Site, occupies the top of a mesa. While it is an extensive site, only five houses were excavated. One of these apparently was a ceremonial house. These, and the depressions indicating other houses, were randomly distributed with no orderly arrangement apparent. All houses excavated were of Pine Lawn Phase. Rubbish was deposited sheetwise over the surface of the site. Three crude boulder walls, perhaps for defense, cross the south end of the site where the mesa merges with higher hills beyond.

Turkey Foot Ridge Site (Martin et al. 1949, 1950a) lies
on a high, narrow ridge shaped like a turkey foot, hence the
name. It is located in Pine Lawn Valley some four miles south
of SU Site. Dominant trees of the area are Western Yellow
Pine, pinyon, and juniper, characteristic of the Transitional
life zone. Rubbish was of the sheet variety. Of the 16
scattered pithouses excavated, one was tentatively assigned
to Georgetown Phase, the others to San Francisco and Three
Circle. One pithouse seems clearly a ceremonial structure;
another had been rebuilt to change an entryway into a
ventilator, perhaps for use as a "kiva".

Twin Bridges Site (Martin et al. 1949) is located atop a
gently sloping, narrow ridge in Pine Lawn Valley. Details
concerning the exact location and immediate environment are
not given, but presumably the general environment is like
that of SU Site. It is a small site containing only four
pithouses, all assigned to Three Circle Phase. No ceremonial
house was found.

The remaining two pithouse sites were discovered during
excavations in later sites (Martin and Rinaldo 1950b). Three
Pines pithouse was found near a small Reserve Phase pueblo of
the same name, located just southeast of Pine Lawn Tourist
Court and overlooking Leggett Creek to the east. It was
assigned to Pine Lawn Phase. Like Three Pines pithouse, South
Leggett pithouse was near a small Reserve Phase pueblo. It
is located just west of Leggett Creek about three miles south
of SU Site. This pithouse, which may not have been occupied,
was assigned to Three Circle Phase. Both of these sites
differ from other pithouse sites of the adjacent area in being

located near the stream rather than on a ridge or mesa
overlooking the valley. One other pit structure was found
near a later site at Wet Leggett Pueblo, located on a ridge
above Wet Leggett Creek, about two miles west of SU Site.
The nature of the pit suggests that it may have been a
roofed walk-in well rather than a pithouse, and since no
phase assignment could be made, it will not be further
considered here.

While they do not contain pithouse structures, three
other excavated sites in this area are important. These
are the cave sites, Cordova, Tularosa, and Bat Cave.
Cordova Cave (Martin et al. 1952) is located some six miles
south of Reserve, New Mexico, high in a cliff about 1,000
feet above the San Francisco River. Access to the cave is
extremely difficult; nevertheless, it seems to have been
used as a dwelling place from preceramic times, but only
sporadically after about A. D. 500.

Tularosa Cave (Martin et al. 1952) is located about a
mile east of Aragon, New Mexico, in a cliff near the end of
a long sloping ridge. It is about 100 feet above the west
bank of Tularosa River, along which is good agricultural land.
The importance of this site lies in the complete cultural
range from preceramic times---Pine Lawn, Georgetown to San
Francisco, and Tularosa phases; Three Circle being almost, if
not entirely, absent; and in the remarkable collection of dry
materials. The Mogollon artifactual materials from this cave
make possible, for the first time, a direct comparison with
many categories of Anasazi material. Plant remains enabled a
direct analysis of food habits of the cave dwellers.

Bat Cave (Manglesdorf and Smith 1949) is situated on the

eastern edge of the Plains of San Augustin in Catron County, New Mexico. The cave, or rather caves, for there were several, were carved in the base of an almost vertical cliff by wave action of a now extinct lake. A complete stratigraphic sequence demonstrates clearly the presence of preceramic agriculture. The cultural complex is Mogollon, but further details must await publication by the excavator, Herbert Dick.

North of Mimbres Branch lies Cibola Branch. Here only one site has been excavated. Danson's recent survey for Peabody Museum of Harvard University has added considerable data, but much of this is necessarily limited (Danson 1952). One of the more important results of this survey is the definition of boundaries between Cibola and Mimbres branches (Fig. 1).

Mimbres sites occur along Blue River to latitude 33°35' N., where the river flows through a deep, narrow, box canyon. North of this canyon only Cibola Branch sites occur. East, across the San Francisco Mountains, Mimbres Branch sites occur as far north as latitude 33°40' N., in Pine Lawn Valley. A few miles north of Reserve, New Mexico, San Francisco River Valley narrows to a box canyon which seems to have been a cultural frontier with Cibola sites to the north and Mimbres sites to the south. Northeast of the confluence of the San Francisco and Tularosa rivers the Tularosa Valley is constricted by a box canyon which here, as in the Blue and San Francisco, divides the Mimbres and Cibola areas.

This last division is especially significant in view of recent excavation at Tularosa Cave. Danson (1952:309) states that, "None of the sites in the upper Tularosa Valley can be considered typical Mimbres. They differ in architectural features and in ceramics from those of the Mimbres Branch."

Martin et al. (1952) consider Tularosa Cave, which lies some
20 miles north of the box canyon, to be a typical Mimbres
site. Architecture is, of course, not present in the cave;
but the ceramic complex does not seem to vary greatly from
other Mimbres sites. The difficulty in assessing this situation at present lies in the fact that we do not have excavated
open sites from the same area and covering the same time span
as Tularosa Cave. When these become available it may be possible to determine with greater assurance the precise affiliation of the site. Two possibilities that should be considered
in this connection are (1) that the border fluctuated from
early to late, and (2) that the branches differentiated long
after the occupation of Tularosa Cave began.

East of the Tularosa Mountains the border appears to run
through the central part of the San Augustin Plains. Bat
Cave, which has a Mimbres Branch ceramic complex, lies on the
southern edge of the Plains, while sites along the northern
edge appear to belong to Cibola Branch, according to Danson
(1952), who found no permanent sites in the basin proper.

The northern, eastern, and western boundaries of Cibola
Branch are less well defined. All in all, the northern edge
of the mountain belt that extends from the Gallos eastward to
the Datils and Gallinas marks the Mogollon frontier toward
the plateau area. However, some brown ware occurs in the
earlier sites north of Quemado, New Mexico (Danson 1952),
which appear predominantly Anasazi after Basketmaker times.
Furthermore, at sites in the Cebolleta Mesa area to the north,
a brown ware complex seems to underlie a northern gray ware
complex, on a Pueblo I level (Ruppé and Dittert, preliminary
reports for 1950 and 1951 seasons). Whether these prove to

be Mogollon, or some other pattern not yet delineated, can be
answered only when further work in the area becomes available.
East of the Continental Divide, which runs along the crest of
the Tularosa Mountains, there are few, if any, permanent
sites, probably because of the arid nature of the San
Augustin Plains. The western boundary has not been defined,
but perhaps is marked by the White Mountains. It seems clear
that early sites along the headwaters of the Little Colorado
River in the Alpine, Nutrioso, and Springerville area are
Cibola Branch Mogollon (Danson 1952).

In general, the culture in the mountain area is of
essentially Mogollon people who seem to have preferred a
mountain environment to that of the plateau. The earlier
peoples lived on high mesas or isolated ridges, well back
from the main streams of travel. Because of geographical
nearness to the plateau with its Anasazi culture pattern,
these Mogollon groups were among the first to receive the
northern traits which, blended and changed, marked the later
stages of the Mogollon pattern.

The single excavated site in this vast area is Luna
Village (Hough 1919). It occupies the gentle southeast slope
of the third terrace above the north bank of San Francisco
River, near Luna, New Mexico. Low hills rise to the north,
while the river is about 1½ miles south. Small north-south
drainages flank the site on either side; the eastern one, fed
by a spring a few miles to the north, has permanent water.
The site is nearly 30 acres in extent, and in former days was
covered by Western Yellow Pine. The soil is alluvial, overlying clay. Hough estimated the village at nearly 100 pithouses. Eight structures were dug, seven domestic houses and

one large ceremonial feature.  There has been some question
as to the age of Luna Village.  Gladwin (1948) suggests that
it was Georgetown Phase.  However, the pottery excavated by
Hough (1919) is Three Circle Phase with a few northern Pueblo
I intrusives.  No pottery which can be positively identified
as an earlier type has been found in any of the modern surveys
(Danson 1952).  Therefore, until such evidence is procured,
the site might best be considered the Cibola Branch equivalent
of Three Circle Phase.

West of the Cibola area, and north and west of the White
Mountains, is Forestdale Branch.  Like Cibola Branch, which
it resembles in many respects, its frontier position caused
it early to receive acculturative influences from the Anasazi.
For the same reason, it may have been an important agency in
passing certain southern traits northward.

The northern boundary of Forestdale Branch probably lies
along the middle course of the Little Colorado.  Although
such placement is partly speculative, it is based on the
close relationship of the ceramic complex of Woodruff Butte
(Mera 1934) to that of the Forestdale sites.  Woodruff Butte
remains one of the most important unexcavated sites in the
Southwest, and there can be little doubt that its excavation
will fill many important gaps in our knowledge of Mogollon -
Anasazi relationships.  Other northern frontier sites whose
positions are not clear include those where the indigenous
pottery is Adamana Brown (Mera 1934; Colton and Hargrave
1937).  Haury and Sayles (1947) suggest that it might be a
regional variant of Mogollon brown ware, although the actual
genesis is not known.  The question of such identification
rests on whether or not the Mogollon are to be credited with

localized production of paddle-and-anvil finished pottery,
or whether some other groups are involved.  Because our
knowledge is scant, this situation is better left as a
question than as a speculation, for the present time.  One
Adamana site, the Flattop, dug by Wendorf (1950a) presents
unusual architectural features as well as a pure Adamana
Brown pottery complex.

To the east, Forestdale Branch seems to merge with the
Cibola.  This appearance may be due to lack of data rather
than to actuality, but in any event these branches seem
superficially closer to each other than to other branches
to the south.

The western boundary has not been defined; indeed, it
has hardly been explored.  Thus, we do not know the nature
of relationships between the central Mogollon area and the
important brown ware complexes of the Flagstaff area, some
of which have sometimes been included as Mogollon.  This
problem will be considered in a later section.

Two pithouse horizon sites have been excavated in the
Forestdale area.  It is on these that definition of the
Forestdale Branch is based.

Bluff Site (Haury and Sayles 1947) is located about nine
miles south of Showlow, Arizona.  It occupies the top of a
high bluff some 50 m. above the south bank of Forestdale
Creek.  The north face of the bluff is nearly vertical; the
east and west sides may be approached more easily over old
trails; to the south the country rises to higher hills.
Grass, manzanita, live oak, juniper, and pine cover the bluff
and surrounding countryside.  Good agricultural land is
available in small plots along the valley.

Twenty-three houses were wholly or partly excavated, and perhaps a dozen remain in the area not fully tested. Houses were distributed at random over the bluff top, with a large ceremonial structure near the village. Sheet rubbish ranged from a few centimeters to more than a meter in thickness on the down-slope of the site. Two phases, Hilltop and Cottonwood, mark the main occupation, followed by abandonment and reoccupation during Corduroy Phase, the local version of Pueblo I.

Bear Ruin lies about 1½ miles northeast and upstream from Bluff Site. The Mogollon Rim is just four miles to the north. The main part of the village occupies the highest of five terraces on the south bank of Forestdale Creek. The elevation is about 6,560 feet above sea level. This area lies in the heart of the Western Yellow Pine belt. Along the valley floor agricultural land occurs.

Seventeen pit structures, representing perhaps half of the total number present, were excavated. Houses occurred at random about a centrally located ceremonial house. Sheet rubbish averaging about 24 cm. in thickness was scattered throughout the village. Only a single phase, Forestdale, was represented.

South and east of Forestdale Branch is the area drained by Black River and Eagle Creek. Only one site, Crooked Ridge Village (Wheat 1954), has been excavated in this area, termed the Black River Branch. Boundaries of this branch have not been defined, but a few surmises may be made. Gila Pueblo's limited surveys north of Black River on the southern flanks of the White Mountains show similarities of the pottery to that of Crooked Ridge Village. It is not clear how far the

branch extends north and east toward the headwaters of Black
River. To the east, Blue Range, the divide between Eagle
Creek and Blue River, probably forms the border between Black
River Branch and Mimbres Branch. Westward there is little
data on early horizons, but the area about the confluence of
the Gila and San Carlos rivers was Hohokam territory. Indeed,
the Gila Valley contained Hohokam sites as far east as Safford
and Clifton, although some Mogollon sites occur there also.
Thus it might appear that the southern boundary of Black River
Branch was along the Gila Mountains north of Gila River.

Crooked Ridge Village is located about three miles east
of Point of Pines ranch on the San Carlos Apache Indian
Reservation, and some 10 miles south of the big bend of Black
River. It occupies the crest of a meandering ridge jutting
northward from Nantack Ridge. The elevation is about 6,200
feet above sea level. A small creek, with good agricultural
land along its bottoms, parallels the site on the east and
drains into Willow Creek, the master stream of the valley,
about three miles to the north. Pinyon, juniper, live oak,
and pine grow along the ridge; the higher hills are forested
with Western Yellow Pine. Great Circle Prairie lies a short
distance to the northwest.

Twenty-four pithouses were excavated. These occurred at
random along the crest of the ridge. Perhaps as many as 75
houses remain to be dug. Two large ceremonial structures
form central features of the village. Rubbish was scattered
sheetwise around the village and in the pits of abandoned
houses. Two, or perhaps three, phases are represented:
Circle Prairie, San Francisco, and Three Circle.

Farthest south and west of any Mogollon branch yet

defined is the San Simon area. The northern extent of this branch is the Gila River. There is no sharp boundary to the east. Here, roughly along the Arizona - New Mexico state line, sites of San Simon Branch are interspersed with Mimbres Branch sites. Sayles (1945, Fig. 1) shows many San Simon Branch sites along the San Pedro River, but, as I shall attempt to show later, most if not all of these actually represent a Mogollon - Hohokam blend. This is evident in such sites as Gleeson (Fulton and Tuthill 1940) and the sites near Dragoon (Fulton 1934a, 1934b, 1938). This merging of features is especially well demonstrated in ceramics, where techniques of manufacture and finishing are typically Mogollon while vessel forms and decoration are essentially Hohokam. Disposal of the dead, architecture, and stone work likewise show mixture of cultural traits. In addition to blend sites, occasional pure Hohokam sites and even a few Mimbres Branch Mogollon sites occur in this area. The southern extent of San Simon Branch has not been defined. It may possibly extend into adjacent parts of Mexico. There is no geographical barrier, and it seems likely that some sites do exist across the international border.

Two sites have been excavated which seem beyond question to be Mogollon, although one shows considerable influence from the Hohokam in its latest phase.

Cave Creek (Sayles 1945) is located on the east side of the Chiricahua Mountains overlooking San Simon Valley. The site occupies part of an outwash alluvial fan at the mouth of Cave Creek, an intermittent tributary of San Simon Creek. Prior to the recent erosion cycle the valley was grassy and cienegas or swamps were numerous. Desert shrubs occupy the

lower slopes of the hills to the west, but pines and other
trees grow on nearby mountain crests.

Seven houses were excavated. These were distributed at
random, and no ceremonial house was found. All of the houses
represent a single phase, Penasco.

San Simon Village is located some 10 miles west of Bowie,
Arizona, on the western margin of San Simon Valley. It lies
on a low terrace above an arroyo on the eastern slope of a
broad pass leading westward to Sulphur Spring Valley. The
Pinaleno Mountains are to the north and the Dos Cabezas
Mountains to the south. The elevation is about 3,600 feet,
the environment much like that of Cave Creek Village.

Sixty-six structures were located, most of which were
excavated. It is probable that more houses remain unlocated.
The houses were distributed at random. No house was found
which could be positively identified as ceremonial in nature.
However, during the latest occupation a ball court was built,
undoubtedly as a result of influence from the Hohokam. Trash
was disposed sheetwise throughout the village. Six phases
were defined: Penasco, Dos Cabezas, Pinaleno, Galiuro, Cerros,
and Encinas.

East of Mimbres Branch is Jornada Branch, which occupies
an environment similar to that of San Simon Branch. Lehmer
(1948) defined its limits as from north of Carrizozo, New
Mexico, to south of Villa Ahumada, Chihuahua, Mexico; and
from 75 miles west to 150 miles east of El Paso, Texas. As
defined, this branch is contiguous to Mimbres Branch only at
the extreme southwestern extension. Mera (1943) defined a
brown ware area bounded on the west by the eastern foothills
of the Magdalena, San Mateo, and Black ranges, with a northern

boundary extending generally eastward from the Magdalena
Mountains. This boundary corresponds to the eastern boundary
of Mimbres Branch. It should be noted that this area is
considerably more inclusive than that defined by Lehmer as
Jornada Branch. Thus, Jornada Branch would constitute only
a part of the southeastern brown ware area. In the north-
western part of the area, excluded by Lehmer, Mera describes
what has since been known as San Marcial Phase, characterized
by a brown ware utility complex together with San Marcial
Black-on-white, a late Basketmaker III decorated ware. The
eastern border is an indefinite one, fading out in open camp
sites of the western Staked Plains and Trans-Pecos area of
Texas. The southern boundary may be taken as the limit of
consistent presence of El Paso Brown wares.

In addition to the geographic problems concerned, there
are cultural ones. In defining Jornada Branch as Mogollon,
Lehmer derives it from the Hueco Cave Dweller Phase, which he
considers a regional variant of Cochise. I do not believe
this cultural identification can be maintained. The Hueco
Cave Dweller group has its principal connection with other
groups to the east and south. It differs in many important
ways from the Cochise as defined farther west. Mera (1943)
shows that the brown ware ceramic complex was diffused east
and north from the Mimbres area beginning probably in San
Francisco Phase times. This apparently was the movement of
certain traits, even though groups of people may also be
involved. Lehmer concurs that the ceramic complex was superimposed on the prevailing cave dweller pattern. Thus, the
problem resolves itself into two parts: (1) Are the Hueco
Cave Dwellers correctly identified as an eastern variant of

Cochise Culture without rendering that term meaningless; and (2) Are we to consider the area a Mogollon branch or simply a Mogollonized branch. The answer to this second problem may be only a semantic one, but it must be provided before the situation can be viewed in its true light. One further question also requires solution. Should we enlarge Jornada Branch, as defined by Lehmer, to include the entire eastern brown ware expansion, or should we seek a more inclusive name in which Jornada Branch is simply a subunit? I do not believe we control sufficient data at present to provide answers to these questions. Therefore, any final decision regarding the cultural alignment of Jornada Branch must await further study, particularly of the preceramic horizons upon which it has been superimposed.

Lehmer (1948:11) proposed the following phase sequence for the northern and southern subareas of Jornada Branch:

| North | South |
|---|---|
| San Andres | El Paso |
| Three Rivers | Dona Ana |
| Capitan | Mesilla |

Hueco

Of these phases, Hueco is preceramic, and those following Capitan and Mesilla are usually associated with surface architecture.

The following sites of the pithouse horizon have been excavated in the Jornada Branch area.

Los Tules is located about 1½ miles upstream from the Mesilla Diversion Dam near Las Cruces, New Mexico. It occupies a terrace some 7 m. above the flood plain, on the west bank of the Rio Grande. The site is divided into two parts by a broad arroyo. Creosote bush, mesquite, and shortgrass, characteristic of the Lower Sonoran Desert, grow on the site, but along the river grow abundant cattails, or tules, hence the name of the site.

Eleven houses and two storage pits were excavated, but because of the nature of the site it is not known whether this is the total village. Houses were scattered at random. One house, although small, was considered to be ceremonial in function. Trash was of the sheet variety. Only one phase, Mesilla, was represented.

La Cueva is, as the name implies, a cave site. It is situated about 10 miles east of Las Cruces, New Mexico, in the south side of an isolated erosional remnant from the Organ Mountains. A stream draining Dripping Springs Canyon flows about 60 m. below the mouth of the cave.

No aboriginal architectural features were present, but a stratitest showed the lower portion of the refuse to belong to Mesilla Phase.

In the northern part of the Jornada area Jennings and Neumann (1940) excavated Site LA 2000, the earliest occupation of which Lehmer (1948:85) places in Capitan Phase. This site is located 40 miles west of Hope, New Mexico, in the valley of the Rio Penasco, a tributary of Pecos River. It is semi-arid country with a Lower Sonoran plant complex.

This site occupies a sloping terrace west of the wide bend of Rio Peñasco. Hills rise steeply to the west. The site is extensive, and surface indications consist of four large, flattened areas produced by leveling off the hillside and disposing the earth along the lower side to make a crescentic embankment. These "flats" are 200 to 300 feet in diameter.  A number of smaller "flats" apparently mark the earlier occupation.

Two houses were excavated, one of which showed a superimposed floor of a later occupation.  A bell-shaped or olla-shaped pit was stratified below the embankment of one of the large "flats."  As previously mentioned, this site is placed in Capitan Phase.

The Bonnell Site (Holden 1952) is located about 14 miles northeast of Ruidoso, New Mexico.  It occupies a low mesa overlooking Ruidoso Valley.  Pinyon and juniper grow in clumps, with blue grama grass and small scrub bushes in between.  The valley of the Ruidoso afforded agricultural land in the alluvial bottoms.  Fifteen houses were defined. Other house floors were found but, because of poor preserva- tion, were not completely defined.  Fourteen of the houses belong to an earlier phase of occupation, and all of these were partly subterranean.  Some were definitely contiguous, sharing a common wall; others, while independent units, were grouped in such a way that they appear to form a more or less cellular arrangement similar to that at Galaz Ruin.  Holden (1952:127) places the site in San Andres Phase, but judging from the presence of about 50 percent of brown ware, it would be early in this phase or possibly late Three Rivers.

## IV / VILLAGE PATTERN AND ARCHITECTURE

Having briefly considered the location, environment, and layout of the various Mogollon villages, we may now analyze them to determine whether or not they follow a pattern.

### Village Location

In their choice of village sites, it is clear that, with few exceptions, the Mogollon chose places of some elevation and isolation. Twelve of 24 villages were located on a mesa, a bluff, or a ridge; 10 others occupied terraces well above valley bottoms; and one was situated on the outwash fan of nearby mountains. Only one was located in a valley bottom. Furthermore, Danson (1952) found in his survey that the early people built their villages on mesas or isolated ridges well back from the main stream of travel. Without exception, sites were located in mountainous country or near to mountains. Whether by preference or for some other reason, it was in the mountain country that the Mogollon people had their ecological niche. Many sites lie in secluded valleys on tributary streams; but except, perhaps, in the northernmost sites, the availability of agricultural land seems to have been one of the deciding factors in selecting a village site.

It has been suggested that the choice of high ridges, bluffs, and similar locations may have been for protection. Certainly, defense may have been a consideration. Promontory Site in Pine Lawn Valley has crude stone walls which may have served a defensive purpose. However, in most cases, other factors would seem to be of greater importance---better

34

drainage, more moderate temperatures, or as Martin and Rinaldo (1947:288) suggested, simply the desire for a view. Another important reason for selecting a ridge or mesa relates to the matter of agricultural land. In most mountain valleys such land is at a premium, and it would be short-sighted to encumber potential farm land with a village if an elevated site were nearby. Probably several factors, rather than a single one, determined the choice.

One of the strongest impressions to be derived from a study of Mogollon villages is their stability. Nearly every excavated site which was first occupied during early or intermediate times was continuously occupied through later pithouse horizons which often were succeeded by a stone pueblo phase. Some sites must have been occupied for nearly a thousand years.

Another characteristic of Mogollon villages is general lack of plan. Houses were built wherever it was convenient to build them, with little regard for village organization. Only two sites, Cameron Creek Village and the Bonnell Site, both in late phases, show any relation of individual houses to a community plan. Nearly every village where there are more than three or four houses contains a large ceremonial structure. The exceptions to this are villages of San Simon Branch, neither of which has a structure which can be clearly identified as ceremonial by its size, arrangement, or design.

## Architecture

Domestic architecture of the Mogollon has its origins in the last stages of the Cochise Culture. In the San Pedro area Sayles has defined hearths and large undercut storage pits on an old habitation surface at Benson:5:10 (Sayles and Antevs

1941:21-23, 26). At the same site large depressions, thought
to be house floors, were exposed in the face of the arroyo
but were not excavated. Further evidence was found in two
house sites of the San Pedro Stage excavated at Benson:5:10,
and another at Pearce:8:11 (Sayles 1945:1-4). Still another
Cochise dwelling is reported by Martin and Rinaldo (1950b:
430, Fig. 157) in Pine Lawn Valley. This structure is assigned to Chiricahua Stage; but although typologically
equivalent to this stage in the San Pedro area, it equates
chronologically with the San Pedro Stage. The Pine Lawn
situation appears to be a prime example of cultural lag in
an isolated area, for it would seem that the changes marking
San Pedro Stage never fully penetrated the Pine Lawn area.
Finally, a number of pits, some undercut and some with
straight sides, and lacking pottery, were found by Haury
(1936b) underlying the earliest ceramic horizon at Mogollon
Village.

This preceramic architectural tradition clearly gives
rise to the houses of early Mogollon. Outside hearths at
Benson:5:10 are simple depressions, a meter or little more
in diameter, filled with fire-cracked stones. The use of
undercut pits has not been fully determined as yet. Those
at Benson:5:10 were bell-shaped in section, up to 2 m. in
diameter and about the same in depth. Some hearth stones
occur in them, but whether these result from use of the pits
as earth ovens or simply represent refuse from the open
hearths is not certain. Perhaps the pits were used primarily
for storage. This seems clearly to be the case at Mogollon
Village where the pits were never burned. Secondarily, they
were occasionally used for burial.

The houses are simple in plan. Those at Benson:8:3 and Pearce:8:4 (Sayles 1945:1-4) are oval pits excavated into native clay about half a meter. Both are small, one being about 2.5 by 4.0 m., the other 2.4 by 3.0 m. One end of each house contained a floor pit 1.5 m. in diameter and 50 cm. deep. The central part of one house was covered with ashes and charcoal, but an irregular fire pit depression on the east side of the floor occurred at Pearce:8:4. Here, too, three shallow holes, presumably for roof supports, were found around the base of the unplastered walls. A short step entry on the west side completed the house. The Chiricahua Stage house is not so clearly defined (Martin and Rinaldo 1950b: 430-431). It apparently consisted of a round floor area 2.5 by 2.6 m., at an old ground surface (?). No post holes, hearth, or other floor features were found. A photograph (ibid., Fig. 157) appears to show a rectanguloid shallow pit occupying much of the floor area, but since no mention of it is made, it is not possible to determine its nature. Did these houses develop from storage pits? Whether or not they did, the storage pit seems to have constituted an important element, both as a unit structure and as a part of the Cochise houses.

Whatever uniformities there may have been in late Cochise architecture, and we do not have sufficient data to establish them, definite regional variations appear by Mogollon 1 times. Several house forms, rather than a single type, are characteristic of the period. During the succeeding periods there is a trend toward uniformity in architecture, but it is by no means complete. In order to objectify these trends, data on 248 domestic houses and 18 ceremonial houses have been tabulated.  All houses, where basic data are available, have been utilized in preparing tables 2, 3, 4, and 5.

In the tables for each period, the following data have been assembled: Site and house number; house description, including shape and type of entry; floor area in square meters; depth of house; kind of entry; orientation of entry; location and type of hearth; number of large and small floor pits; and post hole arrangement and probable roof plan.

These tables are neither so complete nor so accurate as might be desired.  Much information has had to be extracted from small-scale maps and diagrams.  Data on floor and other features are frequently not given at all, or are so vaguely generalized as to leave much doubt.  In some reports, phase assignment of many houses was not given, thus eliminating them from consideration.  It will be noted that in the matter of defining house form I have sometimes varied from the definition originally given by the excavator.  There are several reasons for this.  It was felt that a uniform point of view was more important in synthesizing the data than following the minutely detailed breakdown possible when dealing with single houses or sites.  Therefore, under the term "quadrangular houses" are several variations, from rectanguloid to square, and from rounded corners to square corners.  In some cases the designations applied by the excavator seem clearly in error.  For example, Nesbitt terms Starkweather houses K and N circilar; yet his map shows N as an ovoid with flattened sides, and photographs (Nesbitt 1938) show both to be rectangular with, perhaps, slightly curving walls, but certainly not circular.  In this study I have used the term "roundish" rather than the more precise "circular"

because most houses vary enough from true circular to justify
the less precise term.  Size is given in square meters because
this seems to give a clearer impression than the raw dimen-
sional measurements.  These data should be considered as
approximations, for many of them have had to be computed from
measurements abstracted from small-scale maps.  Depth measurements, likewise, are not very satisfactory.  Some are given
from present surface level, which may vary considerably from
the original depth; but it is often difficult to determine
where the surface was at the time the house was constructed.
In general, however, the figures do give some idea of the
original depth of the house pits.  Entryways less than a
meter long have been considered here as short, those exceeding a meter, long.  Other data on entries have been given
when available, but the tables obviously are not complete in
this respect.  The same may be said for details on hearths.
Floor pits less than 50 cm. in diameter are here considered
small, those more than 50 cm., large.  I have attempted, by
study of post hole patterns of many houses, to postulate roof
construction.  Admittedly, this is less than satisfactory,
but in many houses the data seem clear enough to warrant such
an attempt.  In any event, in seeking to determine architectural customs of a long dead people, such a trial seems necessary.  In Table 6, summarizing data for ceremonial houses,
floor grooves have been added to features considered in domestic houses.  Other details might have been included in the
tables but were not because of lack of data or because they
appear to be restricted in range or time.  Finally, it should
be added that I assume responsibility for any misinterpreta-
tions of data where I have varied from that originally given

by the excavator.

## Mogollon 1

Analyzing tables 2-5, certain trends are immediately apparent. At least 18 types of domestic houses were used during Mogollon 1 (Table 2, at rear). Houses without a lateral entry composed 38.5% of all houses, including 21.4% roundish in form. This does not mean that all of these structures were entered by a ladder, since most are shallow enough that a side entry consisting of a simple step could have sufficed. Such an entry would, in many respects, be like that of the group designated "short entry" houses, which comprise an additional 15.1%. Houses with long lateral entries constituted the largest group, but only by a margin of less than 2%. Of these, most were quadrangular. The remaining fraction is made up of houses, all from Crooked Ridge Village, with vestibule entries or southern annexes.

Considerable variation between branches may be noted. In Penasco Phase of San Simon Branch, 60% of the houses were roundish or had one or more sides flattened, and were without lateral entries. Another 15% were quadrangular, also lacking lateral entries. Most of the remaining houses had only a short entry. In Mimbres Branch, leaving aside Pine Lawn Valley for a moment, only 10% (1 house) of the total did not have a long, narrow entry. D-shaped, ovoid, roundish, and quadrangular houses with long entries were the predominant forms. Pine Lawn Phase is characterized by 41.4% of its houses lacking a definite entry. Houses with short side entrances comprised 34.4%, of which most were roundish in shape or lacked any readily definable outline. The largest remaining group, 17.2%, consisted of roundish houses with

large, broad entries imparting a pear shape.  These houses
are especially characteristic of SU Site.  Only two houses
had long, narrow entryways.

Hilltop Phase houses are likewise varied, but the
predominant form is a roundish pit without a lateral entry
(46.2%).  Another 46.2% constitute a miscellaneous group
with long entries, including one pear-shaped house so typical
of SU Site.  Circle Prairie Phase houses, as a group, differ
markedly from those of the other phases of Mogollon 1.
Quadrangular houses with long lateral entries constitute
52.9% of all houses excavated.  D-shaped and bean-shaped
houses with long entries comprise 17.7% and, as mentioned
above, the remaining group consists of houses with vestibule
entries or southern annexes.  In summary, each branch or
subarea shares some house forms with each of the others, yet
each has its own characteristic composition.

In the matters of size and depth, there are clear branch
variations.  Floor areas (in square meters) average 9.9 for
Penasco Phase, 14.9 for Georgetown, 16.1 for Hilltop, 20.7
for Circle Prairie (Early), and 27.1 for Pine Lawn Phase.
When compared with Mogollon 1 houses of all other areas,
those of Pine Lawn Valley are clearly aberrant.  In these
houses much space is taken up by floor pits.  It is clear that
if the floor areas of these houses be calculated excluding the
pits, they would more nearly accord with the Mogollon 1 houses
of the other areas.  Martin and Rinaldo (1950b:560) have
suggested that the larger Pine Lawn Valley houses were correlated with larger social units, which had emerged from smaller
Cochise social units and later returned to a smaller social
grouping.  Even if the pits in these houses were floored over

and all space thus made usable, as Martin suggests (personal
communication), an alternative to the social unit interpretation would correlate the larger size and number of floor pits
with a specialized solution to the storage problems.

Average depth of houses in the various branches differs,
also. Those of San Simon Branch, averaging only 39 cm., are
of the least depth, as well as being the smallest. The other
areas follow in order of increasing average depth: Pine Lawn
Valley, 46 cm., Black River Branch, 86 cm., Mimbres, 88 cm.,
and Forestdale, with its very deep houses, 121 cm.

The entryways of those houses possessing them are
remarkably uniform, even though some variation does occur.
Almost all are inclined, but a few begin or end with a step,
and some have a step at both ends. Still fewer entries are
simple step arrangements, no ramp being involved. Orientation
is overwhelmingly to the eastern quadrant, 48 of the 55 houses
having lateral entryways open to the east or nearly so. Three
of the houses are oriented to the south, two to the west, and
two to the north.

Hearths are usually present in the houses, but not in
all. For those houses where data are available, the hearth
most frequently consists of a simple unlined depression
between the center of the room and the entry. A few hearths
are centrally located, and fewer, still, occur at some other
position. In some houses no definite fire pit was made, and
in these the fire apparently was built directly on the floor
but in its customary place. Stones were used occasionally to
line the fire pit and sometimes were embedded in the floor,
at floor level or slightly above it, on the side nearest the
entrance. Two houses at Crooked Ridge Village had fire pits

curbed with clay. Other floor features consist of pits for storage, for sleeping (?), and possibly for other uses. Few houses, outside Pine Lawn Valley; have many floor pits; and where pits are present, they are usually less than 50 cm. in diameter. The localized concern with floor pits by the Pine Lawn Valley Mogollon has already been mentioned. In houses of Crooked Ridge Village and Bluff Site, pits sometimes occur filled with fire-cracked stones and sand but showing little evidence of having actually contained fire. These have been interpreted as warming pits or ovens.

Considerable variation is to be observed in methods of roofing the pithouses of Mogollon 1 times. Data are lacking on many houses and obscure on others. However, of 44 houses where a postulated reconstruction is feasible, seven have both central and marginal post holes, suggesting an umbrella-like arrangement of uprights and radiating beams. Another six have central post holes only, and must have been roofed the same way. Six houses had marginal post holes only, perhaps implying a flat or domed roof. Twenty houses, including most of those at Crooked Ridge Village, had some form of quadrilateral roof support, while four appear to have had a gable roof supported either on a single main cross beam or on three. All evidence recovered demonstrates that the main framework was covered with transversely attached small branches or reeds and then coated with heavy plaster.

## Mogollon 2

Only nine houses assignable to Mogollon 2 are available for study; three each from San Simon Village (Dos Cabezas Phase), Bluff Site (Cottonwood Phase), and Crooked Ridge Village (Circle Prairie Phase, Late) (Table 3). While the number

Table 3

| HOUSE DESCRIPTION | San Simon | | | Bluff | | | Crooked Ridge | | |
|---|---|---|---|---|---|---|---|---|---|
| | House No. 28 | 32 | 50 | House No. 11 | 14 | 19 | House No. 20 | 24 | 5 |
| **Quadrangular** | | | | | | | | | |
| No lateral entry | | | | | ? | | | | |
| Long entry | | | | x | x | x | x | | |
| Southern annex | | | | | | | | | x |
| **One or more sides flat** | | | | | | | | | |
| Short entry | x | | | | | | | | |
| **Ovoid** | | | | | | | | | |
| Entry at end | | | x | | | | | | |
| Entry at side | | | | | | | | x | |
| **D-shaped** | | | | | | | | | |
| Short entry | | x | | | | | | | |
| Floor area in sq. m. | 9 | 8 | 15 | 21 | 34 | 44 | 24 | 11 | 45 |
| Depth in cm. | | | | 120 | 70 | 40 | 48 | 50 | 120 |
| **Entry** | | | | | | | | | |
| Inclined | | | x | ? | ? | ? | x | x | ? |
| Starting with step | x | x | x | | | | | | ? |
| Ending with step | x | x | | | | | | | ? |
| Orientation | E | E | | E | SE | E | E | SE | NE |
| **Location of hearth** | | | | | | | | | |
| Near entry | | x | x | | x | | x | x | x |
| Near center | | | | x | | | | | x |
| Elsewhere | x | | | | | | | | |
| **Type of hearth** | | | | | | | | | |
| Depression | x | x | x | x | | | | x | |
| Fire area | | | | | | | x | | x |
| Stone-lined | | | | | x | | | | |
| **Floor pits** | | | | | | | | | |
| Large | | | | 1 | | | | | |
| Small | | | | | | | | 1 | 1 |
| **Post hole and roof plan** | | | | | | | | | |
| Central | | | x | | | | | | |
| Quadrilateral | | | x | ? | x | | x | | x |
| Gable | | | | | | | | x | |

Table 3. Domestic architecture of Mogollon 2: Dos Cabezas Phase, Cottonwood Phase, Circle Prairie Phase (Late). No houses are known for the postulated San Lorenzo Phase.

of houses is too small to be of great significance for analysis, it is interesting to note that the nine houses represent
six different types. No houses have been reported which do
not have lateral entries, but this is possibly because we
have too little information rather than because the type was
not present. Perhaps some houses at San Simon Village were
of types with no lateral entry, but inasmuch as Sayles (1945)
has not given phase assignments for the majority of his
houses, nor pottery associations, so that we may make independent assignments, it is not possible to judge. Four of
the nine houses, including all three from Bluff Site, are
quadrangular with long lateral entryways. The remaining five
represent as many types. One of these, the L-shaped house
with short lateral entry, dies out in this period, but the
other types carry on into later periods.

Because of the smallness of the sample, there seems
little advantage in further analysis of the houses of Mogollon 2. It may be worthwhile, however, to raise a few questions concerning this period. So far as local manufacture of
the characteristic broad-line red-on-brown pottery is concerned, only San Simon Branch has a clearly defined complex.
A few sherds from Mogollon Village in late Georgetown Phase,
and a few more from Crooked Ridge Village, seem to indicate
local manifestations of the period. Cottonwood Phase is so
placed because of its intermediate chronological and typological position with regard to Hilltop and the later Forestdale
phases. Mogollon 2 is the least well defined period in Mogollon history. Because of the scarcity of its representation,
we should ask whether it existed at all as a widely spread
period or whether it was confined, at least so far as its

pottery is concerned, to the southern and western parts of
the Mogollon area.  Another question which might be asked
concerns the length of the period.  From data now at hand,
it seems possible that Mogollon 2 was, in the southern part
of the area, a short transitional period.  The postulated
San Lorenzo Phase has yet to be isolated stratigraphically,
but the isolation of an equivalent period in both San Simon
and Black River branches lends weight to the idea that it
will sometime be demonstrated.

## Mogollon 3

Sixty-five houses may be assigned to Mogollon 3 (Table
4, at rear).  Twelve varied types were used during this period.  Houses lacking a lateral entry comprise 35.4% of all
houses, while 10.7% have short side entries.  Houses with long
lateral entries comprise nearly 50% of the total.  The remaining 4.6% are roundish houses with vestibule entries, and one
has a southern annex.  Perhaps the most important trend to
note is that 70.7% of all houses are basically quadrangular in
plan in contrast to 21.2% of this same plan during Mogollon 1.

Regional variation is still to be noted but is not so
marked as in earlier times.  The picture presented by Pinaleno
and Galiuro phases of San Simon Branch may, or may not, be an
accurate representation of its architectural variations.  Here
quadrangular houses with short lateral entries appear early,
followed closely by quadrangular houses with long side entries.  In Mimbres Branch, exclusive of Pine Lawn Valley,
nearly 52% of all houses lacked lateral entries, many of these
houses occurring at one site, Cameron Creek Village.  About
40% of the remainder are quadrangular with long lateral
entries.  Pine Lawn Valley has a few carry-overs of archaic

types such as the roundish houses with large, broad entries, and ovoid houses with the entry at the end rather than at the side. Fifty percent of the houses, however, are quadrangular with long lateral entries. Forestdale Phase presents a variety of forms. Roundish or quadrangular houses without lateral entries composed 32.2% of the architectural complex, roundish houses with long lateral passageways, 18.7%. Roundish houses with vestibules comprise another 12.5%. Only one house from Black River Branch has been tentatively assigned to Mogollon 3, and it is quadrangular.

Both size and depth trends show increasing uniformity throughout the Mogollon area. Excepting one house from Crooked Ridge Village, which, with 26.7 square meters of floor area, may be aberrant, the houses of Pine Lawn Valley, averaging 22.2 square meters in floor area, are the largest of their time. This still seems to be, in some measure, correlated with the presence of large floor pits, but not so much so as in earlier phases. Next in order of size are the Forestdale houses at 19.4 square meters. It is interesting to note that more storage pits are included within the houses here, perhaps explaining their increased average size. Mimbres area houses remain about the same average size, 15.0 square meters, as compared to 14.9 for houses of Mogollon 1 period. Houses in the San Simon area increase from 9.9 to 13.2 square meters, bringing them more into line with the other areas. There is a marked tendency throughout the area, except in the Forestdale region, toward deepening the house pits, and again, the tendency is toward uniformity. Listed in order of increasing average depth of houses, the areas are San Simon, 68 cm.; Black River, 100 cm.; Mimbres, 105 cm.;

and Forestdale and Pine Lawn Valley, 114 cm.

Entry passages, where they occur, are all of the ramp variety, but perhaps half of them begin, and many also end, with a step. The stepped entry, as such, is not often used, if at all. Of 42 houses having lateral entryways, 32 are oriented to the east, southeast, or northeast; one is to the north, seven to the west, and two to the south. Four houses of Forestdale Phase had ventilators in place of, or in addition to, the entryway.

Hearths are more common in houses of this period. There seems a definite correlation between the presence of an entry and the location of the hearth. Nearly all houses lacking an entryway have the hearth near the center of the house, while in most houses with a lateral entry the hearth is between the center and the entrance. A simple unlined depression is the most common type of hearth, but occasionally pits are lined with stones or have stones embedded in the floor on the side nearest the entrance. Fire areas, as distinguished from formalized hearths, and clay-lined or clay-curbed pits occur sporadically.

Large intramural storage pits appear less often than in Mogollon 1, but as mentioned above, continue to occur in the houses of both Pine Lawn Valley and the Forestdale area. Small pits also are less frequent than they were previously. Warming ovens continue in the Forestdale area and probably in the Black River area as well, since they occur later in Mogollon 4 period.

The central and marginal roof support plan occurs in only five of the 39 houses where such assessment can be made. No houses had only the central roof support, and only two had a definite marginal support plan. Twenty houses had post hole patterns suggesting a quadrilateral flat roof, and 13 appear to have had a gable roof supported on one or three beams parallel to the long axis of the room.

## Mogollon 4

Architecturally, Mogollon 4 is dominated by quadrilateral houses with a long lateral entryway (Table 5, at rear). About 63% of all houses constructed during this period are of this type, as compared to about 37% during the preceding period. Both houses at San Simon Village, said by Sayles (1945:26) to typify the trend there, are of this type, as are 86.6% in the Mimbres, exclusive of Pine Lawn Valley where only 20% (two houses) occurred. It should be remembered, however, that several houses assigned by Martin and Rinaldo (1950a) to San Francisco Phase (Mogollon 3) were considered by them to have been occupied also during Three Circle Phase (Mogollon 4), a fact which would increase the predominance of quadrangular, long-entry houses. In the Jornada area 41.6% of the houses were of the same type. However, another 41.6% were roundish, lacking a lateral entry.

Round pithouses appear to be the dominant type in Cibola Branch, where 77.8% of the houses at Luna were of this type. Danson (1952) also reports this the prevalent type recorded by his survey in the same area. Two round houses (20%) occurred in Pine Lawn Valley, apparently a carry-over from earlier times. These data indicate that in the nuclear Mogollon area round houses without lateral entries had been largely replaced by quadrangular houses with long entries, but in the peripheral areas the round house was still a preferred type.

One point that should be remembered is that most of the houses reported for this period are in the Mimbres area; when we know more of the period elsewhere the ratio of house types may be changed. Roundish houses with vestibules were still being built in Pine Lawn Valley and in the Black River area, and at Starkweather Ruin houses with a southern annex were a continuing form. In the peripheral areas, Cibola and Jornada, quadrangular houses without lateral entries accompanied the round houses.

A trend toward smallness continued in Pine Lawn Valley, houses averaging 19.8 square meters of floor area. House D at SU Site was not computed in this average because its size, 69.1 square meters, would have skewed the result. Houses were somewhat less deep, also, averaging just less than a meter. Elsewhere in the Mimbres area houses increase in size (19.4 square meters) and depth (114 cm.). In San Simon Branch, judging by the two houses for which we have data, size increased to an average 14.1 square meters, but depth decreased to an average 50 cm. In the Black River area the one house possibly assignable to Mogollon 4 is large (29.4 square meters) and deep (130 cm.) but is not statistically significant.

Two branches, Cibola and Jornada, are first known architecturally during Mogollon 4. As pointed out above, their structural complex is in some ways similar, as is the size of their dwellings. Cibola houses, as known from Luna Village, average 13.1 square meters in floor area and 134 cm. in depth, while Jornada houses average a little larger (15.0 square meters) but more shallow (95 cm.). However, three very small houses, perhaps used primarily for storage, averaged 5.9 square meters in floor area and were not computed with the other houses.

The majority of Mogollon 4 houses (79%) have lateral entries, most of which are simple ramps, although a few have a step at one or both ends. Some houses have two entries, but in most cases these represent later modification of the original plan. Of 66 houses where entry orientation is shown, 46 are to the east, northeast, or southeast; 9 to the north, 8 west, and 12 south. (Houses with two entries account for the orientation total exceeding the total number of houses with lateral entrances.)

As noted for Mogollon 3, it appears that houses with no lateral entry have a centrally placed hearth, while in lateral entry houses the hearth is between the entry and the center of the house. A simple unlined depression is the common form of hearth, but embedding of a stone on the entrance side of the fire pit continues into this period at Harris Village. The peculiar portable hearths from Luna should also be mentioned. These consist of two divergent arms of clay which terminate in knobs or bosses and are joined together in another knob, the whole resembling a letter V.

Large storage pits within houses are rare except in Pine Lawn Valley, where their use is generally diminished from earlier phases. Small floor pits are likewise less frequent, a fact to be correlated, perhaps, with an increase in some form of perishable container.

Quadrilateral and gable roofs are clearly the predominant types in Mogollon 4. One notable exception is Luna Village where, according to Hough (1919), a central and marginal roof support plan was used.

## Mogollon 5

Although the Mogollon 5 period lies beyond the scope of this study, a few remarks concerning the architectural manifestations may be made. In general, the period was one of transition from villages of scattered unit pithouses, often clustered about a large ceremonial house, to masonry pueblos. In the Mimbres this transition was made through a series of short-lived house forms. Mostly these were semi-subterranean with walls of masonry extending to and supporting the roofs. Many of these rooms were contiguous, and probably reflect a true blending of pithouse and pueblo traditions. Swarts, Cameron Creek, Mattock, and Galaz ruins represent this phase, which some term Mangus Phase. This trend culminates in the pueblos of Mimbres Phase. In the upper Blue River area, Pine Lawn Valley, and the Reserve area---that is, in the northern subarea of Mimbres Branch---the transition was to Reserve Phase with masonry pueblos similar in most respects to those farther south. The transition, however, seems to have been accomplished through an intermediate stage of jacal structures. Martin and Rinaldo (1950b:432-437) report one such structure, and Danson (1952), on the basis of his survey, believes that to be the common type of house structure just preceding the first masonry pueblos. Cibola and Forestdale branches were the first Mogollon areas to receive acculturative influences spreading southward from the Anasazi area. Details are generally lacking in the Cibola area, but in the Forestdale area a northern pithouse tradition blended with the southern to form Corduroy Phase. In the Black River area the Mogollon pithouse horizon was replaced by a Reserve Phase pueblo horizon, but it is interesting that the pithouse village pattern maintained itself alongside the newer pueblo pattern until well into the thirteenth century (Wendorf 1950b). The Hohokam Culture was the chief influence in San Simon Branch. The Mogollon pithouse tradition continued but was heavily influenced by contemporaneous Hohokam. East of the Mimbres, aberrant pueblos of adobe were replacing the late Mogollon pithouse tradition. The Alamogordo and Bradfield sites of Lehmer (1948), Twelve-Room House (Moore 1947), and Bonnell Site (Holden 1952) exemplify the architectural changes and varieties of this area during Mogollon 5 times.

## Discussion of Mogollon Domestic Architecture

Some general architectural trends may now be examined. Data extracted or computed from tables 2, 4, and 5, have been regrouped into bar graphs to show these trends (Fig. 2). Mogollon 2 has been omitted because the sample is too small to be other than a distorting influence in the apparent trends. Roundish, ovoid, or irregular houses were clearly the predominant form during Mogollon 1, followed by bean-shaped or D-shaped houses; quadrangular houses were clearly a minority form (Fig. 2, a). By Mogollon 3, quadrangular forms constitute some 70% of all houses; bean- or D-shaped houses have almost disappeared, and roundish houses are still common. The sharp break between Mogollon 1 and Mogollon 3 suggests that Mogollon 2, when adequately known, would have roundish and quadrangular houses in about equal proportions. The trend begun in Mogollon 3 continues into Mogollon 4, where about 75% of all houses are quadrangular. There tends to be regional difference in the ratio of quadrilateral to roundish houses, the latter being more common in the eastern and north-ern parts of the Mogollon area. However, quadrilateral houses

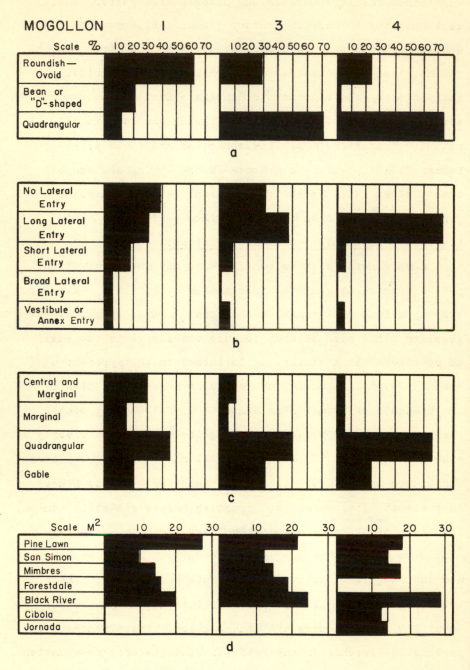

Figure 2. Mogollon architectural trends: a, house form;
b, type of entry; c, type of roof structure; d, floor area in
square meters.

are plainly a typical Mogollon architectural form from the earliest times.

An equally sharp trend is apparent in the presence or absence of lateral entrances and in the nature of the entry-ways (Fig. 2, b). Houses lacking side passageways compose only about 40% of all houses during Mogollon 1, but as such, are the largest single group. Long lateral entries are next most common, but short side entries occur nearly as often. Large, broad entrances, which impart a pear-shape to the house, and vestibules or antechambers and southern annexes form a small percentage of the total.

Mogollon 3 shows increasing frequency of long lateral entries (nearly 50%) and decreasing occurrence of short entries and of houses lacking entrance passageways. Large, broad entries die out during this period, but vestibules and southern annexes continue as an infrequent but characteristic type. By Mogollon 4, long side entries occur in nearly 70% of all houses, while about 20% of the rooms have no passage-way. Short side entrances began to take on a new meaning as one of the types transitional to surface dwellings. Vesti-bules and annexes continued but were never common. It is clear that houses without lateral rampways are a part of the Mogollon architectural tradition.

Everywhere except in Pine Lawn Valley there was a small but consistent increase in house size from Mogollon 1 through Mogollon 4 (Fig. 2, d). In Pine Lawn Valley, where large house size correlates, at least partly, with the presence of large floor pits, house size decreased proportionately with the number of floor pits. In general, also, earlier houses tended to be more shallow than later ones, but this trend was neither constant nor uniform throughout the Mogollon area.

One other general trend may be noted in the type of roof construction (Fig. 2, c). Quadrilateral roof support was the most common type, even in Mogollon 1, but increased until during Mogollon 4 about 67% of all houses were roofed in this manner. A central and marginal support plan (or central only, which is functionally the same) was nearly as common as the quadrilateral form in Mogollon 1, but decreased markedly until it was used only in the peripheral areas during Mogollon 4. The marginal post arrangement also decreased from early to late. Gable roofs, supported either on a single beam or on three parallel beams, increased from Mogollon 1 to maximum use in Mogollon 3, then decreased during Mogollon 4. By Mogollon 5 the function of roof support was commonly taken over by the masonry walls of the structures except in the San Simon area, where pithouses continued to prevail. There appears something of a regional specialization in roof support, for the quadrilateral roof is definitely more common in the western and southern parts of the Mogollon area than in the eastern. However, it is important to note that each form occurs in all branches and subareas and is therefore to be considered a standard Mogollon technique when it occurs.

## Mogollon Ceremonial Architecture

Ceremonial houses appear as consistent features in Mogollon villages everywhere except in San Simon Branch. What took their place there, if anything, or if they just have not been excavated, cannot be said on the basis of present knowledge. Data on 18 ceremonial houses are available for study (Table 6.)

Of six ceremonial houses assignable to Mogollon 1, two

House Description

| POST HOLE AND ROOF PLAN | | Bluff 5 | Crooked Ridge 9 | SU A | SU V | Promontory B | Harris 14 | Crooked Ridge 19 | Bear Ruin Kiva K | Turkey Foot Ridge 3 | Mogollon Village 8 | Harris 5a | Mogollon Village B | Starkweather | Luna Dance Pit Y | SU 10 | Harris 23 | Harris | Cameron Creek Kiva |
|---|---|---|---|---|---|---|---|---|---|---|---|---|---|---|---|---|---|---|---|
| | Gable | | | | | | | | | | | | | | ? | x | x | x | x |
| | Quadrilateral | x | x | | | | x | x | x | | | | | | | | | | |
| | Marginal | | | x | x | | x | | x | | | | x | | | | | | |
| | Central | 1 | | x | x | | x | | | | | | x | | | | | | |
| Single major floor groove | | | | | | | | x | | | | | | | | | | | |
| Groove encircling floor | | x | | | ? | | | | | | | | | | | | | | |
| Grooves isolating center | | | x | | | | | x | | x | | | | | | | | | |
| Marginal floor grooves | | | x | | | | | | | | | | | | | | | | |
| Number of small floor pits | | | | | | | | 1 | 2 | | | | | | | | | | |
| Number of large floor pits | | 1 | 3 | 1 | 3 | 4 | | 1 | 1 | 3 | | | | | | | | | |
| LOCATION AND TYPE OF HEARTH | Elsewhere | S | D | | | | | | | | | | | | 2 | | | | |
| | Near center | S | S | | | | | D | D | D | | | | | | | | | |
| | Near entry | | | | | E | D | | | | E | D | | C | D | D | S | D | |
| ENTRY | Orientation | SW | | E | | SE | E | E | E | | | E | ED | NE | N | | SE | SE | S |
| | Ends with step | x | | ? | | x | x | | | | | | x | | | | | | x |
| | Starts with step | x | | | x | x | x | x | | | | x | x | | | x | | x | x |
| | Inclined | x | x | x | ? | x | | | x | x | x | | | | | x | x | x | x |
| Depth in centimeters | | 145 | 150 | 70 | 115 | 70 | 100 | 170 | 175 | 140 | 110 | 90 | 110 | 170 | 304 | 180 | 190 | 80 | |
| Floor area in square meters | | 83 | 64 | 74 | 79 | 86 | 38 | 112 | 86 | 60 | 71 | 82 | 86 | 99 | 330 | 13 | 135 | 50 | 87 |
| Quadrangular, long entry | | | | | | | | | | | | | | | | | x | x | x |
| D-shape, long lateral entry | | | | | | | x | | | | x | | | | | | | | |
| Bean-shape, long lat. entry | | | | | | | | | | | | x | | | | | | | |
| Ovoid, long lateral entry | | | | | | | | | | x | | | | | | | | | |
| Quadrangular, short entry | | | | | | | | x | | | | | | | | | | | |
| Bean-shape, short entry | | | | x | x | x | | | | | | | | | | | | | |
| Roundish, short lat. entry | | x | | | | | | | | | | | x | | | | | | |
| Quadrangular, no lat. entry | | | | | | | | | x | | | | | | | x | | | |
| Roundish, no lateral entry | | x | | | | | x | | | | | | | | x | | | | |
| House No. | | 5 | 9 | A | V | B | 14 | 19 | K | 3 | 8 | 5a | B | | Y | 10 | 23 | | |
| SITE | | Bluff | Crooked Ridge | SU | SU | Promontory | Harris | Crooked Ridge | Bear Ruin Kiva | Turkey Foot Ridge | Mogollon Village | Harris | Mogollon Village | Starkweather | Luna Dance Pit | SU | Harris | Harris | Cameron Creek Kiva |
| MOGOLLON PERIOD | | | | 1 | | | | 2 | | 3 | | | | | | 4 | | | |

Table 6. Mogollon Ceremonial Architecture. Legend for Location and Type of Hearth: C = clay-lined, D = depression, S = stone-lined.

are roundish, three (in Pine Lawn Valley) are bean-shaped, and one is D-shaped. House 5 at Bluff Site had no lateral entry, and House 14 at Harris Village had a long lateral entry; the others had short side entries. Most entries had steps incorporated in them. Excepting House 14 at Harris Village, whose floor area was only 38.4 square meters, the ceremonial houses range from 63.6 to 86.5 (average 77.1) square meters in area, and average 108 cm. in depth. Four are oriented to the east and one to the southwest, the latter apparently opening toward the domestic houses which it served. Hearths occurred in most ceremonial houses, but none was found in House V at SU Site. Three hearths were lined with small stones and all were pits. Large floor pits occurred in both House A and House V at SU Site, and one occurred in House 9 at Crooked Ridge Village. Three houses of this period are distinguished by floor grooves of various sorts. House 5 at Bluff Site had a groove cut in solid sandstone completely around the floor, inward from the wall. That this groove had nothing to do with wall construction seems proved in that the pit wall itself was plastered. House A at SU Site had five elongated pits shaped like a half-log (two were double), located evenly about the margins of the room. House 9 at Crooked Ridge Village had four grooves, one of which was double, also shaped like half-logs, forming a square and iso-lating the central part of the house. The hearth was located within this restricted area. Central and marginal post hole patterns prevailed except at Bluff Site and Crooked Ridge Village ceremonial houses, which had a quadrilateral roof plan. House B at Promontory Site was not completely excava-ted, so details of floor features and roof supports are not known.

Only one ceremonial house, No. 19 at Crooked Ridge Village, is known for Mogollon 2 period. It is quadrilateral with a short stepped entry to the east. It contained 111.6 square meters of floor area and was 170 cm. in depth. The central portion of the house is isolated by half-log shaped grooves which completely enclose the space. A large double fire hearth divided by an upright stone slab is located in the center of the enclosed area. The roof was constructed on a quadrilateral plan.

Six ceremonial houses are known for Mogollon 3 period, and each is a different type. One is roundish with a short lateral entry oriented north. Three have long lateral entryways oriented to the east, but one is ovoid, one bean-shaped, and one D-shaped. One is quadrangular with no lateral entry; and the other, the Bear Ruin Kiva, although roundish and without a lateral entryway, is distinguished by a southeastern annex and four directional recesses apparently structural in nature.

In size, the ceremonial houses of this period range from 60.0 to 99.5 square meters of floor area (average, 80.8), and in depth, from 90 to 170 cm. (average 132 cm.). Only three contained hearths: two centrally located, unlined fire pits were in houses lacking lateral entries; House 8 at Harris Village had a depression between the house center and the entry, with a stone embedded in the floor clay on the entrance side. Large floor pits occurred in Bear Ruin Kiva and in House 3 at Mogollon Village, and some small ones in the Bear Ruin structure and in House K at Turkey Foot Ridge. Floor grooves occurred in two houses: Bear Ruin Kiva had a single

large groove somewhat isolating the rear part of the house,
and House K at Turkey Foot Ridge contained four grooves iso-
lating the center.  Remains of a log which had been plastered
in position were found in one of the grooves.  Two houses had
quadrilateral roof plans, and one had a central and marginal
plan.  Data as to roofing are not available for the other
houses.  Pithouse B at Starkweather is classed by Nesbitt
(1938:90) as late San Francisco.  If this assignment is correct (and there is some reason to doubt it), this would mark
the first major use of stone masonry by the Mogollon.

Masonry is common, however, in ceremonial and domestic
houses of Mogollon 4 in the Mimbres area.  Five ceremonial
structures of this period are available for study.  Three,
all from the Mimbres area, are of the same type, large rectangular houses with long lateral entries oriented southeast
or south and having a gable type roof.  Masonry was used to
support weak places in the walls of each house.

Fire hearths consisted of a simple depression, in the
Cameron Creek house, with a stone embedded in the floor on
the entrance side in the two houses at Harris Village.
Essentially, these three ceremonial houses are overgrown
domestic houses.  They range from 48.9 to 135.5 square meters
in floor area, and from 80 to 190 cm. in depth.  The remaining two structures are very different.  Pithouse Y at SU Site
was a small (12.5 square meters), deep, rectangular room with
a ventilator in place of a lateral entry, and was undoubtedly
entered through a roof hatchway.  A rectangular, clay-curbed
fire pit and probably a deflector were located in front of
the ventilator.  A gable roof, or perhaps a flat roof supported
by the walls, covered the structure.  The last structure is

the huge "dance pit" uncovered by Hough (1919) at Luna. This
was a circular pit with sloping walls interrupted by a bench
around a "dance floor" 181.4 square meters in area. The
whole excavation covered about 330 square meters (diameter,
25.6 m.). Total depth of the pit was 3.04 m. Hough surmised
that the structure was too large to be roofed and that it was
surrounded by a palisade instead. No suggestion is made regarding shelter during rainy weather. Since the pit was only
trenched, details of construction and floor features are not
known. No floor grooves are reported for any Mogollon 4
ceremonial structure.

In ceremonial architecture, as in domestic, it is clear
that there was not one type of structure, but several. In
general, the basic plan of ceremonial houses is similar to
that of dwelling and storage houses. It is their size and
floor features, primarily, that distinguish them. In floor
area most are three or four times the size of domestic houses
and are consistently deep. A house of such size surely should
be regarded as a communal project. In many such houses domestic furniture is scarce or lacking. Six of the 18 houses
had floor grooves, suggesting some special use; their purpose
can only be surmised. Haury (1940:47) suggested that the
grooves in Bear Ruin Kiva might be a form of loom anchor; but
the grouping of grooves to form central quadrangles at Turkey
Foot Ridge and Crooked Ridge Village suggests some other
function. It will be recalled that fragments of a log were
found plastered into the grooves at Turkey Foot Ridge House K
(Martin and Rinaldo 1950a:284). These logs may have served
either as a visual barrier or as the foundation for a physical
barrier to divide the hearth area from the rest of the house.

However, it is possible that hollow logs embedded in the grooves served as primitive foot drums. Wooden slabs fitted over the encircling groove of the Bluff Site ceremonial house would have served the same purpose, the grooves acting as resonators. Although smaller floor grooves are sometimes found in domestic houses, it seems clear that the large ones are primarily connected with the ceremonial complex of the Mogollon. Further, it can hardly be doubted that some form of community activity was carried on in these large houses.

## Storage Pits and Outside Hearths

Two characteristic features of Mogollon sites are extramural storage pits and hearths or earth ovens. However, on the basis of present knowledge it is not possible to determine how consistently these features occur. This is because practically the entire site would have to be stripped to native clay in order to discover them, a fact which largely accounts, also, for the comparatively small number of burials recovered. With this condition in mind, we may first examine the distribution of extramural storage pits.

The occurrence of multiple pits with undercut sides at Mogollon Village has already been mentioned. Although the evidence is not conclusive, it seems probable that most, if not all, of these pits are preceramic. In any case, such undercut pits are clearly a feature of San Pedro Stage, as evidenced at Benson:5:10. This type of pit continued into later Mogollon phases.

During Mogollon 1 extramural pits occur at San Simon, SU, and perhaps at Harris Village. Some of the thirty pits excavated at San Simon probably belong to this horizon. The early pits were either undercut or straight-sided. Some pits

were cut through the floor of earlier houses, and a few were
large enough that they could have been used as houses, although no floor features were found other than occasional
ashes and burned stones. Nine pits, representing both undercut and straight-sided types, were found at SU Site. These
ranged in diameter from 1.0 to 2.0 m., and from 95 to 135 cm.
in depth. Since it is not clear whether some of the Harris
Village pits belong to this horizon, they will be considered
as Mogollon 3.

Presumably some of the extramural pits belong to the Dos
Cabezas Phase of Mogollon 2, but no details are available,
and characteristics noted above probably are valid for these,
as well. They have not been noted at other sites of the
period as yet.

Extramural storage pits of Mogollon 3 occurred at San
Simon, Harris, and Bear Ruin. At San Simon Village the undercut variety seems to have died out and straight-sided pits
predominate. The same is true of the Harris Village pits,
which are neither so numerous nor so well made as those of
Mogollon Village. They range in diameter from 1.0 to 2.0 m.,
and are seldom more than a meter in depth. Two storage pits
occurred at Bear Ruin; both were round with straight sides,
and were about a meter in diameter and in depth.

Mogollon 4 storage pits are known only from San Simon
and from Los Tules in the Jornada Branch. Those at San Simon
were straight-sided, but the two at Los Tules were undercut
pits 50 to 75 cm. in diameter and the same in depth.

Several varieties of extramural hearths are associated
with Mogollon villages. Even in sites where actual hearths
were not located, fire-fractured stones are so common in the

refuse, it seems clear that such hearths were in use.

Extramural hearths of Mogollon 1 are reported from Cave Creek and Bluff sites. At Cave Creek several hearths, some in shallow depressions, others on the old surface level, appear to be associated with well-trodden floor areas, suggesting a definite outdoor kitchen. These hearths range up to 2.0 m. in diameter. At Bluff Site two earth ovens were found, one assignable to Hilltop Phase, the other to Corduroy Phase, the local equivalent of Pueblo I. The early hearth was an oval pit about 1.5 by 3.0 m., and about 1.0 m. in depth. The out-sloping sides were plastered and heavily burned. Many fire-cracked sandstone rocks, debris from the hearth, formed a small midden nearby. From the number of these middens located, but not excavated, it appears they may be associated with each domestic unit as an outdoor kitchen.

No outdoor hearths definitely assignable to Mogollon 2 have been reported, but some of those at San Simon Village may belong to Dos Cabezas Phase.

Mogollon 3 extramural hearths are reported from San Simon Village and Bear Ruin. Those at San Simon were straight-sided pits dug into earlier debris. These were filled with fire-cracked stones. At Bear Ruin 16 hearths of four types were excavated. Nine were shallow basins from 25 to 100 cm. in diameter, while two pits resembled the previously described Bluff Site hearth. A third type, represented by a single example, has straight sides and a rounded bottom, and would appear to be much like those of San Simon Village. These pits were not plastered but all contained numerous hearth stones and showed heavy burning. The fourth type, represented by four examples, is a specialized earth oven with undercut sides, ranging in depth from 1.5 to 2.0 m., and averaging 1.75 m. in diameter at the bottom.  They had been dug through sterile clay into sand, and heavily plastered with clay.  All showed very heavy firing.  They were filled with hearth stones and fragments of calcined animal bone, but no carbonized vegetal remains were found, suggesting that they were used principally for the preparation of meat.

While some hearths at San Simon Village may be assigned to Mogollon 4, they do not differ from those of the preceding period.  A single hearth is reported from Los Tules.  It is an oval depression 45 by 60 cm., and was filled with hearth stones, charcoal, and charred animal bones, again suggesting that meat was the main food cooked in these outdoor hearths.

Judging from the occurrences enumerated, the range in time and space, and the invariable presence of hearth stones in the refuse of sites where specific examples have not been excavated, there is little doubt that the extramural hearth, like the extramural storage pit, was a common, if not invariable, part of the structural complex of Mogollon villages.

Somewhat more than 221 burials have been recovered from Mogollon sites which can be assigned to the periods covered by this study. The precise number cannot be given, nor is it important other than as an index to the validity of our reconstruction of the burial customs represented.

Burials of Mogollon 1 have been found at Cave Creek, Chiricahua:3:25, San Simon, SU, Bluff, Crooked Ridge Village, and Tularosa Cave. At Cave Creek two burials, flexed on the side, occurred in pits cut through the floor of an abandoned pithouse; a third, that of an infant, came from a shallow pit outside the house. Two additional burials, an infant and an adult, were placed in shallow depressions in the silt at Chiricahua:3:25. None of these burials, all Penasco Phase, contained grave furniture. Numerical data are not available on Penasco Phase burials at San Simon Village, but according to Sayles (1945:62-64) the body was commonly flexed on the side and placed in a pit sometimes cut through the house floor, but usually outside the house. Offerings were rare, but quartz crystals were occasionally found, and in some cases the bodies were covered by cairns consisting of unworked stones, broken metates, hand stones, and the like. In the Mimbres, excluding Pine Lawn Valley, no burials dating surely to this period were reported. At SU Site 54 burials were recovered, all but one of which were assigned to Pine Lawn Phase. Sixteen of these were in extramural pits scattered at random through the village, and 10 were on the floor or in

the fill a few centimeters above the floor of abandoned
houses. The majority (27), however, had been placed in
abandoned floor pits within the houses. It seems clear that
in some cases the houses had also been abandoned at the time
the inhumations were made; but in others, the pits had been
plastered over and the houses continued in use, the first
appearance of this trait. Bodies were usually flexed, and
those in pits were placed in a reclining position, while
those in floors or floor fill were laid on their backs.
Two possible bundle burials were found. Only one burial
was extended. Orientation to the east was perhaps most
common, but no clear-cut pattern is apparent.

The two Mogollon 1 burials from Tularosa Cave are of
special interest because they show the nature of accompanying
artifacts which would not survive in an open site. Both had
been placed on a bed of grass. Burial 1, a male, was in a
semi-sitting position on a deer or antelope hide, and a
bundle of feathers tied on a stick had been placed on the
chest. The hair was cropped short. Orientation was south,
toward the mouth of the cave. The second burial, a female
wearing a string apron, lay on a rush mat with a coil of
fibers at the feet. The hair was cropped shorter than that
of the male. The head was oriented toward the southwest.

Bluff Site yielded only two burials; both had been
placed in extramural pits and were not apparently associated
with any fixed village feature. Both were semi-flexed on the
side. One was oriented east, the other south. No burial
offerings were found.

Six burials assignable to the Mogollon occupation were
recovered at Crooked Ridge Village, but it is not possible to

determine whether they belong to the early, or to the late, part of Circle Prairie Phase, although four were located in the generally early part of the village. The remaining two were cut through the floor of a house tentatively considered late Circle Prairie. Since the burial pattern is the same for all, they will be summarized here. Two burials occupied individual extramural pits cut into native clay, while two pits contained two bodies each, probably interred at the same time. All bodies were flexed. Those in individual pits were on the back in a semi-reclining position; those in double pits were placed on the side. There was no preferred orientation. Burial furniture, which occurred with three of the burials, consisted of whole or fragmentary pottery vessels.

Unless some of the burials of Crooked Ridge Village belong to Mogollon 2, this period is represented only by those of Dos Cabezas Phase at San Simon Village, and we do not possess numerical data on these. According to Sayles (1945: 63), the earlier flexed-on-the-side position continued, as did the occasional use of rock fill in the pits over the bodies. During Dos Cabezas Phase, burials begin to occur in a sitting position in the grave pit, and offerings of pottery become more common. No preferred orientation is apparent.

During Mogollon 3, both side-flexed and seated-flexed burials continued in San Simon Branch, but offerings became more prevalent toward the end of the period. In Mimbres Branch, excepting Pine Lawn Valley (for which we have no data), a considerable number of burials are recorded. At Harris and Mogollon villages 56 burials and three cremations were recovered, most of them assignable to San Francisco Phase. These were scattered through the villages in extramural pits, occasionally in abandoned storage pits, and in the fill of abandoned houses. Usually they were flexed in a semi-sitting position, but occasionally on the back, and two extended prone burials were found. Fractional burials were frequent at Harris Village, the skulls missing in eight cases. Orientation was usually to the east but might be in any direction. Offerings occurred in about 30% of the burials and consisted of pottery, seed and shell beads, bracelets, and a carved bone talisman or die. The first evidence of killing of offerings occurs here in the breaking and scattering of pottery vessels through the grave. The three cremations, two of which contained offerings, were found in deep pits.

Many burials were found at Cameron Creek, scattered throughout the village in pits and in trash, but lacking specific data, it can only be surmised that some of these belong to Mogollon 3 period. Three burials assignable to the pithouse occupation were found at Starkweather Ruin, all in sub-floor pits which presumably had been plastered over while the house continued in use, a trait that did not become common until late Mogollon 4 in the Mimbres. Both extended and flexed-on-the-side burials were found, but orientation is not given. Offerings consisting of pottery, shell bracelets, and an arrowhead occurred with two of the burials.

At Bear Ruin in Forestdale Branch 40 burials were recovered, about 10 scattered at random in shallow pits throughout the village, the remainder concentrated in two burial areas. No burials were found beneath floors nor in room fill trash. Three of the burials were tightly flexed and 24 semi-flexed; 22 were placed on the back, and four on the side. Orientation was principally to the northeast or east, less commonly in

other directions. There was no evidence of cremations, nor of
fractional or multiple burial. Grave offerings, usually of
pottery, occurred with 36 of the burials. This is clearly at
variance with the usual Mogollon practice, as is concentration
of the burials into what might be termed cemetery areas.

Mogollon 4 was marked by a number of changes in burial
customs, or crystallizations of patterns begun earlier. In
San Simon Branch, simple flexed-on-the-side burial in a pit
continued, but extended burials with only the knees flexed
were an innovation during Cerros Phase. One bundle burial
was also found. Offerings were usually placed with the
bodies. In the Mimbres area as a whole, burials continued to
be placed in old storage pits, in deep trash, or in extramural
pits; but subfloor burials, especially of infants, became
increasingly common. Some of the deep pithouses at Cameron
Creek had as many as 12 subfloor burials. The bodies were
semi-flexed on the back, flexed on the side, and some were
still buried in the sitting posture. Cremation was rare but
did occur. There seems to have been no preferred orientation
of bodies. Offerings were common, most of the pottery having
been killed by breaking or by punching a hole through the
bottom of the vessel. In Pine Lawn Valley only one burial
was assigned to Three Circle Phase. This was semi-flexed
on the back, in a shallow pit in an abandoned pithouse.
Orientation was to the southwest. Several offerings were
included with the body.

In Cibola Branch, Hough (1919) found four or five infant
burials concentrated in a cemetery near one of the houses.
No details are given as to position or orientation, but offerings of small pottery vessels and the peculiar portable clay

hearths accompanied the bodies. In the eastern periphery Lehmer (1948) reported three burials from Los Tules. Two of these were in extramural pits, placed in a flexed reclining position, unaccompanied by offerings. The third burial came from the fill of an abandoned house and had a fragment of a pottery jar placed over the head.

A few general statements seem justified on the basis of our present knowledge. Throughout most of their history the Mogollon buried their dead in pits scattered at random through the villages. Often the pits were dug in the fill of abandoned houses, but perhaps as frequently they were between or near houses. Occasionally, abandoned storage or cooking pits were put to secondary use as graves, but this custom seems to have varied regionally, being more common in Pine Lawn Valley than elsewhere. Bodies were sometimes placed on the floor of an abandoned house. Does this mean that the house was abandoned because of the death of the individual? No answer is evident, but in any event, the house must still have been standing when such placement was made. Flexed inhumation was the prevailing mode, on the side, the back, or characteristically in a half-sitting position in the burial pit. Orientation to the east and northeast seems to have been slightly preferred, but there was no dominant directional predilection. Offerings were, as a rule, rare in early times, becoming somewhat more frequent in later phases, but seem never to have been numerous.

The Mogollon Culture begins with the addition of pottery
to the last phase of the Cochise Culture.  Pottery was the
last distinctive element to be added, for architecture and
agriculture had been a functioning part of the culture for
perhaps a thousand years or more.  There can be little doubt
that pottery was introduced from outside the area, for the
earliest ceramic complex appears as a thriving industry with
well established techniques.  Technically this pottery is well
made, and although only a limited number of shapes occur, it
is by no means primitive.

The main outline of Mogollon pottery development can be
summarized briefly.  The earliest horizon yet known contains
polished brown and polished red wares.  These wares, or variations of them, continue as basic wares of the ceramic
complex throughout Mogollon history.  Techniques of texturing
and neck-banding are introduced late in this plain ware horizon (Mogollon 1), perhaps from an area apart from the source
from which the Mogollon got their original pottery complex.
The first painted wares consist essentially of plain ware
bowls in which crudely executed broad-line red designs are
painted.  Later developments of this red-on-brown painting
are mainly refinements of technique and increasing complexity
of design elements and layout.  This evolution can be broken
into several technological stages, and at times, into chronologically sequent stages.  The technique of adding a lighter
slip to increase the contrast between painted decoration and

72

background is introduced during Mogollon 3.  The red-on-brown
period is terminated, or interrupted, by the innovation of a
white slip, thus producing a red-on-white pottery series.  In
the eastern and northern parts of the area, this is followed
by black-on-white pottery, while in the San Simon area there
is a return to red-on-brown.  The later phases of this ceramic
development evidence a degree of influence from neighboring
cultural provinces, but nonetheless maintain their own
integrity to a certain extent.

Gladwin (1948:127-145) called the earliest Mogollon
horizon the "stage of polished red pottery."  Reed (1948a:
383) called it "the first general Mogollon period or horizon."
For the purpose of this study, I have used the term "Mogollon
1."  Ceramically, this period is characterized by both the
polished and unpolished varieties of brown ware, and in the
southern areas, by polished red ware.  Indigenous red ware
does not occur at some of the northern sites of this period.

The following Mogollon sites have phases characterized
primarily by plain wares:

Cave Creek and San Simon Village (Sayles 1945)

SU, Promontory, Turkey Foot Ridge, Three Pines Pithouse,
Tularosa and Cordova caves (Martin and associates,
1940, 1943, 1947, 1949, 1950a, 1950b, 1952)

Bluff Site (Haury and Sayles 1947)

Mogollon and Harris villages (Haury 1936a, 1936b)

Starkweather Ruin (Nesbitt 1938)

Crooked Ridge Village (Wheat 1954)

To these sites Gladwin adds Cameron Creek Village, Vahki
Phase at Snaketown, and Luna Village.  Perhaps these should
be considered briefly before entering into a description of
the pottery of Mogollon 1.  Vahki Phase is now thought by

Gladwin to represent a Mogollon site. Since it is ordinarily classified as Hohokam, Mogollon - Vahki Phase relationships will be discussed in a later section. Luna is placed here by Gladwin purely on guesswork (Gladwin 1948:144-145). Inasmuch as architectural and ceramic evidence indicate a local variant of Three Circle Phase, Luna Village will be further discussed there. Cameron Creek, on the other hand, may have had a plain ware horizon. Since Gladwin misquotes Bradfield in order to establish this phase there, it seems necessary to examine the situation as actually reported by Bradfield.

Bradfield (1931:13-20) defined six at least partly sequent types of house structures: (1) shallow floor areas; (2) shallow pithouses without lateral entrys; (3) shallow pithouses with ramp entrys; (4) deep pithouses with ramp entrys; (5) semi-surface rooms; and (6) surface pueblos. Gladwin (1948:133) states that Bradfield did not attempt to correlate house types with pottery types. Nevertheless, Bradfield (1931:52-53) did discuss this correlation, listing a number of specific vessels associated with the second and succeeding house types, and suggests assigning earlier forms and sherds to the earlier stratigraphic positions. By close examination of Bradfield's plates and the detailed notes on each specimen in Appendix A, it is possible to identify the types with considerable accuracy.

These vessels, as listed by Bradfield, with my own identifications as to type, are as follows. For House Type 2, vessels 215 and 223 (Alma Neck-banded), and 258 (Mogollon Red-on-brown), obviously a San Francisco Phase association. Bradfield (1931:52) also states, "This places the well developed rubbed corrugated vessels principally within this

period, at this site," apparently referring to Three Circle
Neck-corrugated or Alma Neck-banded types.  For the later
years of Type 3 and the earlier occupation of Type 4 houses,
Bradfield lists vessels 419 (Alma Plain); 101-28 and 430
(Alma Scored); 214, 373, 375, 103-28, and 106-28 (Three Circle
Neck-corrugated); 159, 284, 410, 102-28, and 103-28 (San
Francisco Red); 378 and 131-28 (Three Circle Red-on-white or
early Bold Face Black-on-white); 271, 289, 333, 376, 377,
412, 428, 429, 96-28, 104-28, 105-28, and 108-28 (Bold Face
Black-on-white); and 110-28 (Mogollon Red-on-brown).  With
the exception of the last, this is a consistent Three Circle
Phase association.  The Mogollon Red-on-brown is out of
context, and from its locus in the site might well be earlier
than the house beneath whose floor it was found.  Moreover,
some of the Bold Face Black-on-white is clearly late and
transitional to Mimbres Black-on-white.

For late occupation of Type 4 and Type 5 houses,
Bradfield lists vessels 24, 91, 147, and 421 (Mimbres
Corrugated); 101, 113 (Mimbres Black-on-white); 248 and 384
(Mimbres Black-on-white zoomorphic bowls), a Mangus or
Mimbres Phase association.  Type 6 houses contained Mimbres
Black-on-white and its associated types.

Bradfield does not identify the ceramic complex of the
Type 1 houses.  By default, these may be Pine Lawn, Georgetown,
San Lorenzo, or may even be preceramic, as Gladwin (1948:131)
suggests earlier.  However, Type 2 houses differ from Type 1
only in being slightly deeper, and therefore, probably belong
to the same period, San Francisco Phase, where I have
considered them in this study.

Gladwin quotes Bradfield as saying that red ware sherds

were the first type to find lodgement in the rock crevices
below the trash mound, implying that this is the type, San
Francisco Red; but Bradfield (1931:32-33) is talking about
his Early Red Paste type, not San Francisco Red.  It is important to note that Early Red Paste includes Alma Plain and
its variations (Bradfield's vessels 244, 328, 430, 106-28,
etc.), Three Circle Neck-corrugated (vessels 212, 268, 288,
etc.), Mogollon Red-on-brown (vessel 110-28), Bold Face Black-
on-white (259, 300, 429, etc.), and Mimbres Black-on-white
(186), as well as San Francisco Red (284, 97-28, etc.).
Gladwin's misinterpretation arises from his mistaken assumption that Bradfield's paste types correspond to pottery types
as used by Southwestern archeologists today when, in fact,
they cross-cut them.  Significant, also, is the pottery complex of the lowest refuse stratum immediately overlying the
rock crevices mentioned above.  Here, plain ware constituted
about 91%; plain coiled, 2%; red ware, 5%; and early decorated
ware, 2% (Bradfield 1931:40-41).

The only statement made by Bradfield (and one which Gladwin does not quote) to support the presence of a plain ware
horizon is as follows: "We find that entirely plain vessels
were the first to be made here.  Bowls covered with a red
wash were then introduced, and many sherds are found showing
its use on bowls that had evidently been made without other
pottery-making tools than the hands and fingers themselves."
(Bradfield 1931:44).  This statement has tantalizing implications, but as the evidence on which it is based is not given,
it is not possible to determine its precise significance.
Nevertheless, it seems possible that Cameron Creek was occupied during the plain ware stage.

### Pottery of Mogollon 1

Many uniformities mark the ceramic complex of the various branches during this period.  But there are also well-defined regional variations which make it possible in some cases to determine readily the origin of specific plain ware sherds. Since adequate type descriptions are available for all but the San Simon series, it is necessary here only to point out similarities and differences between the various branches and to trace the general development of Mogollon ceramics.

During Mogollon 1 six basic pottery types were produced. Plain brown ware, either polished or unpolished, constitutes the dominant pottery of all Mogollon horizons.  During Mogollon 1 about 85% of all pottery produced belongs to one or another of the variants of Alma Plain.  Typologically, the simplest of these are the unpolished varieties termed Alma Rough (Martin and Rinaldo 1941), Alma Plain, Early (Sayles 1945), and Alma Plain, Bluff Variety (Haury and Sayles 1947). All of these types are characterized by hand-smoothing resulting in somewhat irregular surfaces.  Some vessels may well have been hand-molded rather than built up by coiling.  The predominant color is some shade of brown.  Each type, however, is individualized by particular forms and by the nature of paste inclusions.  In this latter respect the principal point to note is that in southern types angular particles predominate, while in northern varieties roundish particles are more common.  It seems probable that these differences are primarily the result of local geologic conditions.

Although technologically superior to the pottery types just considered, the stone-polished varieties of Alma Plain constitute the bulk of pottery recovered at every site yet

known, including Bluff Site where polished fine-paste brown
ware constituted an additional minority type. The finish is
smoother, the paste more compact, the color varies more, and
there is a greater range of forms. Surface color of the several varieties of Alma Plain ranges from light tan through
reddish-brown to dark brown and gray. Again, the varieties
reflect local geologic conditions in the matter of paste inclusions. Southern varieties are generally characterized by
angular temper particles, northern ones by rounded particles
of sand.

In every branch except Forestdale, an indigenous red
ware, San Francisco Red, was a normal part of the ceramic
complex during Mogollon 1. Most of this pottery was well
made and polished, but local varieties can sometimes be recognized by surface finish, slip color, or paste differences.
Sayles (1945:39) recognized an early variant in which the slip
color usually is a dark purplish-red or magenta. The slip is
usually thin and the vessels are seldom highly polished. In
most respects the normal San Simon variant of San Francisco
Red is similar to the Mimbres variety but lacks the "hammered"
or finger-dented surface of the latter. The color is typically a rosy hue. In Pine Lawn Valley, Martin (1941:240) notes
the following differences from the Mimbres type in his Saliz
variety: "lack of finger-dented surfaces, deeper rose color,
rarity of marks of polishing tool, coarser paste, less highly
polished and less lustrous surface." Most San Francisco Red
of the Black River Branch cannot be distinguished from that
of the Mimbres, although the dimpled form is perhaps less
prevalent. However, a local variety showing the characteristic gold mica and other inclusions, in which the slip is

both thinner and not so well fired, does occur.

Some time during Mogollon 1, probably near the end, several innovations in pottery technology occur. These are smudging; texturing by incising, scoring, or brushing; and neck-banding. None of these traits was widespread during this time, and all except, perhaps, smudging, may well have been confined to Mimbres Branch as far as actual manufacture is concerned. Texturing and neck-banding do not occur in Penasco or Pine Lawn Phase. No neck-banded sherds were found in Circle Prairie Phase, and so few textured sherds occurred that they very probably represent trade with Georgetown Phase of the Mimbres rather than local production. The evidence is not so clear in regard to smudging. Haury (1936a:32) mentions the occurrence of occasional smudged sherds in Georgetown Phase associations. Smudged ware was not found in Penasco Phase nor in Pine Lawn Phase, but Martin and his co-workers (1952:58) record its occurrence in Georgetown Phase levels in Tularosa Cave. On the basis of statistical tests, they regard the smudged sherds as intrusive from later levels, but the presence of two whole bowls in floor contact and a number of sherds from early Circle Prairie Phase at Black River Branch, the equivalent of Georgetown, leaves little doubt that smudged ware was a consistent, if minor, product of the times. In the Forestdale area Woodruff Smudged, in small quantities which suggest either trade or the beginning steps in the manufacture of smudged ware, was found associated with Hilltop Phase houses. The precise relationships of Woodruff Smudged are not known, but it is presumably a Mogollon type and may be ancestral to the more evolved Forestdale Smudged of Mogollon 2 and 3.

While paste variations between the different branches may well reflect environmental resources, differences in vessel forms must reflect cultural factors. Twenty-three vessel forms and numerous intergrade shapes were made during Mogollon 1 (Fig. 3). For the most part, these are simple in character, although a few compound forms were also produced. The distribution of these pottery shapes by ware and branch is given in chart form in Figure 3. While not produced in as great numbers, the most prevalent form in Mogollon 1 times was the hemispherical bowl (Fig. 3, a). Excepting neck-banded ware, it was made in every ware in every branch at this time. Smudged wares, because of the technique involved, were produced only in bowl form. A globular jar with outdrawn neck (Fig. 3, b), made in all branches and in most wares, was probably more numerous, since jars out-numbered bowls about four or five to one. A modified form of the globular jar, with a smaller orifice (Fig. 3, d), and a somewhat flattened spherical "seed" jar (Fig. 3, c) were produced in all branches except Forestdale, usually in polished brown or red ware. Three forms, a shallow plate-like bowl (Fig. 3, e), a globular wide-mouthed jar with slightly outcurved neck (Fig. 3, f), and a globular jar with strongly outcurved or flaring neck (Fig. 3, g), were shared by San Simon, Mimbres, and Black River branches. The shallow bowl was made usually in red ware, while the other shapes were most frequently polished brown ware. In San Simon Branch, however, both shallow bowl and wide-mouthed jar forms were made in unpolished brown ware as well. A barrel-shaped jar (Fig. 3, h), made in both polished and unpolished brown ware, was shared by San Simon and Pine Lawn Valley. Black River and San Simon potters produced a

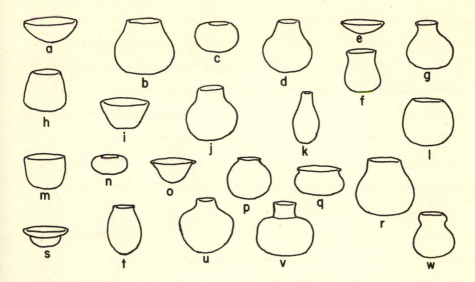

POTTERY TYPE                                        VESSEL SHAPE

| | a | b | c | d | e | f | g | h | i | j | k | l | m | n | o | p | q | r | s | t | u | v | w |
|---|---|---|---|---|---|---|---|---|---|---|---|---|---|---|---|---|---|---|---|---|---|---|---|
| **San Simon** | | | | | | | | | | | | | | | | | | | | | | | |
| Unpolished Brown | x | x | x | | x | x | | x | x | | | | x | x | | | | | | | | | |
| Polished Brown | x | x | x | | x | x | x | x | x | | | | x | x | | | | | | | | | |
| Polished Red | x | x | | x | x | | | | | | | | | x | | | | | | | | | |
| **Mimbres** | | | | | | | | | | | | | | | | | | | | | | | |
| Polished Brown | x | x | x | x | | x | x | | | x | | | | | x | | | | | | | | |
| Polished Red | x | x | | x | x | | | | | | | | | | | x | x | | | | | | |
| Neck-banded | | | | | | | | | | | | | | | | | | x | | | | | |
| Textured | x | | | | | | | | | x | | | | | | | | | | | | | |
| Smudged | x | | | | | | | | | | | | | | | | | | | | | | |
| **Pine Lawn Valley** | | | | | | | | | | | | | | | | | | | | | | | |
| Unpolished Brown | x | x | x | | | | | x | | | | | | | | | | | | | | | |
| Polished Brown | x | x | x | | | | | x | | | | | | | | | | | | | | | |
| Polished Red | x | | | x | | | | | | | x | | | | | | | x | | | | | |
| Smudged | x | | | | | | | | | | | | | | | | | | | | | | |
| **Forestdale** | | | | | | | | | | | | | | | | | | | | | | | |
| Unpolished Brown | x | | | | | | | | | | x | | | | | | | | | x | | | |
| Polished Brown | x | x | | | | | | | | | x | | | | | | | | | | | | |
| Smudged | x | | | | | | | | | | | | | | | | | | | | | | |
| **Black River** | | | | | | | | | | | | | | | | | | | | | | | |
| Polished Brown | x | x | x | x | | x | x | | | x | x | x | | | | | | | | | x | x | x |
| Polished Red | x | x | | | x | | | x | | | | | | | | | | | | | | | |
| Smudged | x | | | | | | | | | | | | | | | | | | | | | | |
| **Total Forms** | | | | | | | | | | | | | | | | | | | | | | | |
| San Simon | x | x | x | x | x | x | x | x | x | | | | x | x | | | | | | | | | |
| Mimbres | x | x | x | x | x | x | x | | | x | | | | | x | x | x | x | | | | | |
| Pine Lawn | x | x | x | x | | | | x | | | x | | | | | | | x | | | | | |
| Forestdale | x | x | | | | | | | | | x | | | | | | | | | x | | | |
| Black River | x | x | x | x | x | x | x | | x | x | x | x | | | | | | | | | x | x | x |

Figure 3. Mogollon Vessel Forms and their Distribution,
during Mogollon 1.

flat-bottomed bowl with straight flaring sides (Fig. 3, i),
but while made in brown ware in San Simon, it has been noted
only in red ware in Black River Branch. Small-mouthed globular jars with vertical necks (Fig. 3, j) were made in polished
brown and textured wares in the Mimbres area, and in polished
brown ware in Black River Branch. Slender-necked bottles
(Fig. 3, k) were produced in red ware in Pine Lawn Valley and
in polished brown ware in Black River Branch. Forestdale and
Black River branches shared the spherical "seed" jar made in
brown ware (Fig. 3, l).

In addition to the various forms shared by two or more
branches, certain forms were peculiar to only one branch. In
San Simon Branch, a deep cup-like bowl (Fig. 3, m) and a flattened "seed" jar (Fig. 3, n) were made in brown ware, while
the latter was produced also in red ware. Four shapes are
reported only from Mimbres Branch excluding Pine Lawn Valley.
These are a deep bowl with somewhat flaring rim (Fig. 3, o)
made in polished brown ware; a globular jar with low outcurved
rim (Fig. 3, p) and a bowl with recurved rim (Fig. 3, q) produced in polished red ware; and neck-banded jars (Fig. 3, r)
which otherwise are very similar in shape to Fig. 3, b. A
bowl of compound silhouette with broad concave flaring rim
(Fig. 3, s) made in red ware, has been reported only from
Pine Lawn Valley. Forestdale Branch also had one peculiar
form, an egg-shaped jar with slightly everted rim (Fig. 3, t)
produced in unpolished brown ware. Three vessel forms have
been reported only from Black River Branch from a Mogollon 1
horizon. One (Fig. 3, u) is a high-shouldered variant of
Fig. 3, b, another is a flattened spherical jar with a high
cylindrical neck (Fig. 3, v), and the third is a type

constricted above the center, for which I propose the name "strangulated jar" (Fig. 3, w). All of these forms were made in polished brown ware.

No site with a pure unpolished brown ware pottery complex has yet been found. The greatest variety of unpolished brown ware shapes was made in San Simon Branch where Alma Plain, Early, was produced in nine shapes. In Pine Lawn Valley four forms occur in Alma Rough, and in Forestdale three shapes were made in the Bluff variety of Alma Plain. Thus it is clear that as the north is approached the ceramic complex becomes simpler. When the polished varieties of Alma Plain, San Francisco Red, smudged, textured, and neck-banded wares are added to the unpolished varieties, the picture is changed. Twelve vessel forms were made in the Mimbres area, eleven in the San Simon, seven in Pine Lawn Valley, and four in Forestdale. Black River Branch is characterized by fourteen vessel forms, but it may well be that the few idiosyncratic shapes should be discounted. Or, this may reflect a greater influence from outside the Mogollon area.

Table 7 shows the number of pottery shapes shared by the various branches, the number of forms peculiar to each branch, and the total number of vessel shapes produced in each branch.

Table 7

| BRANCH | San Simon | Mimbres | Pine Lawn | Forestdale | Black River |
|---|---|---|---|---|---|
| San Simon | (11) 2 | 7 | 5 | 2 | 8 |
| Mimbres | 7 | (12) 4 | 4 | 2 | 8 |
| Pine Lawn | 5 | 4 | (7) 1 | 2 | 5 |
| Forestdale | 2 | 2 | 2 | (4) 1 | 3 |
| Black River | 8 | 8 | 5 | 3 | (14) 3 |

Table 7. Number of shared pottery forms between branches; number of unique forms, and total number of vessel shapes produced (in parentheses), at column intersections. Mogollon 1.

Analysis of this table suggests that, so far as vessel forms are concerned, San Simon, Mimbres, and Black River branches are closely related ceramically, while Pine Lawn Valley and Forestdale appear somewhat peripheral. Nevertheless, the majority of forms produced in any one area are shared with one or more of the other areas, further suggesting a common complex for Mogollon 1 times. In all probability, as additional excavation is carried on in the early Mogollon horizons most of the vessel forms which now appear peculiar will prove to be commonly produced shapes.

Data for analysis of vessel size in the various branches are inadequate, but the general impression is that vessels of San Simon, Mimbres, and Pine Lawn Valley average about the same size; those of Forestdale Branch are smaller, and those of Black River are larger. Finally, it may be reiterated that while these branches clearly belong to the same basic ceramic complex, each maintains a distinctive combination of traits within the general group.

### Pottery of Mogollon 2

The most important innovation in the pottery of Mogollon 2 is painted decoration. It is true that four sherds of a broad-line red-on-brown pottery occurred in Georgetown Phase at Harris Village, but whether these are from the floor, or the fill, is not stated. Six similar sherds occurred in the fill of early Circle Prairie Phase houses at Crooked Ridge Village. Thus, it cannot be stated with certainty whether these types should be considered as indigenous painted types of Mogollon 1 period, or if they are stray sherds of a Mogollon 2 type as yet undefined. Typologically they are similar to Dos Cabezas Red-on-brown, the only surely defined painted type of Mogollon 2.

Dos Cabezas Red-on-brown is the index type for Dos Cabezas Phase in San Simon Branch, for although it continued into Pinaleno Phase (Mogollon 3), it occurred stratigraphically below Pinaleno Red-on-brown in pure associations. Furthermore, a variant of the type with decoration in specular iron paint was confined to Dos Cabezas Phase. There is a question as to whether Dos Cabezas Red-on-brown should be considered a decorated version of Alma Plain or of San Francisco Red, for although the exterior is slipped with the magenta color of early San Francisco Red, it is not polished as in the case of San Francisco Red. Design elements consist of broad rectilinear lines in red pigment on the interior of bowls which were polished over after painting, so that the line edges are streaked and blurred. Sectional patterns are built up of "pendant rim triangles and bordering lines; pendant rim triangles joined in the center and bordering lines; bordering lines may form either chevrons or join the main section lines." (Sayles 1945:42) Firing clouds are frequent. Deep hemispherical bowls (Fig. 3, a) seem to have been the only form produced.

Neither Black River nor Forestdale, the two other branches where a Mogollon 2 horizon has been established, has a clearly defined painted type, although, as mentioned above, the broad-line red-on-brown sherds from Crooked Ridge Village may represent such a type.

There are insufficient data to trace, with any degree of certainty, the development of plain wares, red wares, and textured types during Mogollon 2, but a few observations may be made. In San Simon Branch the early variant of Alma Plain

became less common and the rather straight-sided bowl form
(Fig. 3, m) appears to have died out, while the flat-bottomed
conoid form (Fig. 3, i) continued only in miniature size.  In
Black River Branch no changes have been defined, except that
during Mogollon 2 there seems to have been a great deal more
commerce with other areas.  In Forestdale Branch the Bluff
variety of Alma Plain died out, having been completely sup-
planted by the Forestdale variety.  More vessel forms were
made, including spherical "seed" jars (Fig. 3, l); low-necked,
everted-rim jars (Fig. 3, p); vertical-rim jars (Fig. 3, b);
and hemispherical bowls (Fig. 3, a, e).  Applique' decoration
was occasionally used around the mouth of "seed" jar forms.

Fine-paste brown ware continued as a minor element in
the ceramic complex and apparently was ancestral to Forestdale Smudged and Forestdale Red types, which became dominant
only in Mogollon 3.  However, the smudging technique appears
during Mogollon 2, but probably was derived from Woodruff
Smudged, which is stratigraphically earlier.  A few sherds of
red ware were also recovered, but whether these are indigenous
or intrusive is not clear.  They may well represent the unnamed red ware which also occurred as an intrusive at Crooked
Ridge Village.

Thus it may be seen that the ceramic complex of Mogollon
2 confronts us with several important problems.  Some of these
concern relationships of Woodruff smudged and red wares to
those of Forestdale Branch, and to Mogollon pottery in general.
Origin and relationships of Adamana Brown constitute another
problem which can be solved only by more excavation in the
northern periphery of the Mogollon area.  Another major problem demanding investigation is the position of San Lorenzo

Red-on-brown pottery. On the basis of typology, it appears
intermediate between Dos Cabezas Red-on-brown and Mogollon
Red-on-brown. Much of it is broad-lined and comparatively
crudely drawn, in which respect it resembles Dos Cabezas; but
other sherds more closely resemble Pinaleno Red-on-brown of
the Mogollon 3 period. The type has not been isolated stratigraphically in the Mimbres, but it occurs in small amounts in
San Francisco Phase houses and not at all in houses of Georgetown Phase. It has been found intrusive in Mogollon 2 horizons in both San Simon and Black River branches. This would
argue for the reality of a phase, as yet undefined, in which
San Lorenzo Red-on-brown would be the principal decorated
type; but convincing proof of such a period has not yet been
given. Martin and his associates (1949:199, 201) have con-
cluded that there was no San Lorenzo Phase in Pine Lawn Valley, nor in the Reserve area; but its absence there does not
disprove its existence elsewhere. This remains a problem to
be argued with the shovel. Purely on the basis of typology,
the pottery type and perhaps the phase, also, if it can be
defined, would appear to be transitional between Mogollon 2
and Mogollon 3.

Available ceramic evidence seems to indicate that Mogollon 2, as a well defined complex, was confined to the southern
part of the Mogollon area. The placing of late Circle Prairie
Phase in Mogollon 2 is on a basis of trade relationships,
while the inclusion of Cottonwood Phase here is because of its
stratigraphic position between the clearly defined Mogollon 1
Hilltop Phase and the equally well established Mogollon 3
Forestdale Phase. It would be equally plausible to consider
Cottonwood Phase simply as late Mogollon 1, but the number of

new traits which appear at this time make the Mogollon 2 placement more convenient. The situation in Pine Lawn Valley is susceptible to several interpretations. It will be recalled that only one house in the valley has been tentatively assigned to Georgetown Phase. Thus, there is almost no evidence of outside influence in the area from the beginning of Pine Lawn Phase until the sudden appearance of San Francisco Phase (Mogollon 3). While such could not be proved at present, it seems logical that Pine Lawn Phase continued until some time in Mogollon 3, without having passed through a Mogollon 2 period at all.

### Pottery of Mogollon 3

Ceramics of Mogollon 3 are marked primarily by continuation of earlier traditions. Such changes as did occur emerge largely as developments of pre-existing norms, but certain innovations appear as clear departures, and almost certainly represent influences from outside sources. While plain, textured, neck-banded, and red wares continue with few modifications, painted ware was rapidly developing on the broad-line red-on-brown base of Mogollon 2. Painted pottery types belonging to Mogollon 3 are Pinaleno and Galiuro Red-on-brown of San Simon Branch, San Lorenzo Red-on-brown (in part), Mogollon Red-on-brown, and Three Circle Red-on-white. There is evidence pointing to a sequential development, but the picture is by no means clear. In San Simon Branch Pinaleno and Galiuro red-on-brown types appear as sequent peaks in a single continuous development. Their isolation as types was based on stratigraphy and clearly shows Pinaleno to be a transitional type between Dos Cabezas Red-on-brown, which occurs with decreasing frequency through Pinaleno Phase, and Galiuro

Red-on-brown.  The general trend is refinement of design and painting techniques.  Line work becomes more narrow and more precise, with fine lines predominating in Galiuro Phase.  Layout and design elements also exemplify the continuous refinement that was taking place.  Sectional layouts continued, with offset quartered sectioning appearing in Galiuro Phase.  During Pinaleno Phase a modification of the pendant triangle layout began, in which an encircling band of triangles pendant from the rim was opposed by triangles separated by a series of zig-zag lines.  Further modification of the pendant triangle layout occurred in Galiuro Red-on-brown.  Design elements became increasingly complex with the innovation of hatching and cross-hatching in Pinaleno Phase, followed by checkerboard patterns and various combinations of other existing elements in Galiuro Phase.  Polishing over the decoration was commonly, but not universally, practised, while the general overall finish of decorated wares was better than that of Dos Cabezas Red-on-brown.  Bowls were the most common painted forms, but painted jars increase in frequency as we come up in time.

If it is remembered that San Lorenzo Red-on-brown shares typological similarities with both Dos Cabezas and Pinaleno Red-on-brown, then it can be seen that the developmental sequence of painted pottery in the Mimbres followed much the same course as in the San Simon.  It should be reiterated, however, that such a development in the Mimbres is based only on typology, inasmuch as its stratigraphic placement has not yet been demonstrated.  In any event, the typological range of Mogollon 3 red-on-brown pottery closely follows that of the San Simon.  The same range of layout was practised, with quartered and otherwise sectioned fields and pendant rim triangles with variations constituting the principal types. Most design elements are similar, with perhaps a greater variety in Mimbres Branch.

In addition to those elements described for San Simon Branch are serrate lines and borders, rectilinear simple scrolls, and very rarely curvilinear elements. Although the exterior of both San Lorenzo and Mogollon red-on-brown was red-slipped and polished, the interior treatment of bowls differed somewhat. On all of San Lorenzo and some of Mogollon red-on-brown, design elements were painted directly on the polished but unslipped base clay of the vessel, then polished over the decoration. The background color was dark, leaving little contrast between design and base. This was remedied in most Mogollon Red-on-brown by using a light tan or pinkish interior slip as a base for the red designs. With the technique of interior slipping firmly established, no great change is needed for the introduction of a white slip to produce Three Circle Red-on-white, for as Martin and Rinaldo (1950a: 362-368) have shown, there is a direct continuity of design elements, the white slip being the only exotic element.

There are a number of problems concerned with the introduction of Three Circle Red-on-white. Presumably, use of a white slip was introduced from the Anasazi; but it should be recalled that white slips were just coming into use in the north at about the same time that Three Circle Red-on-white was coming into use. There is also a question as to when this type was introduced in San Francisco Phase. Haury (1936a:42, Fig. 9) indicates a late introduction, with the type carrying over into early Three Circle Phase.

This placement was based on the fact that while Three Circle Red-on-white was common in San Francisco Phase houses at Harris Village, it was rare in what Haury considered to be early San Francisco Phase houses at Mogollon Village. On the other hand, Nesbitt (1938) found Three Circle Red-on-white in what he termed early San Francisco Phase houses, which, if correct, would place the beginning of both Mogollon Red-on-brown and Three Circle Red-on-white at about the same time. However, it should be noted that Nesbitt did not follow the usual archeological practice of dating stratigraphic levels by the latest sherds in them, nor in assigning phases. Therefore, there is some question as to whether his early San Francisco Phase houses are that, or are just early for the site. For the same reason, the consistent occurrence of Mimbres Bold Face Black-on-white in some of the houses assigned by Nesbitt to San Francisco Phase would rather seem to justify a Three Circle Phase placement, which is where I have considered them in this study.

Finally, there is a question as to the center of origin of Three Circle Red-on-white. Haury (1936a:20) believed its focus was in the Mimbres drainage proper, but the abundant representation of the type in Pine Lawn Valley makes it clear that a secondary focus existed there. None of these questions can be settled without further stratigraphic excavation, but the problem of the relative chronological relationship of Mogollon Red-on-brown and Three Circle Red-on-white should be a primary one when future excavation is undertaken in the Mimbres area.

Martin and Rinaldo (1950a:368-369) have concisely summarized some of the similarities and differences between San

Lorenzo Red-on-brown, Mogollon Red-on-brown, Three Circle Red-on-white, and Mimbres Bold Face Black-on-white, and have traced the development of design elements from Mogollon Red-on-brown through Mimbres Bold Face Black-on-white (ibid.:362-367). Their study shows that parallel medium-width lines constituted the primary design element in all three types considered, but declined from about 65 to 44 percent from early to late. Solid triangles remained fairly constant at about 22 percent, although being somewhat less popular in the decoration of Three Circle Red-on-white. Serrate lines increased in frequency from early to late (7.11% to 13.46%), as did serrate-edged triangles (0.44% to 5.94%). On the other hand, pennants decreased from early to late (3.11% to 0.17%), followed by ticked triangles (2.66% to 0.14%) in Three Circle Red-on-white, none in Mimbres Bold Face Black-on-white. Zig-zag lines or spaces, diamond cross-hatching, and checkerboard elements were not found by Martin and Rinaldo for Mogollon Red-on-brown, but Haury (1936a:10-17) shows examples of all these, so they must be included in the design roster. However, all of these appear to culminate in Three Circle Red-on-white and to decrease slightly in favor in Mimbres Bold Face Black-on-white. Haury (ibid.:15) also shows a spiral element from Mogollon Red-on-brown, but this, too, increases sharply in Three Circle Red-on-white and Mimbres Bold Face Black-on-white. Thus the continuity of design and layout, as well, seems clearly established.

In the matter of paste characteristics, San Lorenzo and Mogollon red-on-brown are tempered with crushed rock and a few rounded quartz grains; but the paste of Mogollon Red-on-brown is finer, harder, and also is sometimes tempered with

crushed sherds.  Three Circle Red-on-white has finer hetero-
geneous inclusions and is somewhat harder.  Firing control
seems to have been better in the earlier wares, for fire
clouds become increasingly common in the later wares.

There are few changes in the plain ware of Mogollon 3,
and these are primarily changes of relative proportions in
the ceramic complex.  Alma Plain, Early, and Alma Rough almost
disappear but continue as minor elements.  Alma Plain de-
creases in frequency as Alma Textured and Alma Neck-banded
become more common.  Finally, with the increasing popularity
of painted wares, San Francisco Red decreased in frequency.
In San Simon Branch a late variant of Alma Plain appeared,
characterized by heavier fire clouding and poor finish, while
in Forestdale Branch a new type, Forestdale Plain, sharing
characteristics of Alma Plain and the Anasazi type, Lino Gray,
came into being.  Forestdale Red, an unslipped red ware
achieved by firing, and Forestdale Smudged developed and were
widely traded during Mogollon 3.

Many of the vessel forms manufactured during Mogollon 1
continued without change into Mogollon 3, but some died out
(Fig. 3, g, i-k, o, p, r, s, u-w) and a few new ones took
their place (Fig. 4, f, g, k, m, n, r-t).  The pottery complex of Mogollon 3 is detailed in Figure 4.  Twenty vessel
shapes were made, of which five (Fig. 4, a-e) were produced
in most wares and in all branches where we control sufficient
data for analysis.  All of these shapes except one (Fig. 4, e)
were also produced in painted ware, as were two new forms,
Figure 4, f, a deep wide-mouthed jar, and Figure 4, g, a bottle form.  Two jar forms, the spherical "seed" bowl (Fig. 4,
h) and a wide-mouthed jar (Fig. 4, i) were shared by Mimbres,

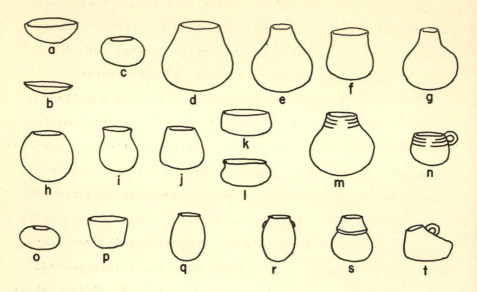

| POTTERY TYPE | a | b | c | d | e | f | g | h | i | j | k | l | m | n | o | p | q | r | s | t |
|---|---|---|---|---|---|---|---|---|---|---|---|---|---|---|---|---|---|---|---|---|
| **San Simon** | | | | | | | | | | | | | | | | | | | | |
| Alma Plain | x | x | x | x | | | | | | x | | | | | x | | | | | |
| Red Ware | x | x | | | x | | | | | | | | | | x | | | | | |
| Painted Ware | x | x | | | | | | | | | | | | | | | | | | |
| **Mimbres** | | | | | | | | | | | | | | | | | | | | |
| Alma Plain | x | | x | x | x | | | x | x | | x | | | | | | | | | |
| Alma Textured | | | x | | | | | | | | | | | | | | | | | |
| Alma Neck-banded | | | | | | | | | | | | | x | x | | | | | | |
| Smudged | x | | | | | | | | | | | | | | | | | | | |
| Red Ware | x | x | x | x | | | | | | | | x | | | | | | | | |
| Painted Ware | x | x | x | x | | x | x | | | | | | | | | | | | | |
| **Pine Lawn** | | | | | | | | | | | | | | | | | | | | |
| Alma Plain | x | | x | | | | | x | | x | | | | | | | | | | |
| Alma Textured | | | | x | | | | | x | | | | | | | | | | | |
| Alma Neck-banded | | | | | | | | | | | | | x | x | | | | | | |
| Smudged | x | x | | | | | | | | | | | | | | | | | | |
| Red Ware | x | x | x | | x | | | | | | | x | | | | | | | | |
| Painted Ware | x | x | | | | | | | | | | | | | | | | | | |
| **Forestdale** | | | | | | | | | | | | | | | | | | | | |
| Alma Plain | x | | x | x | x | | | x | x | | | | | | | | x | x | x | |
| Forestdale Plain | | x | | x | | | | | x | | | x | | | | | | x | x | x |
| Smudged | x | x | | | | | | | | | | | x | | | x | | x | x | x |
| Red Ware | x | x | | | | | | | | | | x | x | | | | x | | | |
| **Total Forms** | | | | | | | | | | | | | | | | | | | | |
| San Simon | x | x | x | x | x | | | | x | | | | | x | | | | | | |
| Mimbres | x | x | x | x | x | x | x | x | x | | x | x | x | x | | | | | | |
| Pine Lawn | x | x | x | x | x | | | x | x | x | | x | x | x | | | | | | |
| Forestdale | x | x | x | x | x | | | x | x | x | | x | x | | | x | x | x | x | x |

Figure 4. Mogollon Vessel Forms and their Distribution during Mogollon 3.

Pine Lawn, and Forestdale potters who made them in polished brown and textured wares. The simple barrel-like jar (Fig. 4, j) was made of plain or red ware in both San Simon and Pine Lawn. Two deep bowl forms, one with incurved rim (Fig. 4, k) and one with recurved rim (Fig. 4, l) were shared by Mimbres and Forestdale branches. Neck-banded jars (Fig. 4, m) and handled pitchers (Fig. 4, n) were made in the Mimbres and in Pine Lawn Valley. Flattened "seed" bowls (Fig. 4, o) of plain and red wares are reported only from San Simon. Five vessel shapes, cup-shaped bowls (Fig. 4, p), the egg-shaped jar (Fig. 4, q) and a variant with vertical lugs (Fig. 4, r), a jar with compound silhouette (Fig. 4, s), and a bird form or shoe-shaped jar (Fig. 4, t) were confined to Forestdale Branch.

The number of pottery shapes shared by each of the branches, the total number of forms produced, and the number of peculiar forms in each branch are presented in Table 8. From this it is clear that, despite the number of forms peculiar to Forestdale Branch, fewer shapes were being made during Mogollon 3. Furthermore, there is an evident trend toward uniformity in the Mogollon pottery complex. The exotic forms (Fig. 4, s and t) made in Forestdale Branch probably reflect influence from nearby Anasazi potters.

Table 8

| BRANCH | San Simon | Mimbres | Pine Lawn | Forestdale |
|---|---|---|---|---|
| San Simon | (7)   1 | 5 | 6 | 5 |
| Mimbres | 5 | (13)  2 | 9 | 9 |
| Pine Lawn | 6 | 9 | (10)  0 | 7 |
| Forestdale | 5 | 9 | 7 | (14)  5 |

Table 8. Number of shared pottery forms between branches; number of unique forms, and total number of vessel shapes produced (in parentheses) at column intersections. Mogollon 3.

One further item needs to be noted. It was during Mogollon 3, judging from the occasional accompanying Mogollon
Red-on-brown sherd, that a Mogollon ceramic complex began to
move eastward into the adjacent Rio Grande drainage. Mera
(1943) has traced this movement in as great detail as possible, lacking adequate excavation. The brown ware complex
moving north and east came into contact with a southward-
moving Basketmaker influence. The combination of these two
influences resulted in San Marcial Phase, of which little is
known. Another significant result of this eastward movement
of brown ware pottery was a progressive coarsening of the
original Alma Plain through a series of short-lived local
types which eventuated in the Mogollon 4 types, Jornada Brown
and El Paso Brown.

### Pottery of Mogollon 4

Both continuity and change mark the pottery of Mogollon
4. In Mimbres Branch the period is begun when Mimbres Bold
Face Black-on-white is developed from Three Circle Red-on-
white, a type which originated in Mogollon 3 and carried over
into Mogollon 4. The relationships and characteristics of
these types have already been discussed.

In San Simon Branch a surviving Galiuro Red-on-brown was
supplemented by Cerros Red-on-white. The chief reason for
including Cerros Phase in Mogollon 4 is that, although the
situation is similar to that of Mogollon Red-on-brown and
Three Circle Red-on-white in Mimbres Branch, Sayles was able
to isolate a phase characterized by architectural and other
components, as well as by pottery. Furthermore, there was
reason to believe that Cerros Red-on-white, as a type, continued longer than Three Circle Red-on-white and was not

merely a transitional type. Nevertheless, there is some con-
fusion existing, and it may be that future investigations
would divide Cerros Phase between Galiuro and Encinas to correspond with the situation as it is known in the Mimbres. The
pottery type, Cerros Red-on-white, appears as a regional variant of Three Circle Red-on-white.

There are few innovations in the non-painted pottery of
Mogollon 4. The trend, noted in Mogollon 3, toward reduction
of Alma Plain and its variants and of San Francisco Red, as
texturing, neck-corrugation, and painted pottery increase in
percentile frequency, was continued in Mogollon 4. The most
important change was the evolution of Three Circle Neck-corrugated from Alma Neck-banded, which died out early in Mogollon 4. With this shift there was a general coarsening of
paste which became even more pronounced in succeeding periods.
While texturing continued, the specific variation of scoring
died out during Three Circle Phase. Smudging was preserved
in such types as Reserve Smudged, which was ancestral to Reserve Fillet Rim, a rare type associated with Three Circle
Phase in Pine Lawn Valley; and this, in turn, gave rise to
Tularosa Fillet Rim of Mogollon 5. No major changes occurred
in San Francisco Red. An analysis of the pottery complex of
Mogollon 4 is presented in Figure 5.

During Mogollon 4 vessels were made in twenty main shapes
with numerous intergrading forms between. Adequate data are
available only for San Simon, Mimbres, and Pine Lawn. Deep
hemispherical and shallow bowls (Fig. 5, a and b) and globular
jars with outdrawn necks (Fig. 5, c) are noted for all
branches and nearly all wares. It is likely that several
other shapes were made in all branches, but our data are not

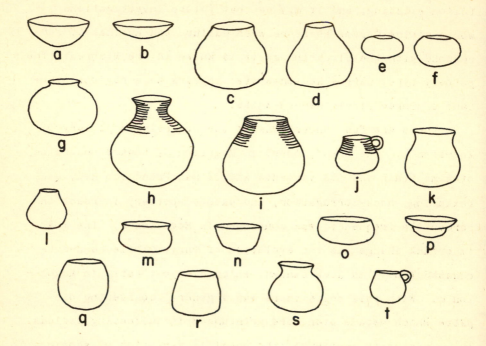

Figure 5. Mogollon Vessel Forms and their Distribution during Mogollon 4.

| POTTERY TYPE | VESSEL SHAPE | | | | | | | | | | | | | | | | | | | |
|---|---|---|---|---|---|---|---|---|---|---|---|---|---|---|---|---|---|---|---|---|
| | a | b | c | d | e | f | g | h | i | j | k | l | m | n | o | p | q | r | s | t |
| **San Simon** | | | | | | | | | | | | | | | | | | | | |
| Alma Plain | | x | x | x | x | | | | | | | | | | | | | | | |
| Polished Red | x | x | x | x | | | | | | | | | | | | | | | | |
| Painted Ware | x | x | | x | | | | | | | | | | | | | | | | |
| **Mimbres** | | | | | | | | | | | | | | | | | | | | |
| Alma Plain | x | x | x | x | x | | x | | | | | | | | | | | | | |
| Alma Textured | | | x | | | | | | | | | | | | | | | | | |
| Neck-corrugated | | | | | | | | x | x | x | | | | | | | | | | |
| San Francisco Red | x | x | x | | | | | | | | x | x | | | | | | | | |
| Painted Ware | x | | | x | | x | | | | | | x | x | x | x | x | | | | |
| **Pine Lawn Valley** | | | | | | | | | | | | | | | | | | | | |
| Alma Plain | x | x | | | | x | x | | | | | | | | | | x | | x | x |
| Alma Textured | | | x | | | | | | | | x | | | | | | | | | |
| Neck-corrugated | | | | | | | | x | x | x | | | | | | | | | | |
| Smudged | x | x | | | | | | | | | | | | | | | | | | |
| San Francisco Red | x | x | | | | | | | | | | | | | | | | x | | |
| Painted Ware | x | | | | | | | | | | | x | | | | | | | | |
| **Total Forms** | | | | | | | | | | | | | | | | | | | | |
| San Simon | x | x | x | x | x | | | | | | | | | | | | | | | |
| Mimbres | x | x | x | x | x | x | x | x | x | x | x | x | x | x | x | x | | | | |
| Pine Lawn Valley | x | x | x | | | x | x | x | x | x | x | x | | | | | x | x | x | x |

complete. Narrow-mouthed globular jars (Fig. 5, d) and squat "seed" bowls (Fig. 5, e) were manufactured in both San Simon and Mimbres branches. Seven shapes were shared by Mimbres and Pine Lawn Valley. These are "seed" jars (Fig. 5, f); globular jars with low recurved rims (Fig. 5, g); the neck-corrugated jars (Fig. 5, h and i) and pitchers (Fig. 5, j); wide-mouthed jars with outcurved neck (Fig. 5, k); and the small-mouthed pitcher (Fig. 5, l). Four forms, flare rim bowls (Fig. 5, m), deep straight-sided bowls (Fig. 5, n), bowls with incurved rim (Fig. 5, o), and compound "double" bowls (Fig. 5, p) are reported only from Mimbres Branch. Another group of four forms, globular "seed" bowls (Fig. 5, q), the archaic barrel-shaped jar (Fig. 5, r), globular jars with wide flaring necks (Fig. 5, s), and the wide-mouthed pitcher (Fig. 5, t) are noted only for Pine Lawn Valley. Most vessel shapes were produced in plain, textured, or red ware, but a surprising number (Fig. 5, a, b, d, f, k, l, m, o, and p) were also painted.

Table 9

| BRANCH | San Simon | Mimbres | Pine Lawn |
|---|---|---|---|
| San Simon | (5)   0 | 5 | 3 |
| Mimbres | 5 | (16) 4 | 10 |
| Pine Lawn | 3 | 10 | (14) 4 |

Table 9. Number of shared pottery forms between branches; Number of unique forms, and total number of vessel shapes produced (in parentheses) at column intersections. Mogollon 4.

An analysis of Table 9 suggests that Mimbres and Pine Lawn Valley are closely related ceramically during Mogollon 4. It also suggests that San Simon Branch was relatively stagnant so far as pottery is concerned. Not sufficiently brought out by Figure 5 or Table 9 is a continuation of the trend toward replacement of plain ware by increasing use of corrugation, and of San Francisco Red by painted wares, a change that became virtually complete during Mogollon 5.

We do not control sufficient data to analyze the ceramic complex at Luna, but a few general remarks may be made. The prevailing type was a coarse, fragile, unpolished brown ware, in all probability a derivative of Alma Plain, which also occurred. Another type is reported simply as polished brown, but recent surveys have shown it to be Alma Plain. Neck-coiled brown ware, which can be identified primarily as Three Circle Neck-corrugated; and incised ware, which appears to be a variety of Mimbres Incised rather than the earlier Alma Incised, also were found. Only one red ware sherd was reported by Hough (1919), but surveys have shown it to be abundant on the surface (Danson 1952). The same is true of Three Circle Red-on-white. Judging from the figures and descriptions, Figure 36 and perhaps 37 (Hough 1919) are Mimbres Bold Face Black-on-white. Associated trade wares appear to be either Kiatuthlanna Black-on-white or, according to Danson (1952) could be an early variant of Reserve Black-on-white. In either case they would indicate a Pueblo I time level. Vessel shapes include Figure 5, a, c, d, t, and variants of Figure 4, t. Thus the ceramic complex almost certainly is equivalent to Three Circle Phase of Mogollon 4.

From the nature of intrusive pottery, it is clear that Mesilla Phase of Jornada Branch should be considered late Mogollon 4, if indeed, not early Mogollon 5.

Intrusives are chiefly a late variety of Mimbres Bold Face Black-on-white and Mimbres Classic Black-on-white, plus minor amounts of Mimbres Corrugated, San Francisco Red, and Alma Plain. The indigenous ware is El Paso Brown, one of the stabilized end products of the coarsening of Alma Plain as

described by Mera (1943).  The type has been described by
Lehmer (1948:94).  Little is known of the forms, but round-
bottomed neckless jars (Fig. 5, q (?)), simple necked jars
(Fig. 5, c (?)), and rarely bowl forms (Fig. 5, a and b)
occurred.

### Summary of Mogollon Ceramic Development

Certain general trends in the history of Mogollon ceramics may now be noted.  Martin and Rinaldo (1949:190-201;
1950a:370-374; 1950b:530-532) have proposed, and applied, an
ingenious technique for seriation of houses within phases of
the Mimbres Branch, in which they include Pine Lawn Valley,
on the basis of percentile differences of pottery types recovered from floor fill of those houses.  I have elsewhere
criticized the basic assumption of this scheme insofar as it
applies to more than extremely general relative dating of
houses within phases (Wheat 1954).  Regardless of whether
their reconstruction of intraphase relationships is correct,
it clearly brings out the basic trends in the ceramic complex
to the extent to which it is represented in Mimbres Branch
and in Pine Lawn Valley.  Generally, these trends prevailed
throughout the Mogollon area.  Figure 6 shows a schematic
representation of these trends.

In each of the branches where the earliest complex combined polished and unpolished varieties of brown ware, the
polished varieties gradually gained predominance at the ex-
pense of the unpolished varieties.  This is the case with
Alma Plain, Early; Alma Rough; and Alma Plain, Bluff variety;
all of which gave way as Alma Plain increased.  The percentile
increase of Alma Plain continued, probably, into Mogollon 2,
after which it declined slowly as textured wares, including

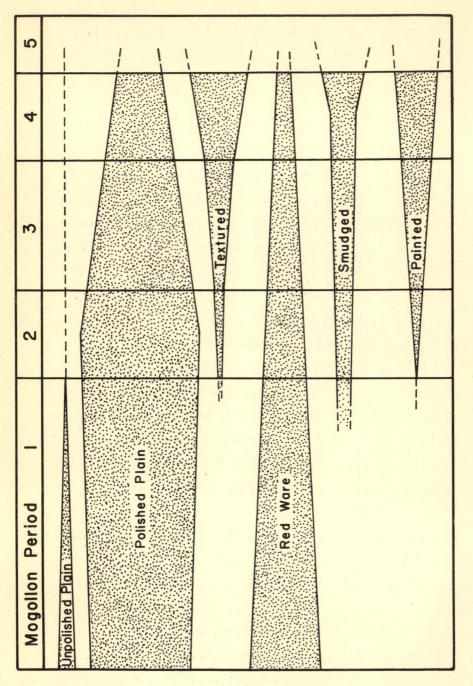

Figure 6. Mogollon Pottery Trends.

neck banding and corrugation, increased. San Francisco Red, a constant companion of the plain wares in southern branches, declined slowly from early to late, a change apparently correlated with increasing popularity of smudged and painted wares. In Forestdale Branch smudging was much more important than elsewhere, while red ware was present but less important, and no local painted Mogollon types were produced.

In San Simon Branch, while general trends were the same, the decline of plain wares was much less pronounced than in the Mimbres and Pine Lawn. In part, this must be attributed to the fact that indigenous smudged and textured wares apparently were not a part of the ceramic complex, at least until very late. In fact, there is no considerable evidence to show that texturing and neck banding were ever much practised during the early phases outside of the Mimbres and Pine Lawn areas. A few textured sherds came from Black River Branch, from the Mogollon 1 horizon, but neck corrugation seemingly did not appear until late Mogollon 3 or in Mogollon 4.

The early horizons are marked by a number of vessel forms, most being variations of hemispherical bowls and simple globular jars, neckless or with a simple vertical neck, and most are wide-mouthed, although a few forms are so constricted as to suggest bottles. There is to be noted, also, a wide diversity of forms, this being especially true of San Simon and Black River branches. Later there is a reduction in number of forms and a trend toward uniformity of the principal shapes manufactured; also, there is a shift in the focus of diversity, first to Forestdale Branch during Mogollon 3, and then to Mimbres and Pine Lawn Valley during Mogollon 4.

In general, it seems clear that Mogollon ceramics form a distinctive complex marked by uniformity in development and by specific techniques of manufacture and treatment. But each branch also developed its own specialties which make it a distinctive complex within the overall cultural pattern.

### Miscellaneous Artifacts of Clay

Throughout the Mogollon area, and during all periods, miscellaneous artifacts were made of fired clay, unfired clay, and sherds (Fig. 7). Data on these traits, as on most others, leave much to be desired. Descriptive material is, for the most part, adequate; but quantitative information is sometimes not given at all and in other cases, where given, is not assigned to phases. For this reason it is possible only to indicate general trends of popularity of specific types and to note local specializations or absences of traits. The available data have been summarized in Table 10.

Miniature vessels (Fig. 7, a) and ladles (Fig. 7, b) occur everywhere in the central part of the Mogollon area. They have not been reported from Forestdale, Cibola, and Jornada branches, but it seems likely that miniature vessels, at least, do occur in these areas. They do not appear to have been abundant anywhere, but they do have a consistent, if minor, representation. Although perhaps more common in Mogollon 1 and 2, they continue into Mogollon 4, and miniature vessels carry over into Mogollon 5.

Like miniature vessels, single-piece pottery pipes (Fig. 7, c) occur during all phases, but unlike them, have a scattered distribution in time and space. Clay pipes are not reported for San Simon nor for Cibola. They occur early in Mimbres, Pine Lawn Valley, and Black River Branch, but do not appear in Forestdale Branch until Mogollon 3, nor in the Jornada area until Mogollon 4. During Mogollon 4 in Mimbres Branch clay pipes fitted with bone stems are reported. At no time were pottery pipes so common as tubular stone pipes, but they seem a consistent part of the Mogollon culture pattern.

Pottery cornucopia-like objects (Fig. 7, d), on the other hand, are so infrequent as to suggest that the idea, if not the actual pieces, was intrusive from outside the Mogollon territory. Only six have been reported; five in Mogollon 3 associations at Mogollon and Harris villages and Tularosa Cave, and the other in mixed Mogollon 3 and 4 association at the last named site, all in Mimbres Branch.

Human figurines (Fig. 7, e) are not common; yet, they occur in five branches and in three periods. While there is some local variation in type, the general form is a flattened torso with legs and arms small, if indicated at all. Coffee-bean eyes occur on those from Pine Lawn Valley and Forestdale, but elsewhere sufficient data for style analysis are not available. In Mogollon 1 these figurines occur in Forestdale, Mimbres, and Black River branches, and probably in Pine Lawn Valley as well. None is reported for Mogollon 2, although it seems likely they were made, since they are reported again from Mogollon 3 at Forestdale and Mimbres, and from Mogollon 4 in San Simon and Black River branches. The distribution is such as to suggest a north to south movement, but the time factor would indicate a Mogollon source unless those of San Simon Branch derived from the Hohokam.

Animal figurines (Fig. 7, f) are even less common than human figurines, for although they are reported from all periods, they have a limited spatial distribution. During

Mogollon 1 they occur in Pine Lawn Valley and Mimbres, during
Mogollon 2 in Forestdale, and during Mogollon 3 in Mimbres and
Forestdale branches.  Hough (1919) reports an animal figurine
from Luna Village, but it is possible this should be considered
later than the Three Circle Phase main occupation of the site.

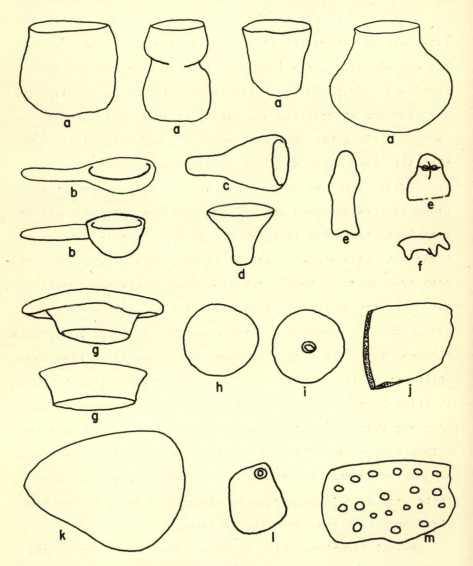

Figure 7. Miscellaneous artifacts of clay.

Unfired clay pot covers (Fig. 7, g) are reported from Pine Lawn Valley, Mimbres, and Black River branches during Mogollon 1 and from Forestdale during Mogollon 3. However, the perishable nature of these artifacts makes it seem likely they were far more common than our limited data indicate.

Potsherd discs (Fig. 7, h, i), both perforate and imperforate, are among the most commonly occurring artifacts in the Mogollon culture pattern. They are reported from every branch and from every period. There are, however, differences in

Table 10

| MOGOLLON PERIOD | BRANCH | Miniature vessels | Miniature ladles | Pottery pipes | Cornucopias | Human figurines | Animal figurines | Clay pot covers | Sherd discs | Perforated discs | Sherd scrapers | Sherd scoops | Sherd pendants | Sherd sieves |
|---|---|---|---|---|---|---|---|---|---|---|---|---|---|---|
| 1 | San Simon | P | P | | | | | | R | | | | P | |
| 1 | Mimbres | ? | ? | P | | P | P | P | P | P | P | | | |
| 1 | Pine Lawn | P | P | P | | ? | P | P | C | R | P | | P | R |
| 1 | Forestdale | | | | | P | | | P | P | | P | | |
| 1 | Black River | P | P | | | P | | P | C | C | P | | ? | |
| 2 | San Simon | P | P | | | | | | R | | P | | | |
| 2 | Forestdale | | | | | | P | | ? | ? | ? | | | |
| 2 | Black River | P | P | P | | | | | P | P | P | | | |
| 3 | San Simon | P | ? | | | | | | P | R | P | | | |
| 3 | Mimbres | P | ? | | P | P | P | | P | C | P | ? | | |
| 3 | Pine Lawn | | P | | P | | | | P | P | P | | | |
| 3 | Forestdale | | | P | | P | P | P | A | A | A | | | |
| 3 | Black River | ? | | | | | | | P | P | P | R | | |
| 4 | San Simon | P | | | | P | | | C | P | P | | | |
| 4 | Mimbres | P | | P | | | | | P | P | | | P | |
| 4 | Pine Lawn | | P | | P | | | | P | P | P | | | |
| 4 | Cibola | | | | | | ? | | | P | | | | |
| 4 | Black River | ? | | | | P | | | P | P | P | | | |
| 4 | Jornada | | | P | | | | | P | P | P | | | |

Table 10. Distribution of miscellaneous clay artifacts. A = abundant, C = common, P = present, R = rare, ? = probable but not reported.

temporal and spatial distribution of the perforate and imperforate types. During Mogollon 1 imperforate discs (Fig. 7,
h) are rare in the San Simon, present but not abundant in the
Mimbres and Forestdale branches, and common in Pine Lawn Valley and Black River Branch. This might suggest a central distribution for the type at this time. During Mogollon 2 they
continue rare in San Simon Branch but occur more often in
Black River; and while data are lacking, they probably occur
also in Forestdale Branch. They are again present in all
branches in Mogollon 3 but are especially abundant in Forestdale Branch. They have not been specifically reported for
Luna Village and Cibola Branch in Mogollon 4, but they occur
everywhere else and become common in San Simon Branch for the
first time.

Perforate sherds (Fig. 7, i) are present everywhere in
Mogollon 1 except in San Simon, and are rare in Pine Lawn Valley. Evidence is not clear for Mogollon 2, but they do occur
in Black River Branch and probably in Forestdale. They do not
occur in San Simon Branch until Mogollon 3, when they are reported for all branches, and are extremely common in the
Forestdale area. During Mogollon 4 they are reported from
all branches.

Sherd scrapers (Fig. 7, j) occur in all periods and are
reported for most of the branches; undoubtedly they are more
common than reports indicate. During Mogollon 1 they occur
in the Mimbres, Pine Lawn Valley, and Black River areas. They
continue at Black River in Mogollon 2, and appear for the
first time in San Simon. In Mogollon 3 they appear in all
branches, and are especially abundant in Forestdale Branch.
Sherd scrapers probably occur in all branches during Mogollon

4 and have been reported from all except Mimbres and Cibola.

Sherd scoops (Fig. 7, k) are reported from Pine Lawn Valley and Forestdale during Mogollon 1, from Black River during Mogollon 3, and from Mimbres in Mogollon 4.

During Mogollon 1 a few other miscellaneous artifacts were made of potsherds but did not become typical. Such are the sherd pendants (Fig. 7, 1) from Crooked Ridge Village and Cave Creek Village, and the peculiar sherd sieve (Fig. 7, m) from SU Site.

Few trends can be derived from the raw data. There appears to be a general decline in the number of miniature vessels and ladles from early to late, but if true, it is not particularly marked. Animal and human figurines occur sporadically throughout the Mogollon area and seem to be a consistent, if not common, trait, as are pottery single-piece pipes. Sherd discs of both varieties appear to increase from Mogollon 1 through Mogollon 3 and then to decline somewhat in Mogollon 4. Neither form seems to have been common in San Simon Branch, but there was a local specialization of discs, especially of the imperforate form, of which 94 were recovered.

## Ground Stone Artifacts

One of the principal characteristics of the Mogollon culture pattern is the relative abundance of ground and pecked
stone artifacts, for the most part of a rather rough-and-ready
nature.  There can be little doubt that this is, in large
measure, a heritage from their Cochise forebears, for often
the same tool types are continued, almost without change, from
preceramic into ceramic Mogollon horizons.  Examples of such
continuation are basin and slab metates and associated mano
types, grinding slabs, pestles and boulder mortars, abrading
stones, stone balls, and the universal hammer stones.  Some
of these artifacts are widespread in the Southwest in both
time and space; others are specifically southern in their distribution.  Data concerning the time and branch distribution
of Mogollon ground stone artifacts are presented in Table 11
and Figure 8.

Several forms of metates were used by the Mogollon, but
definite trends in popularity are apparent.  Basin and slab
metates (Fig. 8, a) occur in all branches during Mogollon 1
and are the most abundant type in Pine Lawn Valley.  They
occur in San Simon Branch during Mogollon 2, and perhaps in
Forestdale and Black River branches as well.  They are not
reported for Forestdale Branch during Mogollon 3, but except
for Black River Branch, where we do not have data, they are
present in all other branches.  They are less common during
Mogollon 4, but continue in San Simon and Pine Lawn Valley,

110

and are one of the types found in Jornada Branch. In the
early periods it is difficult to distinguish between a basin
metate in the first stages of wear and a slab metate; but in
later horizons slab metates, as such, are more common than
basin metates. A type I have called the basin/trough metate
(Fig. 8, b) occurs in all the southern areas during Mogollon
1 but is absent in Forestdale Branch. It is a common type in
Pine Lawn Valley, and although rare, it does occur in Black
River Branch. It continues through Mogollon 2, to become
common in Forestdale Branch in Mogollon 3 and present in Mimbres and San Simon branches. The type carries over into Mogollon 4 in the San Simon but seems to die out elsewhere as
typologically more advanced forms come into use. Judging from
space and time distribution, this was a southern type which
was moving northward during Mogollon 2. Except for the fact
that it does not seem to occur in San Simon Branch at any
time, the one-end-closed trough metate (Fig. 8, c) should be
considered the typical Mogollon form, for the type occurs in
every other branch in every time period. It is the most common type at Crooked Ridge Village and is abundant in Pine Lawn
Valley during Mogollon 1; elsewhere it is less common until
Mogollon 3, when it becomes the most common form. During
Mogollon 4 it is supplemented by the full trough metate.

In the northern half of Mogollon territory (Forestdale,
Black River, Cibola, and Pine Lawn Valley) there occurs a
variant of the one-end-closed trough metate which has a mano
rest or supplementary trough at the closed end (Fig. 8, d).
This is sometimes called the "Utah" type metate. It occurs
in Mogollon 1 and 2 in Forestdale and Black River branches.
By Mogollon 3 it is abundant in Forestdale and appears also

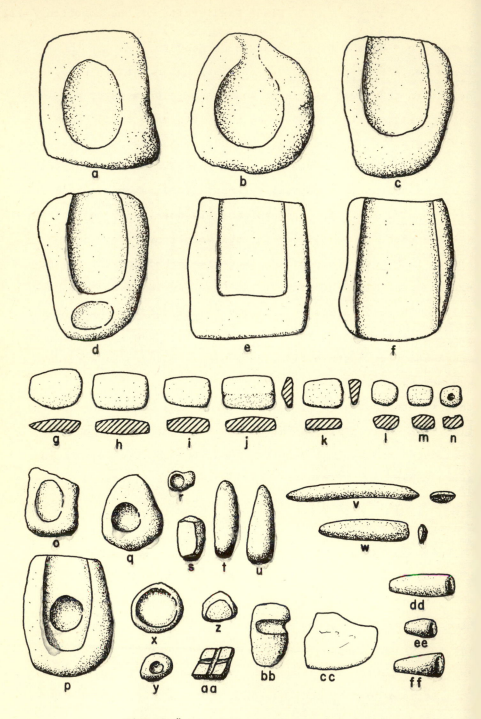

Figure 8. Ground stone artifacts.

Table 11

| MOGOLLON PERIOD / TYPE | 1 | | | | | 2 | | | 3 | | | | | 4 | | | | | |
|---|---|---|---|---|---|---|---|---|---|---|---|---|---|---|---|---|---|---|---|
| BRANCH | San Simon | Mimbres | Pine Lawn | Forestdale | Black River | San Simon | Forestdale | Black River | San Simon | Mimbres | Pine Lawn | Forestdale | Black River | San Simon | Mimbres | Pine Lawn | Cibola | Black River | Jornada |
| **Metates** | | | | | | | | | | | | | | | | | | | |
| Basin | P | P | A | P | P | P | ? | ? | P | P | P | | | P | ? | P | | | P |
| Basin/trough | P | P | A | | R | ? | R | R | P | P | | C | | P | | | | | |
| One-end-closed | | P | A | P | C | | P | R | C | | P | A | P | | P | P | P | P | P |
| "Utah" | | | P | P | | | | R | | | P | A | | | | P | P | | |
| Thin slab | | | | | | R | | | | | | | | | | | | | |
| Full trough | | | | | | | | | | | ? | R | | P | P | P | | | |
| Flat grinding slabs | C | | P | R | P | P | | | P | | P | | | P | | P | | | |
| Basin grinding slabs | P | | | P | P | | P | | P | | | | | P | P | P | | | |
| **Manos** | | | | | | | | | | | | | | | | | | | |
| Type 1a | P | P | A | C | A | C | P | P | A | A | P | A | P | A | P | P | P | P | P |
| Type 1b | | | P | P | P | P | P | | P | P | C | | | | P | P | | | |
| Type 1c | | | | P | | | P | | | | P | | | | | P | | | |
| Type 1d | | | | P | | | R | | | | | | | P | | | | | |
| Wedge | A | | P | | | P | | | | | P | | | | | ? | | | P |
| **Hand stones** | | | | | | | | | | | | | | | | | | | |
| Type 1a | A | P | P | C | C | P | P | P | C | P | P | C | P | | | P | | | P |
| Type 1b | A | P | P | P | A | C | P | P | C | C | P | P | P | P | P | P | | P | P |
| Pitted | P | | P | | | | P | | | | | | | | | P | | | P |
| Palettes | C | R | | R | | | P | P | | | | | | P | P | | P | | |
| **Mortars** | | | | | | | | | | | | | | | | | | | |
| Metate | R | | P | P | R | | ? | R | R | P | P | P | | | | ? | | | |
| Boulder | P | P | P | | P | | P | | P | | | | | | | P | P | | |
| Pebble | R | | A | R | | R | | | | | P | | R | P | | P | | | |
| Small flat | | | | P | | | | | | | | | | | | | | | |
| Thin flat | | | | P | | | | | | | | | | | | | | | |
| Slab | | | | | | | | | | | | R | | | | P | ? | | |
| **Pestles** | | | | | | | | | | | | | | | | | | | |
| Type 1 | C | P | A | P | R | P | ? | P | P | P | P | P | | P | | ? | | | |
| Type 2 | P | | A | P | | | P | P | P | | | P | | P | | P | | | |
| Type 3 | | | P | P | | | | | | | | | | | | | | P | P |
| **Digging tools** | | | | | | | | | | | | | | | | | | | |
| Type 1 | | | | P | | | | | | | | | | | | P | | | |
| Type 2 | | | | P | | | | | P | | | | | P | | | | | |

(Continued on next page)

Table 11 (Continued)

| MOGOLLON PERIOD / TYPE | 1 San Simon | 1 Mimbres | 1 Pine Lawn | 1 Forestdale | 1 Black River | 2 San Simon | 2 Forestdale | 2 Black River | 3 San Simon | 3 Mimbres | 3 Pine Lawn | 3 Forestdale | 3 Black River | 4 San Simon | 4 Mimbres | 4 Pine Lawn | 4 Cibola | 4 Black River | 4 Jornada |
|---|---|---|---|---|---|---|---|---|---|---|---|---|---|---|---|---|---|---|---|
| Stone bowls | P | ? | P | | P | | | R | P | P | P | R | | P | | ? | | | P |
| Pitted Pebbles | | C | | P | | | P | | | P | | | | | P | P | | | P |
| Stone griddles | | | | | R | | | | | | | | | | | P | | | |
| Worked slabs | | | ? | P | | | P | | | | P | | | | | P | | | |
| Stone pot covers | | | P | P | | | | | | | ? | | | | P | P | | | R |
| Polishing stones | P | P | A | P | C | P | P | P | P | P | P | P | C | P | P | P | P | ? | P |
| Abrading stones | P | ? | A | P | C | P | P | P | P | P | P | P | ? | P | P | P | P | ? | ? |
| Grooved abraders | | ? | P | | C | | P | | P | | | | | | | | | | |
| Hammer stones | A | P | A | P | A | P | P | P | P | C | A | A | P | P | C | A | P | P | P |
| Grooved mauls | P | C | A | | C | | | P | | C | P | P | ? | | P | R | P | R | R |
| Axes |  |  |  |  |  |  |  |  |  |  |  |  |  |  |  |  |  |  |  |
|   3/4-grooved | | | | | R | | | | R | | | R | | R | R | | | | |
|   Full-grooved | | | | | | | | | | R | R | | | R | R | | | | |
|   Flaked | | | | | | | | | | P | P | | | ? | | | | | |
| Stone hoes | | ? | P | P | | | | | P | | | | | | | R | | | |
| Pipes |  |  |  |  |  |  |  |  |  |  |  |  |  |  |  |  |  |  |  |
|   Type 1a | | P | P | | P | R | | | | P | P | | | | P | ? | | | |
|   Type 1b | | P | P | | | | | | | P | R | | | | | ? | | | |
|   Type 2 | P | P | P | P | R | | P | | | P | P | | | | | ? | | | |
|   Type 3 | | | | | R | | | | | ? | | | | | | | | | |
|   Type 4 | | | | | R | | | | | | | | | | | | | | |
| Stone tubes | | | | | R | | | | | | | | | | | | | | |
| Medicine stone | | | | | R | | | | | | | | | | | | | | |
| Medicine cylinder | | | | | | | R | | | | | | | | | | | | |
| Stone figurines | | | | | | | | | | | | | | P | | | | | |
| Atlatl stones | P | | | | | | | | | R | | | | | | | | | |
| Stone rings | | | | | | | | | | ? | | | | R | | | | | |
| Stone balls | | P | P | | | | | | | P | P | C | | | | ? | | | P |
| Stone discs | | | P | | | | P | | | | | | | | | P | | | |
| Foot effigies | | | | | | | | | | P | | | | | | | | | |

Table 11. Distribution of ground stone artifacts.
A = abundant, C = common, P = present, R = rare, ? = probable but not reported.

in Pine Lawn Valley where it carries over into Mogollon 4.
The type is found also in Cibola Branch during Mogollon 4.
From the distribution, this would appear as a northern Mogollon form which was spreading southward during Mogollon 3 but which apparently did not penetrate into the Mimbres and San Simon areas.

Still another variant of the one-end-closed trough metate occurred in Forestdale Branch in Mogollon 3. This is the thin slab type metate with squared, flat-bottomed trough (Fig. 8, e). It appears intrusive from the Anasazi.

The full trough metate (Fig. 8, f) does not appear until Mogollon 3 when a single somewhat aberrant example appeared in Bear Ruin in Forestdale Branch. However, during Mogollon 4 true full trough metates begin to occur in San Simon, Mimbres, and Pine Lawn Valley, although they do not become prevalent until Mogollon 5.

Flat grinding slabs and slabs with shallow basins occur sporadically in all periods and in most branches, but no particular trends can be discerned. Their significance is in indicating that grinding or pulverizing various substances was an established part of the Mogollon culture pattern.

Manos go with grinding bases in the sense that they are partly shaped by them and that specific types of metates require, or produce, specific styles of manos. It is possible to isolate many types of manos as used by the Mogollon, but for the purposes of this study I have tried to simplify by combining those types that appear as variants of basic types.

The most common type of mano among the Mogollon was the ovoid to rectangular unifacial stone with slight to moderately convex grinding surface used on basin and one-end-closed trough metates (Fig. 8, g). This type ranges in size from those small enough to be held in one hand, to the larger ones undoubtedly wielded by both hands. Commonly the non-grinding face is unshaped, although the edges and some irregularities might be smoothed. I have termed this Type 1a. It occurs in all periods and in all branches. A few trends in its use may be noted. There is a general increase in length from early to late, although both large and small ones occur at all levels. Late manos tend to be flatter than early ones; and there is a decrease in popularity from early to late, first, as similar but bifacial forms become more common, and second, as the rectanguloid brick-like forms associated with full trough metates come into use during Mogollon 4.

Bifacial manos (Type 1b, Fig. 8, h), with both grinding faces like that of Type 1a, likewise occur in all time per-iods; but their spatial distribution is more limited, for they do not appear until Mogollon 5 in San Simon Branch, nor are they reported for the late horizons in Cibola and Jornada branches. They tend to have an early northern distribution (Pine Lawn Valley, Forestdale, and Black River), spreading southward into the Mimbres area during Mogollon 3.

While types 1a and 1b, and their variations, are the principal forms used by the Mogollon, two other variations occur sporadically. In one of these (Type 1c, Fig. 8, i), a bifacial form, one face is strongly convex on both axes and was probably used in a deep basin metate. This type occurs in Black River Branch during Mogollon 1 and 2, and a slightly less convex form is found at Pine Lawn Valley in Mogollon 3 and 4. The second variant, Type 1d (Fig. 8, j), has one face divided into two facets by a roundish longitudinal ridge. It occurs rarely in Black River Branch during Mogollon 1 and 2, and appears in San Simon in Mogollon 4.

Wedge-shaped manos (Fig. 8, k), both uniface and biface, are typical of early phases in San Simon Branch but also occur in Pine Lawn Valley during Mogollon 1 and 3, and in the Jornada during Mogollon 4.

Hand stones, made for use in one hand, are very common in all Mogollon periods and branches. Both uniface (Type 1a, Fig. 8, 1) and biface (Type 1b, Fig. 8, m) forms were made, the latter being somewhat more common. As with manos, the various types can be established on the basis of outline and degree of convexity of grinding faces. But since outline is largely a happenstance of the shape of the stone selected for use, and because there is continuous intergradation from flat to strongly convex stones, they are here considered as variations of a single basic type.

While both forms are common in early times, bifacial hand stones appear as the dominant form during Mogollon 4. A variant form has a small pit pecked in one face for some purpose unknown (Fig. 8, n). During Mogollon 1 these occur in San Simon and Forestdale branches; they continue in San Simon Branch in Mogollon 3, and are reported from Pine Lawn Valley and Jornada Branch in Mogollon 4. Judging only from this distribution and from their general scarcity, they could be expected to occur occasionally in all branches and periods.

Mogollon palettes (Fig. 8, o) are small flat stone slabs, sometimes with a shallow depression in one face, and frequently stained with pigment. They are not, until Mogollon 4, formalized as were those of the Hohokam. During Mogollon 1 they are common in San Simon Branch, are reported from Pine

Lawn Valley, and occur in Black River Branch where they continue into Mogollon 2. Although not reported for Mogollon 2 in San Simon, they probably occur there inasmuch as they are found in both Mogollon 3 and 4. During the latter period palettes occur in Pine Lawn Valley and in the Mimbres, where the type found suggests either Hohokam influence or actual trade specimens.

Several kinds of mortars are characteristic of the Mogollon culture pattern; however, they seem never to have been abundant. One type consists of a round depression pecked in the bottom of the grinding surface of a metate. During Mogollon 1 this type is reported from every branch except Mimbres, and it probably occurs there also, as does the companion type of boulder mortar.

Metate-mortars (Fig. 8, p) are reported only from Black River Branch in Mogollon 2; but since they are present in Forestdale and San Simon branches both before and after this period, they undoubtedly occur then, also. During Mogollon 3 they are reported everywhere except Black River Branch, where there is insufficient data; and by Mogollon 4 the type seems to have died out, although it may occur in Pine Lawn Valley.

Boulder mortars (Fig. 8, q) follow essentially the same development except that they are not reported from Forestdale Branch at all. They continued into Mogollon 4, however, for they are reported from both Pine Lawn Valley and Cibola Branch.

Similar to boulder mortars, but smaller, are pebble mortars (Fig. 8, r). Technically these should be termed cobble mortars, for their size range falls primarily in that geological classification; but the name pebble mortar is well established in archeological literature and so will be used here. These mortars occur sporadically in all Mogollon periods but are not reported for Mimbres, Black River, Cibola, nor Jornada, although they may have been used there. They occur in San Simon and Forestdale branches and are abundant in Pine Lawn Valley during Mogollon 1. They are not reported for Forestdale after that time, but continue to occur in San Simon Branch and Pine Lawn Valley into Mogollon 5.

Two specialized mortar types were found in Forestdale Branch during Mogollon 1. One resembles the pebble mortar in size but the grinding depression is larger, shallower, and better finished. The other form, less common, is a thin, well finished oval slab with a dish-like depression. Another specialized type is reported from Pine Lawn Valley during Mogollon 3 or 4, and from the Mimbres during the latter period. This type is simply a stone slab with several small mortar depressions pecked in one or both faces.

The most common type of pestle is the short, squat, multifaced stone here termed Type 1 (Fig. 8, s). Usually two or more faces, and both ends, show evidence of use. These occur in all branches and in all periods, but decline in number during Mogollon 4, as the associated mortars also decline.

Type 2 pestles (Fig. 8, t) are selected elongated stones which show, on one or both ends, evidence of use in a mortar. Although their distribution in time and space is essentially the same as that of Type 1, they were less common in most areas. In San Simon Branch, however, they were the predominant form.

Type 3 pestles (Fig. 8, u) differ from Type 2 primarily in that they are shaped by pecking and grinding to a more symmetrical form. Their distribution, although probably wider than reported at present, is more limited than either of the cruder varieties. During Mogollon 1 they are reported from Pine Lawn Valley and Black River Branch, and from Cibola and Jornada branches during Mogollon 4.

Two types of tools which have frequently been called pestles, I have termed digging tools or picks, for reasons given elsewhere (Wheat 1954). As presently reported, their distribution is more restricted than that of the pestles. The longer Type 1 (Fig. 8, v) has been reported only from Black River Branch during Mogollon 1 and from Mimbres Branch in Mogollon 4, but they almost certainly had a greater distribution. The shorter, wedge-shaped tool (Type 2, Fig. 8, w) is reported from Black River Branch in Mogollon 1 and from San Simon in Mogollon 3 and 4.

Morphologically related to pebble mortars, and in some cases probably used as such, are stone bowls (Fig. 8, x). These differ from mortars primarily in usually being made of more durable stone, and in their more careful shaping, finish, and proportions. Sometimes they are decorated by relief carving or by incising. They occur in all periods and in all branches, at one time or another, but are most common in the southern part of the Mogollon area. They do not occur in Forestdale Branch until Mogollon 3, a fact which, together with their general distribution, suggests that they were moving northward during that period.

Pitted pebbles (Fig. 8, y) of unknown use occur sporadically in the central Mogollon area but are not reported from San Simon, Forestdale, and Cibola branches.

Thin stone slabs were used in a number of ways. One from

Black River Branch in Mogollon 1, and six from Pine Lawn Valley in Mogollon 4, show use over fire, perhaps as griddles. Slabs with shaped edges occur sporadically, especially in Pine Lawn Valley, and were probably used for various purposes. They are not reported from San Simon Branch. Slabs worked to circular form are usually called pot covers, although they also occur in preceramic levels at Tularosa Cave. They are reported from Pine Lawn Valley and Forestdale Branch in Mogollon 1, and from Cibola and Jornada branches in addition to Pine Lawn Valley, in Mogollon 4.

Pebbles were commonly utilized as polishing stones for pottery (Fig. 8, z), and many were undoubtedly used for other purposes, since the kind of stone and the nature of wear facets definitely were not suited to pottery polishing. However, since such distinctions usually are not made in the literature, all polishing stones have been considered together in this study. They occur in all branches and in all periods. Similar pebbles sometimes show short, deep scratches, as if used for flaking artifacts.

Abrading stones of gritty sandstone or some other corrasive stone are common in Mogollon sites, occurring in every period. They have been reported from all branches except Cibola and Jornada, and there is no reason to doubt their occurrence in these areas with further investigation. These abrading stones vary in shape but are usually small enough to have been held with the fingers or in one hand.

Grooved abraders are much less common. A specialized type (Fig. 8, aa) which appears to have been used for shaft abrading was common at Crooked Ridge Village in Black River Branch during Mogollon 1. Other types used for sharpening

awls and abrading other substances occurred in both Black
River Branch and Pine Lawn Valley during this period.  Grooved
abraders continue in Mogollon 2 in Black River Branch, and
occur in Mimbres Branch during Mogollon 3.  Nesbitt (1938:104)
reports grooved shaft polishers from San Francisco Phase at
Starkweather Ruin, but it should be noted that they are of
sandstone and limestone, and so may be abraders rather than
polishers.  Specialized abraders in the form of elongate sandstone rasps occurred in Forestdale Branch in Mogollon 1 and 2.

Hammer stones are, of course, among the commonest artifacts at most sites throughout the Southwest, but while different types are sometimes recognized, there has been no general
attempt to discriminate between subtypes.  It would appear
that if there are intercultural differences to be observed in
the distribution of this tool, they will be manifest in the
differing subtype frequencies.  Three principal kinds are
nodular or spheroid, angular or flaked, and discoid stones
which sometimes have pitted faces to serve as finger-grips.
It has not been possible to determine the distribution of subtypes, so all types have been considered together in this
study.  They are abundant to common in every branch and during
every period.

Another typical Mogollon artifact is the grooved stone
maul (Fig. 8, bb).  Several subtypes have been distinguished.
The most common form is a cobble or small boulder, selected
for general shape and heft, and completed with a groove around
all or part of its circumference.  Both full-grooved and
three-quarter-grooved mauls occur, but most typical is an
intermediate form I have termed seven-eighths-grooved, that
is, the groove passes nearly around the stone but a small

wedge is left to interrupt the groove.  Mauls occur in every period, but their branch distribution is interesting and informative.  During Mogollon 1 they occur in every branch except Forestdale, but they appear to be rare in San Simon. They are reported only from Black River Branch in Mogollon 2, apparently having died out in San Simon and not yet having reached Forestdale.  By Mogollon 3 they appear in Forestdale Branch, and during Mogollon 4 they occur in every branch except San Simon.  It seems clear that grooved stone mauls were typical of the central Mogollon area from the earliest times. Sayles (1941:27) reports four from Chiricahua Stage of the Cochise Culture.  Therefore, the trait must go back at least several thousand years in the Mogollon area.  After being present in the earliest phase in San Simon Branch, it died out.  Judging from the time it appeared in Forestdale Branch, the northward movement of the trait took place during Mogollon 2 and 3; and at a time equivalent to early Mogollon 3, it had also reached the Basketmakers in Anasazi territory.  The grooved maul appears as one of the few Southwestern artifact types whose spread can be clearly traced through time and space.

Quite opposite to the maul in their status among the Mogollon are ground stone axes, for they do not become a fixed part of the culture pattern until Mogollon 5.  A few flaked stone axes are reported from Pine Lawn Valley and Mimbres Branch during Mogollon 3.  However, ground stone axes occasionally occur, undoubtedly as intrusives from other areas. A typical three-quarter-grooved Hohokam Snaketown Phase axe was found at Crooked Ridge Village in a house that may be considered late Mogollon 1 or early Mogollon 2.  Rare occurrences of three-quarter-grooved axes are recorded in San Simon and Forestdale branches in Mogollon 3, while full-grooved axes are reported from Mimbres Branch and Pine Lawn Valley. Both full- and three-quarter-grooved axes were intrusive in Pine Lawn Valley and Mimbres Branch in Mogollon 4.

One of the interesting problems in Southwestern archeology is the reason why the Mogollon, living for the most part in a forest environment, did not take over the polished stone axe which presumably would have been a more suitable tool than flaked hand axes and choppers for cutting trees. It is even more remarkable when it is remembered that both Hohokam and Anasazi, neither of whom generally occupied a heavily forested environment, possessed and used the axe. Such a circumstance can only be the result of different cultural traditions.

Stone hoes (Fig. 8, cc) occur sporadically in various Mogollon branches. The earliest variety is made of thin spalls of resistant stone. Most show no indication of having been hafted, and the chief sign of use is the abraded edges. Later hoes, however, show more shaping, and some could have been hafted. They are reported from Pine Lawn Valley and Black River Branch during Mogollon 1; they occur in Mimbres Branch in Mogollon 3, and again in Pine Lawn Valley in Mogollon 4.

Tubular stone pipes of several varieties are typical of most central Mogollon sites. They vary in size and shape, but most, if not all, were made for use with bone or wooden stems. The most common form is elongate ovoid or cylindrical (Type 1a, Fig. 8, dd), followed closely by short versions of the same shapes (Type 1b, Fig. 8, ee). These occur in Mimbres, Black River, and Pine Lawn Valley during Mogollon 1,

while Type la is reported from San Simon Branch during Mogollon 2.  They continue in Pine Lawn Valley and Mimbres Branch
during Mogollon 3 and 4.

Type 2 pipes (Fig. 8, ff) are an elongate, truncate conical form.  This is the only type reported from Forestdale
Branch, where it occurs during Mogollon 1.  For the same period this type is reported from every branch except San Simon,
where it occurs in Mogollon 2.  It also is found at Black
River Branch in Mogollon 2, and in Pine Lawn Valley and Mimbres in Mogollon 3, but it is not surely reported from any
later period.  In any event, its early popularity seems to
die out in Mogollon 3, while the ovoid or cylindrical type
continues into Mogollon 5.

Two other pipe forms were found at Crooked Ridge Village
in Mogollon 1.  One of these (Type 3) is essentially a Type 2
with offset shank.  The other (Type 4) is a slender ovoid form
with cylindrically bored stem.  Hough (1903: pl. 52) reports
a Type 3 pipe from the Mimbres area but the phase association
is not known.

Technologically allied to stone pipes is an engraved
stone tube from Crooked Ridge Village in late Mogollon 1 or
early Mogollon 2.  It is not clear whether this should be considered an indigenous form, or a trade artifact.  In either
case, it appears unique so far as Mogollon is known at the
present time.

A group of miscellaneous specimens completes the catalog
of ground stone artifacts.  Among these are two types of "med-
icine" stone; one, probably a Hohokam intrusive, from late
Mogollon 1 or early 2 at Crooked Ridge Village, the other a
polished cylinder from Bluff Site in Mogollon 2.  A single

stone figurine is reported from San Simon Village in Mogollon 4. Atlatl weights or charm stones occurred in the Mimbres during Mogollon 1 and 3, indicating, together with perishable material from Tularosa Cave, the continuance of the atlatl alongside the bow and arrow until San Francisco Phase of Mogollon 3. Ground stone rings of an essentially Hohokam type are reported from Mimbres and San Simon branches during Mogollon 3 and 4, respectively. Stone balls have a somewhat wider distribution in time and space, for they occur in Mimbres Branch and Pine Lawn Valley in Mogollon 1; in Mimbres, Pine Lawn Valley, and Forestdale in Mogollon 3; and in Jornada and probably Pine Lawn Valley in Mogollon 4. What they were used for is not clear, but some possibilities are: games, sling shots, or bolos (although many are too small to suggest this use). Smooth-edged stone discs have a sporadic distribution, having been reported from Pine Lawn Valley in Mogollon 1, Forestdale in Mogollon 2, and Mimbres in Mogollon 4. Finally, two effigies of the human foot, from a Mogollon 3 horizon in Tularosa Cave, deserve mention.

The use or purpose of many of these miscellaneous objects cannot be assigned with certainty, and there are no particular trends to be noted other than that more of them are reported from Mogollon 3 than from any other period, perhaps suggesting a greater experimentation or fermentation of culture during this time. Our data are too scanty, for the most part, to derive significant conclusions as to trends, cultural movements, and the like, from Mogollon ground stone tools. Those conclusions which seem probable have been given above, and it does not seem worthwhile to further synthesize them here.

## Flaked Stone Artifacts

Although the Mogollon were capable of producing, and upon occasion did produce, finely worked flaked artifacts, most of their implements were made just well enough to do what was necessary. Many were simple flakes with a working edge made by removal of a few chips by percussion or pressure. Often a natural flake was used without modification other than that which occurred as a direct result of usage. Distributional data for flaked stone artifacts have been summarized in Table 12. Some are illustrated in Figure 9.

Projectile points are among the most common flaked arti-facts at most Mogollon sites. The type of greatest frequency is the diagonally notched, medium-sized point here termed Type 5a (Fig. 9, e). Martin and his associates (1952:113) were able to distinguish a slender subtype which had primarily an early distribution in Tularosa and Cordova caves, but since most investigators have not made such distinctions, I have necessarily considered these points as a single category. During Mogollon 1, Type 5a was represented in every branch, but by Mogollon 2 it had died out in San Simon and is not re-ported there at any later time. In Mogollon 3 this type was the most abundant form; it occurred in Forestdale Branch and undoubtedly in Pine Lawn Valley as well, since it is reported there in Mogollon 4. It continued also in the Mimbres, and was found in Jornada Branch. Although Type 5a continued into Mogollon 5, it seems to have reached its popularity peak in Mogollon 3 and to have declined somewhat after that time.

The small version of the diagonally notched type (Type 5b, Fig. 9, f) closely follows the larger in distribution. Martin et al. (1952:113) state that this type is late in

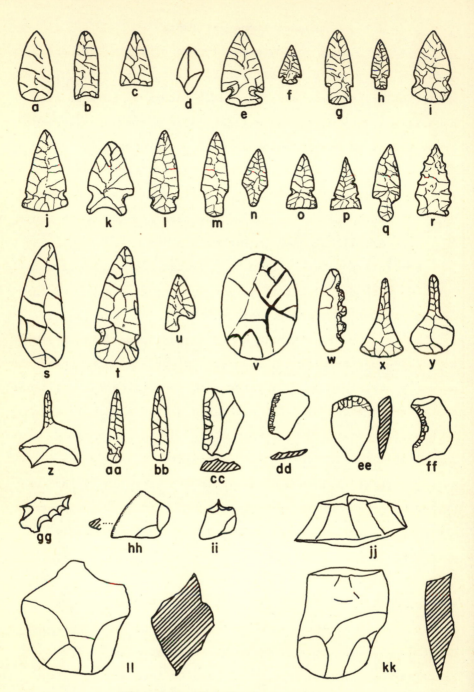

Figure 9. Flaked stone artifacts.

Table 12

| Category | MOGOLLON PERIOD → Type | 1 San Simon | 1 Mimbres | 1 Pine Lawn | 1 Forestdale | 1 Black River | 2 San Simon | 2 Forestdale | 2 Black River | 3 San Simon | 3 Mimbres | 3 Pine Lawn | 3 Forestdale | 3 Black River | 4 San Simon | 4 Mimbres | 4 Pine Lawn | 4 Cibola | 4 Black River | 4 Jornada |
|---|---|---|---|---|---|---|---|---|---|---|---|---|---|---|---|---|---|---|---|---|
| PROJECTILE POINTS | Type 1 |  | C | C | P | P | P |  |  | ? | P |  | P |  |  |  |  |  |  |  |
|  | 2 |  |  |  |  | R |  |  |  |  |  |  |  |  |  |  |  |  |  |  |
|  | 3 |  | P | P | P | P | P |  |  | ? | P |  | C |  |  |  | P |  |  | P |
|  | 4 |  |  |  |  | P |  |  |  |  |  | ? |  |  |  |  |  |  |  |  |
|  | 5a | P | P | P | P | P | P | P |  |  | A | ? | P |  |  | P | P |  |  | P |
|  | 5b | P | P | P | P | P | P | P |  |  | P |  | P | ? |  | ? |  |  | ? | P |
|  | 6a |  |  |  |  | P |  | ? |  |  | P |  |  |  |  | P |  |  |  |  |
|  | 6b |  |  |  |  | P |  |  |  |  | P |  |  |  |  |  |  |  |  |  |
|  | 7 |  | P | P | P | P | P | P | P | P | P |  |  |  | P | P |  |  |  |  |
|  | 8 |  | P | P |  | P |  |  |  |  | P |  |  |  |  | ? |  |  |  |  |
|  | 9 |  | P |  |  | P | ? |  |  |  | P |  |  |  |  |  | P |  |  |  |
|  | 10 |  | P | P | P |  |  | P |  |  | P | P | P | P |  |  | P |  |  |  |
|  | 11 | P |  | P | P |  |  |  |  |  |  | P | P |  |  |  | P |  |  |  |
|  | 12 |  |  |  |  |  |  | ? |  |  |  | P |  |  |  |  |  |  |  |  |
|  | 13 |  |  |  |  |  |  |  |  |  |  |  | P |  |  |  |  |  |  |  |
|  | 14 |  |  |  |  |  |  |  |  |  |  |  |  |  |  | R | R |  |  |  |
|  | 15 |  |  |  |  |  | P |  |  |  | P |  | P |  |  | P |  |  |  |  |
|  | 16 |  | P |  |  |  |  |  |  |  | P |  |  | P | P |  |  |  |  |  |
| KNIVES | Type 1 |  | A | P | C | P |  | P | P | A | P | A | P |  |  | P | P |  | P |  |
|  | 2 | P | P |  | P | P | P |  |  |  | P |  | P |  |  | ? |  |  |  |  |
|  | 3 | P | P | P |  | P |  | P |  |  | P |  |  |  |  |  |  |  |  |  |
|  | 4 |  |  |  | P |  |  |  |  | ? | P |  |  |  |  | ? |  |  |  |  |
|  | 5 |  | P |  |  |  |  |  |  |  | P |  | P |  |  |  |  |  |  |  |
|  | 6 |  |  |  |  | P |  |  |  |  |  |  |  |  |  |  |  |  |  |  |
|  | 7 |  |  | P |  | P |  |  |  |  | P | P |  |  |  |  | P |  |  | P |
|  | 8 |  |  |  |  |  |  |  |  |  | P |  | A |  |  | ? |  |  |  |  |
| DRILLS | Type 1 |  | P | P |  | P |  |  |  |  | P |  |  |  |  |  |  |  |  |  |
|  | 2 |  |  | P | P | P | P |  |  |  | P | P | P |  |  |  | P |  |  |  |
|  | 3 |  |  | P |  | P |  |  |  |  |  |  | P |  |  |  | P |  |  |  |
|  | 4 |  |  |  |  | P |  |  |  |  | P |  | P |  |  |  |  |  |  |  |
|  | 5 |  | P |  | P |  | P |  |  |  | P |  |  |  |  | ? |  |  |  |  |
| SCRAPERS | Type 1a | P | P | P | P | C | ? | P | P | P | P | P | C |  |  | ? | P |  |  | P |
|  | 1b |  | C | ? | P | R | P | P |  | P |  |  |  |  |  |  |  |  |  |  |
|  | 2 | C | P |  | P | P | P |  |  | P | P | P | P |  | P |  | P |  |  |  |
|  | 3 |  | P | P | P | P | P |  |  |  |  | P | P | C |  |  | P |  |  |  |
|  | 4 |  |  | P |  |  |  |  |  |  |  |  |  |  |  |  |  |  |  |  |
|  | 5 |  |  |  |  | P | P |  |  |  |  |  | C |  |  | P |  |  |  |  |
| Gravers, large |  |  | P |  | C | P | P |  |  |  |  |  | P | C |  |  |  |  |  |  |
| Scraper planes |  |  | P | P | C | P | P |  |  | C |  | P |  |  |  | P |  |  |  |  |
| Hand axes |  |  |  | P | P |  |  |  |  |  |  |  |  |  |  |  |  |  |  |  |
| Choppers |  | P | C | P | P | C | ? | P | P | P | A | P |  |  |  | C | P | P |  |  |

Table 12. Distribution of Mogollon flaked stone artifacts.  A = abundant, C = common, P = present, R = rare,
? = probable but not reported.

Tularosa Cave, but their distribution table shows it as occurring in both preceramic and Mogollon 1 levels in Cordova Cave. It also occurs at SU Site in Pine Lawn Valley and in every other branch during the same period. Therefore, it must be considered an early type in general. In fact, although its distribution in later phases largely parallels that of Type 5a, it would appear even less common during Mogollon 4. In most specimens of this type from Crooked Ridge Village the blade edges were worn smooth, as if they had been used as drill tips, which use their size would facilitate. It would be interesting to know whether points of this type from other sites show the same feature.

Another projectile point with wide distribution is Type 7, essentially a small to medium leaf-shaped blade with shallow side notches (Fig. 9, i). During Mogollon 1 and 2 this type occurred in all branches except San Simon, where it did not appear until Mogollon 3, at which time it was disappearing from the more northern sites. However, it continued in Mimbres and San Simon branches through Mogollon 4.

Type 10, a deeply side-notched form with a definite expanding stem and usually a slender blade (Fig. 9, 1) has a central and northern distribution during Mogollon 1. It is not reported from San Simon at any time; does not appear in Black River Branch until Mogollon 3; and after this time seems to decline in all branches, being reported only from Pine Lawn Valley in Mogollon 4. Martin et al. (1952:114) record a similar trend for this type in the Tularosa Cave midden.

Type 8 is another side-notched point, with convex to straight edges and straight to slightly convex base (Fig. 9, j). It has a central Mogollon distribution. It is reported

from Pine Lawn Valley, Mimbres, and Black River during Mogollon 1, from Mimbres in Mogollon 3, and from Pine Lawn Valley
again in Mogollon 4. Types 13 (Fig. 9, o) and 14 (Fig. 9, p)
appear as refinements of Type 8, although they may well be
newly introduced forms. Type 13 is reported only from Forestdale Branch in Mogollon 3 during the pithouse horizon, while
Type 14 occurs as a rare intrusive (?) in Pine Lawn Valley
and in Cordova Cave in Mimbres Branch.

One of the most interesting projectile point groups is
Type 9 (Fig. 9, k), a broad side-notched form with indented
base, for it is distinctly reminiscent of the preceramic
indented-base points which sometimes have serrate edges.
During Mogollon 1 this type is reported from Mimbres and
Black River branches, from Mimbres in Mogollon 3, and from
Pine Lawn Valley in Mogollon 4. A smaller version with ser-
rated edges but lacking the indented base is Type 16 (Fig. 9,
r), reported from Mimbres Branch in Mogollon 1 and again in
Mogollon 3 and 4. During the latter period it also occurs in
San Simon Branch.

Type 15 (Fig. 9, q) is a slender point with a slender
expanding stem. It has a sporadic distribution, occurring in
the San Simon in Mogollon 2, in the Mimbres in Mogollon 3 and
4, and also in Forestdale during Mogollon 3. Types 6a (Fig.
9, g) and 6b (Fig. 9, h) are square-shouldered points with
straight-sided and -based expanding stems. They differ only
in size. Both occur in Black River Branch in Mogollon 1, and
appear in the Mimbres during Mogollon 3, where the larger
type, 6a, continues into Mogollon 4.

Type 11 (Fig. 9, m) is a medium to slender proportioned
point with straight-edged and -based stem. It has a predom-

inantly early distribution even though it continues into Mogollon 4 in Pine Lawn Valley. During Mogollon 1 it occurs in San Simon, Pine Lawn Valley, and Forestdale, and in Pine Lawn Valley and Forestdale in Mogollon 3.

Types 1 (Fig. 9, a) and 3 (Fig. 9, c), stemless types which may be considered either projectile points or small knives, have wide distribution in Mogollon sites. The leaf-shaped Type 1 is reported for all branches except San Simon during Mogollon 1, as is the trianguloid Type 3. Both are reported from Forestdale in Mogollon 2 and from Mimbres and Forestdale in Mogollon 3. Type 3 is reported for Pine Lawn Valley and Jornada Branch in Mogollon 4, but Type 1 does not appear to survive.

Type 2 (Fig. 9, b) is a thin, slender, parallel-sided blade with concave base, occurring in Mogollon 1 at Crooked Ridge Village, probably as an intrusive, for it is not reported for any other site or period.

Type 4 (Fig. 9, d) points are a miscellaneous lot of flake points and undoubtedly are more common than the record indicates. They are reported from Black River Branch in Mogollon 1 and probably occur in Pine Lawn Valley in Mogollon 3.

Blades and knives are frequently classified together with projectile points, and there can be little doubt that it is often impossible to distinguish the specific function of many specimens. Nevertheless, certain forms, because of their nature, could have been used for cutting but not for tipping arrows or darts. These are considered here as knives. I have also restricted the term, knife, to bifacially flaked objects, in accord with our own general technology. Undoubtedly many thin, unifacially chipped tools were used for cutting, but such tools are normally used in the scraping or planing motion for which they are best suited. The distinction is, perhaps, not important so long as all reports carry adequate description or illustration; but the adoption of some such distinction would unquestionably simplify and clarify our terminology.

Type 1 knives are small, thin, selected flakes which are bifacially chipped to produce a cutting edge. They are reported for nearly every branch and time period, and almost certainly occur in all. They are often overlooked or disregarded, however, and so the record shows none for San Simon, Cibola, and Jornada branches.

Type 3 knives are like Type 1 except that they are larger and cruder, and are mostly percussion flaked. Their distribution tends to be southern, in that they are reported for all branches except Forestdale; and early, in that they are not reported for Mogollon 4 at all and only in Mimbres during Mogollon 3. While their actual occurrence may be somewhat greater than reported, their certain decline may suggest that they were used in some definite process that also was declining.

Almost as widely distributed as Type 1 are the leaf-shaped Type 2 knives (Fig. 9, s). These are large, often asymmetric, blades usually showing rather coarse workmanship. They are reported from all areas except Pine Lawn Valley in Mogollon 1; from Forestdale in Mogollon 2 and 3, and also from the Mimbres during the latter period. They are not definitely reported for Mogollon 4, so it seems that the type declined after Mogollon 1.

Type 7 knives (Fig. 9, r) are similar to Type 2 but are ovoid rather than pointed. They occur in Pine Lawn Valley and Black River Branch during Mogollon 1, in Mimbres Branch and Pine Lawn Valley in Mogollon 3, in Jornada and again in Pine Lawn Valley during Mogollon 4. Type 6, discoidal in shape but otherwise like types 2 and 7, is reported only from Crooked Ridge Village in Mogollon 1.

Type 4 knives (Fig. 9, t) are essentially like stemmed projectile points, but because of their size I have considered them as knives. They are not common but occur sporadically in Pine Lawn Valley in Mogollon 1 and in Mimbres Branch during Mogollon 3. They are reported, also, from San Simon, but are not placed temporally.

Single- or corner-notched blades (Type 5, Fig. 9, u), which might be considered either projectile points or knives, are reported from Mimbres Branch in Mogollon 1 and 3, and also from Forestdale during the latter period.

A specialized type of knife is the serrate-edged form, Type 8 (Fig. 9, w), which appears to have a late and more or less northern distribution. These are abundant in Forestdale Branch during Mogollon 3, and are reported also from the northern Mimbres (Tularosa Cave) in this period.

Five main types of drills are reported from Mogollon sites. Type 1 has a small, trianguloid base and a relatively narrow shaft (Fig. 9, x). During Mogollon 1 it is reported for Pine Lawn Valley, Mimbres, and Black River, but only from Mimbres in Mogollon 2. It appears that as a type, this form was declining in popularity.

Type 2 is similar to Type 1, but the base is more ex- panded and the shaft somewhat more lenticular (Fig. 9, y). It is recorded for Pine Lawn Valley, Forestdale, and Black River during Mogollon 1, Forestdale in Mogollon 2, and Pine

Lawn Valley, Mimbres, and Forestdale in Mogollon 3.  It is reported only for Pine Lawn Valley in Mogollon 4.

Type 3 has an irregular, unshaped flake base (Fig. 9, z), and occurs sporadically.  It was found in Black River Branch in Mogollon 1 and in Pine Lawn Valley in Mogollon 1, 3, and 4.

Type 4 is a category rather than a type, for it includes all the stemmed forms, most of which are projectile points used secondarily for drilling (Fig. 9, aa).  They are probably more widespread than the literature indicates, for they are reported only from Black River Branch during Mogollon 1 and from Mimbres and Forestdale in Mogollon 3.

Plain shafted or cylindrical drills (Type 5, Fig. 9, bb) have a sporadic, early northern distribution, being reported from Forestdale and the northern Mimbres (Tularosa Cave) during Mogollon 1 and from Forestdale in Mogollon 2.  By Mogollon 3 the type is reported as far south as Mogollon Village in Mimbres Branch.  It will be noted that there are almost no records of drills occurring in Mogollon 4, but this surely reflects a gap in our data rather than an absence of the tool, for it does occur in all later horizons and areas.

The basis for the discrimination of scrapers has been given above and need not be repeated here.  In Mogollon sites, as in most Southwestern sites, scrapers of various sorts are common artifacts.  At least six basic types or subtypes can be isolated.  Of these, scrapers made from selected random flakes constitute the vast majority.

Thick flake tools with a high-angle scraping edge (Type 1a, Fig. 9, cc) occur through Mogollon 3 in every branch where we have sufficient data, and are reported from Pine Lawn Valley and Jornada Branch in Mogollon 4.  They probably occur in other areas during the latter period, also.

Type 1b consists of smaller and thinner flakes than the preceding type, and the working edge has a low, flat angle of retouch (Fig. 9, dd), sometimes by percussion but more often by pressure or shear flaking. These tools are often called knives, and many were undoubtedly used as such, as well as for scraping. This may account for the fact that Type 1b is less often reported than Type 1a. Nonetheless, they occur in every branch except San Simon during Mogollon 1 and 2; they are reported only from Mimbres Branch in Mogollon 3, and not at all in Mogollon 4.

End scrapers (Type 2) are thick random flakes with a high-angle scraping edge at the end rather than on the side (Fig. 9, ee). Like the foregoing types, they occur in every period and in four branches. They are not recorded for San Simon, Cibola, and Jornada branches, and like types 1a and 1b, seem to decline somewhat after Mogollon 3.

Concave or hollow-edge scrapers (Type 3, Fig. 9, ff) also occur widely, being reported from all branches except San Simon through Mogollon 3, but only from Pine Lawn Valley in Mogollon 4.

Type 4, a deeply serrated edge chipped into a thick random flake (Fig. 9, gg), is reported only from Pine Lawn Valley in Mogollon 1 within the period covered by this study.

Ground-edged scrapers (Type 5, Fig. 9, hh) are usually considered a southern tool type, but for the period under consideration they are reported only for Forestdale Branch in Mogollon 1, 2, and 3, and do not occur elsewhere until Mogollon 4 when they are reported only from Cameron Creek. This probably does not indicate the actual extent of their distribution, for the type is difficult to recognize until one is quite familiar with it; hence, many have probably gone unreported. Nevertheless, future investigators should try to establish the range of this scraper type.

Large gravers (Fig. 9, ii) are occasionally reported from Mogollon sites, and their chief distribution seems to be northern. During Mogollon 1 they are reported from northern Mimbres (Cordova Cave), Black River, and Forestdale branches, being common in the latter area. They continue in Forestdale during Mogollon 2 and 3, and in the latter period are also reported for Pine Lawn Valley.

Other tools commonly occurring in Mogollon sites are those used in a planing motion, the scraper planes or pulping planes (Fig. 9, jj). While it is possible to distinguish subtypes based on size and the amount of perimeter included in the working edge, such distinctions are not always determinable in the literature, for which reason I have combined them here in one type for distributional purposes.

During Mogollon 1 these planes are reported from every branch except San Simon. They probably occur there also, for they are present in San Pedro Stage of the Cochise Culture and are reported there for all later periods. Elsewhere, for later periods they are recorded only for Mimbres Branch during Mogollon 3. Their decline may well be associated with a shift in economy, for the larger planes, at least, are believed to have been used in the preparation of soft pulped plants for food and other uses.

Plano-convex hand axes are large primary flakes with a low-angle cutting edge opposite an untrimmed hand-hold (Fig. 9, kk). Although probably of much wider occurrence in early horizons, they are reported only from Pine Lawn Valley and Black River Branch during Mogollon 1.

Choppers, on the other hand, have a very wide distribution. These are large cores or cobbles with a bifacially percussion-flaked, usually sinuous, cutting edge on about half of the perimeter, the remainder being left untrimmed to serve as a hand-hold (Fig. 9, 11). Subtypes can be recognized on the basis of size, but usually are not; hence, all sizes have been considered together here. They occur in all of the branches during Mogollon 1 and 2, in San Simon, Mimbres, and Pine Lawn Valley in Mogollon 3, and continue into Mogollon 4 in these areas.

### Bone and Antler Artifacts

Bone and antler artifacts are illustrated in Figure 10 and their distribution given in Table 13. Awls are by far the most common bone artifacts recovered in Mogollon sites. At least seven types may be isolated, several of which may be further divided into subtypes. The most widely distributed form is Type 6 (Fig. 10, k), a splinter of bone modified for use by working the end to a sharp point. These occur everywhere except Forestdale during Mogollon 1 and 2, everywhere but Black River in Mogollon 3, and occur in San Simon, Mimbres, and Pine Lawn Valley during Mogollon 4. The absence of splinter awls in the areas where they are not reported would seem to indicate a lack of data rather than actual absence of the artifact.

Another group of awls showing little modification for use consists of various sorts of bones whose unmodified heads served as handles. Such are types 1, 2, and 2a, the difference between them being only the kind of bone used. Deer ulna awls (Type 1, Fig. 10, a) have a consistent distribution and are reported from Mimbres, Pine Lawn Valley, and Black River during Mogollon 1. They are not recorded for Mogollon 2, but in Mogollon 3 are reported from all branches except Black River where there is insufficient evidence. The type is reported only from the Mimbres and Pine Lawn Valley during Mogollon 4.

Type 2 awls are made from turkey or other large bird wing bones, by grinding obliquely across the shaft (Fig. 10, b). The working tip thus produced is more like a chisel than an awl, and the tools may not actually have been awls. This type is reported only from Mogollon 1 in Black River Branch, and from Mogollon 4 in the Mimbres.

Type 2a is made from rabbit humeri and similar bones, and has a sharp point (Fig. 10, c). This type has a late distribution, occurring during Mogollon 3 in Pine Lawn Valley and possibly in San Simon; and in Mimbres and Pine Lawn Valley during Mogollon 4. Sharpened deer rib awls (Type 7, Fig. 10, l) are reported only for San Simon Branch during Mogollon 1.

Awls made of split bones, usually deer metapodials, are found in many Southwestern sites. Characteristic of Mogollon sites are split metapodial awls further modified by notching the shaft to reduce the diameter, or to aid in the manufacture. Two notched awl subtypes may be recognized on the basis of size. Type 3a is a long, slender tool with sharp, gradually tapered point (Fig. 10, d), while Type 3b is short with a broad shaft tapering sharply to a slender point (Fig. 10, e). Whether there was actually a difference in use of these subtypes cannot be said, but the fact that the two size ranges generally do not overlap might indicate such a difference, as

might also the variation in shape of the tip. Most Type 3
awls at Crooked Ridge Village were made from the distal end
of the cannon bone, and although this distinction is not made
in the literature, judging from illustrated specimens it is
also true elsewhere. The reported temporal and spatial distribution of the types is indicative. They do not occur in

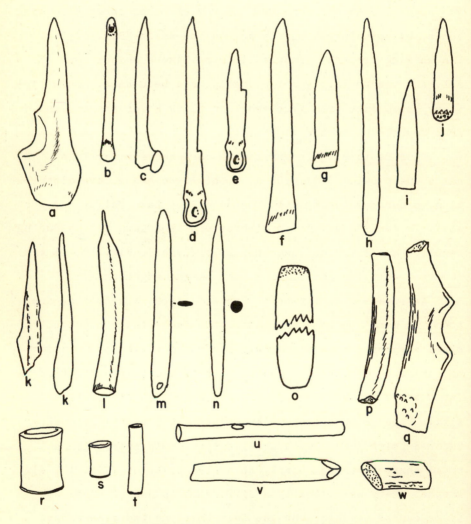

Figure 10. Bone and antler artifacts.

either San Simon or Forestdale branch; hence, their distribution is central in the Mogollon area. They occur in Mimbres, Pine Lawn Valley, and Black River during Mogollon 1, in Black River in Mogollon 2, and in Mimbres and Pine Lawn Valley during Mogollon 3 and 4.

Table 13

| MOGOLLON PERIOD | 1 | | | | | 2 | | | 3 | | | | | 4 | | | | | |
|---|---|---|---|---|---|---|---|---|---|---|---|---|---|---|---|---|---|---|---|
| BRANCH | San Simon | Mimbres | Pine Lawn | Forestdale | Black River | San Simon | Forestdale | Black River | San Simon | Mimbres | Pine Lawn | Forestdale | Black River | San Simon | Mimbres | Pine Lawn | Cibola | Black River | Jornada |
| Awls: Type 1 | | P | P | | P | | | | P | P | P | P | | | P | P | | | |
| 2 | | | | P | | | | | | | | | | | P | | | | |
| 2a | | | | | | | | | ? | | P | | | | P | P | | | |
| 3a | | P | P | P | | | P | | | P | P | | | | P | P | | | |
| 3b | | P | P | P | | | P | | | P | P | | | | P | P | | | |
| 4a | | P | P | P | | | P | | | P | P | P | | | P | P | P | | |
| 4b | P | | P | P | | | | | ? | | | P | | | P | | | | |
| 5a | P | P | P | P | | | | | | | P | | | | P | P | | | P |
| 5b | ? | P | P | | | | | ? | ? | | P | | | ? | P | P | | | |
| 5c | | | | | | | | | | | P | P | | C | | | | | |
| 6 | P | P | P | | P | P | | ? | P | P | P | P | | P | P | P | | | |
| 7 | P | | | | | | | | | | | | | | | | | | |
| Needles | | | P | | | | | | | | P | P | | | P | | | | |
| Pins (or skewers) | | | P | | | | | | | ? | | | | | P | | | | |
| Fleshers | | | P | | | | | | ? | | P | P | | | P | P | | | |
| Rib scrapers | P | | | | | | | | | P | P | | | | | | P | | |
| Pelvis knives | | | | | | | | ? | | | | | | | | | | | |
| Large tubes | P | | | P | P | P | | | | P | P | | | P | | P | | | |
| Small short tubes | | | P | P | | | | | | P | P | | | | | | | | |
| Pipe stems | | | P | | | | | | | ? | | | | | ? | | | | |
| Whistles | | | | ? | | | | | | | P | | | | | | | | |
| Flakers (bone) | | | P | | | | | | | | | | | | | | | | |
| Flakers (antler) | | | P | P | | | | | | P | P | | | | P | | | | |
| Rubber (antler) | | | P | | | | | | | | | | | | | | | | |
| Miscellaneous bone | | | | | | | | | | | P | | | | P | | | | |

Table 13. Distribution of Mogollon bone and antler artifacts by branch and period. C = common, P = present, ? = probable but not reported.

Unnotched bone awls differ from notched types in several respects. Again, there are long and short subtypes (4a, Fig. 10, f, and 4b, Fig. 10, g). They are usually made from the proximal end of the metapodial, and the broad, sturdy shaft tapers evenly to a rather thick point. They have a somewhat different distribution from the notched awls. The long variety (Type 4a) has the same Mogollon 1 and 2 distribution as Type 3 awls, but in Mogollon 3 they occur also in Forestdale Branch, and in Mogollon 4 are reported for Cibola. The short Type 4b occurs at San Simon, Pine Lawn Valley, and Black River during Mogollon 1, and is not recorded for Mogollon 2; in Mogollon 3 it occurs in Forestdale and perhaps in San Simon, and is reported only for Mimbres in Mogollon 4.

Type 5 awls have the articular head of the bone modified or completely removed. Type 5a consists of a long, slender section of bone shaft with the head completely removed (Fig. 10, h). It has a wide distribution, being reported for every branch but Forestdale during Mogollon 1. It is not recorded for Mogollon 2, but in the next period it occurs in Pine Lawn Valley, and in Mogollon 4 is recorded for Mimbres, Pine Lawn Valley, and Jornada.

Type 5b has the articular head removed, but most of the half bone shaft is left (Fig. 10, i). In general form, these are similar to Type 4. During Mogollon 1 they are reported from Mimbres and Pine Lawn Valley; from the latter during Mogollon 3; and from Mimbres and Pine Lawn Valley in Mogollon 4. The type is also reported from San Simon Branch, but the time levels are not known.

Type 5c awls retain part of the articular head, but the end is ground down and smoothed to form a handle (Fig. 10, j).

Distribution of this type is late, being reported for Mimbres and Pine Lawn Valley during Mogollon 3, and for Mimbres only in Mogollon 4 when they are a common type.

Some artifacts termed bone needles very possibly had other functions, for the dull, flat, rounded-tip tools (Fig. 10, m) would not have functioned well for sewing most materials. During Mogollon 1 they are reported only for Pine Lawn Valley; for Mimbres and Pine Lawn Valley in Mogollon 3; and only for Mimbres during Mogollon 4.

Slender, carefully finished bone pins or skewers (Fig. 10, n) are reported only from Pine Lawn Valley during Mogollon 1, and from Mimbres during either Mogollon 3 or 4.

Fleshers are spatulate-edged tools made from long-bone sections or from ribs (Fig. 10, o). They have a sporadic distribution in both time and space. They occur in Pine Lawn Valley during Mogollon 1; in Pine Lawn Valley, Forestdale, and perhaps Mimbres during Mogollon 3; and Mimbres and Pine Lawn Valley in Mogollon 4. Closely allied to fleshers, and perhaps used for the same purpose, are tools termed rib scrapers (Fig. 10, p). The difference is that fleshers have working edges on the ends, rather than on the sides as in the scrapers. Rib scrapers are reported from Mimbres Branch during Mogollon 1 and 3; they occur also in Pine Lawn Valley in Mogollon 3, and in Cibola Branch in Mogollon 4.

Deer-pelvis knives (Fig. 10, q) are reported only from Crooked Ridge Village, but since all occurred in the fill of one pithouse, there is some question as to whether they belong to the Mogollon horizon or to one of the small late Pueblo units on the site. They are tentatively assigned to Mogollon 2.

Several sizes of bone tubes were made by the Mogollon. Large tubes sometimes have signs of wear on the interior and around the mouth, as if they had been used as slides (Fig. 10, r). During Mogollon 1 they occur in Black River and in San Simon, where some have incised designs as they do also in Mogollon 2. Incised and plain tubes continue in San Simon during Mogollon 3, but elsewhere (in Pine Lawn Valley and Forestdale) only plain tubes are reported. During Mogollon 4 plain tubes occurred in both San Simon and Pine Lawn Valley, and the incised variety seems to have died out. Short tubes of small diameter, with cut and polished ends (Fig. 10, s), may have been used as beads. During Mogollon 1 they occur in Pine Lawn Valley and Black River Branch, and in Mimbres and Forestdale during Mogollon 3. They are not reported for later periods, and so, together with the evidence of the large bone tubes, might indicate a decline in popularity of bone tubes. Longer small-diameter tubes occasionally are found in place as stems of tubular stone pipes (Fig. 10, t), so that many, if not all, of these can be identified as such. They occur in Pine Lawn Valley in Mogollon 1, and in Mimbres Branch during either Mogollon 3 or 4.

Bone whistles (Fig. 10, u) have a northern distribution. One specimen from Crooked Ridge Village may have been a whistle; if so, this would place a single occurrence in Mogollon 1. Definite whistles are reported only from Forestdale during Mogollon 3 and probably represent an intrusive northern trait.

Flakers of bone (Fig. 10, v) and antler are reported sporadically, but in all probability had a wider distribution than is indicated. Only one bone flaker is reported from

Pine Lawn Valley during Mogollon 1, where antler flakers are also reported, as they are in Black River Branch during the same period. In Mogollon 3 antler flakers are reported from Mimbres and Forestdale, and from Mimbres in Mogollon 4. Another type of antler tool is the rubbing tool or smoother (Fig. 10, w), reported from Pine Lawn Valley in Mogollon 1.

Miscellaneous bone objects are reported for late periods. These include perforated bird bone beads and a polished bone cylinder from Forestdale during Mogollon 3; and a curved pointed object (perhaps an awl), a blunt-ended tool, and a scraper made of a segment of turtle carapace from Harris Village in Mimbres Branch during Mogollon 3 or 4. None of these has occurred commonly enough to be considered standard artifact categories, but they do indicate a certain amount of experimentation in late times.

## Ornaments of the Mogollon

Ornaments of stone, shell, and bone are characteristic of Mogollon sites, and while more common in late periods, are by no means rare in early phases. (See Table 14 and Figure 11.) This would argue for considerable trade relationships with other peoples, for certain materials, such as shell or finished shell artifacts, must have come from outside sources. Other objects, such as those of bone, undoubtedly were made locally. When ornaments made of perishable materials (discussed below) are added to those of durable substances, it becomes clear that Mogollon ornaments were abundant even if mostly simple in nature.

During Mogollon 1, 11 varieties of ornaments are reported. They occur in all branches except Forestdale. Most common were shell disc beads (Fig. 11, c) and thin shell

bracelets (Fig. 11, j), found in three branches, and stone
pendants (Fig. 11, h), which occurred in four. Ornament
types occurring in two branches were whole olivella shell
beads (Fig. 11, a), shell pendants of various forms (Fig. 11,
g), and bone dice (Fig. 11, n). The remaining five categories
---vermetus tube beads (Fig. 11, b), stone disc beads (Fig.
11, d), bone disc beads (Fig. 11, e), stone zoomorphic pendants (Fig. 11, i), and solid bone discs (Fig. 11, o)---are
each reported from only one branch during Mogollon 1. Nine
categories were reported from Pine Lawn Valley, while each of
the other branches had only three to five types of ornaments.

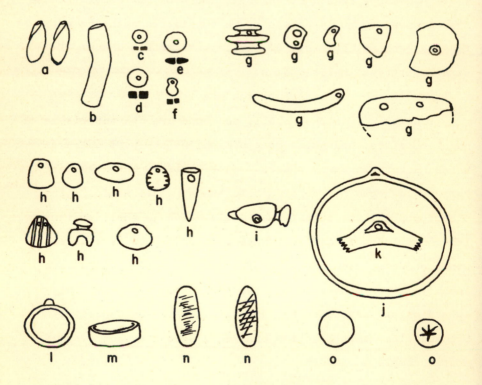

Figure 11. Mogollon ornaments.

Mogollon 2 ornaments are known only from two branches, San Simon and Black River, and only five types of objects are recorded for the period. Stone disc beads and bone dice are reported only for Black River Branch, but stone and shell pendants and thin shell bracelets occurred in both Black River and San Simon branches.

Ornaments of Mogollon 3 are more common and more widespread than in earlier periods. However, only 11 categories are represented. Since the one house from this period at Black River Branch contained no ornaments, data are available for only four of the branches. All of these had some variety

Table 14

| MOGOLLON PERIOD | 1 | | | | | 2 | | | 3 | | | | | 4 | | | | | |
|---|---|---|---|---|---|---|---|---|---|---|---|---|---|---|---|---|---|---|---|
| TYPE \ BRANCH | San Simon | Mimbres | Pine Lawn | Forestdale | Black River | San Simon | Forestdale | Black River | San Simon | Mimbres | Pine Lawn | Forestdale | Black River | San Simon | Mimbres | Pine Lawn | Cibola | Black River | Jornada |
| Olivella beads | | | P | | P | | | | | P | P | | | | P | | | | P |
| Vermetus tubes | | P | | | | | | | | P | | | | | | | ? | | |
| Shell disc beads | P | P | P | | | | | | P | P | | A | | A | | | | | P |
| Stone disc beads | | | P | | | | | P | | | P | | | P | P | | | | |
| Bone disc beads | | | P | | | | | | | | | | | P | | | | | |
| Figure-8 beads | | | | | | | | | | | | | | P | | | | | |
| Shell pendants | | P | | | P | P | | P | P | P | P | P | P | P | P | P | P | | P |
| Stone pendants | P | P | P | | P | P | | P | | | | P | P | P | P | P | P | | P |
| Miscellaneous shell | | | | | | | | | | | P | | P | P | | | | | |
| Zoomorphic pendants | | P | | | | | | | | | | | | | | | ? | | |
| Thin shell bracelets | P | P | ? | | P | P | | P | P | P | P | P | C | P | C | P | P | | P |
| Broad shell bracelets | | | | | | | | | P | | | | | P | | | | | |
| Shell rings | | | | | | | | | | | | | | P | P | | | | |
| Bone rings | | | | | | | | | | | | | | P | | | | | P |
| Bone dice | | | P | | P | | | P | P | P | C | | | P | P | | | | |
| Bone discs | | | P | | | | | | | | P | | | P | | | | | |

Table 14. Distribution of Mogollon ornaments by branch and period. A = abundant, C = common, P = present, ? = probable but not reported.

of shell pendants and thin shell bracelets, and three had
shell disc beads and bone dice. Olivella shell beads occurred
in two branches, Mimbres and Forestdale, which also had miscellaneous peculiar ornaments. Pine Lawn Valley and Forestdale Branch shared stone pendant forms. Stone disc beads,
broad shell bracelets (Fig. 11, k), and bone discs are each
represented in one branch. Forestdale Branch had nine categories of ornaments, Mimbres had seven, San Simon had four,
and Pine Lawn Valley had four.

Fourteen types of ornaments are reported for Mogollon 4,
three of them, figure-8 beads (Fig. 11, f), shell rings (Fig.
11, l), and bone rings (Fig. 11, m), being innovations. As
in Mogollon 3, the most widespread ornament types were thin
shell bracelets and various kinds of shell and stone pendants,
which occur in every branch where we have adequate data.
Olivella shell beads, shell and stone disc beads, shell and
bone rings, and bone dice are each reported for two branches,
while bone disc beads, figure-8 beads, broad shell bracelets,
and solid bone discs occurred in only one branch. Vermetus
tubes and zoomorphic pendants may be associated with Cibola
Branch, but the evidence is not clear. Twelve categories of
ornaments are represented in Mimbres Branch, six in San Simon,
six in Jornada, five in Pine Lawn Valley, and three to five in
Cibola Branch.

Certain trends may be observed. It is clear that ornaments of durable material increased in popularity from early
to late, in part reflecting expanding outside contacts. Shell
bracelets and pendants of shell and stone were rather consistently the most common types of ornaments through all periods.
The pendants of Mogollon 1 are generally simple; yet the

zoomorphic stone pendant from SU Site is surprisingly well conceived and executed. The pendants of later periods become increasingly complex, many being carved in the Hohokam manner. Figure-8 beads, and bone and shell rings are obviously late introductions, probably from the Hohokam, who had each of these at an earlier period. The few miscellaneous shell objects do not, as yet known, constitute significant categories, but may instead reflect the creativeness of individuals.

### Perishable Materials

Open sites seldom yield significant quantities of the perishable goods which usually constitute the greater part of material culture. Mogollon sites are not exceptions to this rule, for ordinarily no such remains are found. The rare find of charred textile, basket, a few grains of corn or beans, or a basketry-impressed sherd, are the only indications of the nature of perishable materials recovered from most sites.

Although Mogollon cave sites had been previously explored, it was not until the stratigraphic excavation of Tularosa and Cordova caves that any considerable body of dry materials became available for study. Because no comparable amount of evidence is available for other sections of the Mogollon area, I can do little more than summarize the significant findings of Martin and his associates (1952). These have been listed in Table 15.

Certain points should be remembered in considering these data. First, the northeasterly position of these caves, in relation to most other Mogollon sites, might indicate some cultural marginality. Certainly, it may reflect local rather than area-wide ecological conditions; and to the extent that it does, the subsistence pattern indicated must be considered a local variation. Finally, in view of individual variation between Mogollon sites (incidentally, clearly evident between Tularosa and Cordova caves), some of the traits and trends apparent may not apply to the whole of Mogollon Culture, nor even to all of Mimbres Branch. Nevertheless, the basic culture traits established there are, in all probability, to be considered basic for the entire culture.

Table 15

| ARTIFACT TYPE | MOGOLLON PERIOD | | |
|---|---|---|---|
| | 1, Early | 1, Late | 3 |
| Sandals | | | |
| Wicker work | Predominant | Predominant | Important |
| Plaited | | Introduced | Present |
| Multiple warp | | Present | Decrease |
| Continuous outer warp | Present | | Predominant |
| Concentric warp | Present | Present | Present |
| Scuffer toe | | | Present |
| Leather, plain | | Present | |
| Leather, winter | Present | | Present |
| Ornaments | | | |
| Feather | | | Present |
| Fig-beetle femora | | | Present |
| Twig ring | | | Present |
| Clothing | | | |
| String apron | | Present | |
| Sash, twisted cord | Present | | |
| Blankets | | | |
| Fur cord | Present | Present | Present |
| Fur and feather cord | | Present | |
| Feather cord | Present | Present | |
| Snares | | | |
| Forked stick | Present | | |
| Trigger (?) | | Present | |
| Digging stick | Present | Present | Present |
| Grass beds | Present | Present | Present |
| Plant fiber scouring pad | Present | Decrease | Decrease |
| Cradles, flexible | Present | Present | |
| Netted carrying bags | Present | Present | Present |
| Twined flexible carrying basket | Present | | |
| Toggles for tump lines | Present | Present | Present |
| Burden strap | | Present | |
| Fire drill hearths | Present | Present | Present |
| Fire drills, simple | | Present | Present |
| Fire drills, compound | | | Present |
| Fire tongs | | | Present |
| Atlatls and darts | Present | Present | Decrease |
| Atlatl dart bunts | Present | Present | Decrease |
| Atlatl charm stones | | Present | Decrease |

(Continued on next page)

Table 15 (Continued)

| ARTIFACT TYPE | MOGOLLON PERIOD | | |
|---|---|---|---|
| | 1, Early | 1, Late | 3 |
| Hunting bows and arrows | Present | Present | Increase |
| Wooden scoop | | Present | |
| Wood and bark trowels | Present | | Decrease |
| Feather carding burred sticks | Present | Present | Present |
| Wooden awls | Present | | |
| Lap boards | Present | | Present |
| Pot rests | Present | Present | Present |
| Brushes | Present | | Present |
| Wooden spindles | | Present | |
| Corncob pottery smoother | Present | | |
| Wooden weaving tool | | Present | |
| Wooden spatula | | Present | |
| Shouldered, pointed charred sticks | | Rare | Present |
| Wooden spoon | | | Present |
| Coiled basketry 2-rod-and-bundle | Dominant | Dominant | Dominant |
| Bundle-with-rod-core | Present | | Present |
| Bundle | | Present | Present |
| Half-rod-and-bundle | | | Present |
| Twined flexible basket | Present | | |
| Twilled matting | | Present | Present |
| Twined and sewed matting | Present | Present | |
| Cotton cloth, over-one-under-one weave | | | Present |
| Bast fiber cloth, over-one-under-one weave | | | Present |
| Knotless netting | | Present | |
| Coiled netting on warps | | | Present |
| Netting tied with square knots | | Present | |
| Netting tied with overhand knots | Present | | |
| Twined fabric, bast fiber | | | Present |
| Twined fabric, bast, hard, and hair fiber | | | Present |
| Leather bags | | Present | |
| Leather quiver | | | Present |
| Yucca leaf container for pitch | | Present | |
| Unfired pottery | Present | Present | Increase |
| Reed flutes | Present | Present | |
| Wooden dice | Present | Present | Decrease |
| Reed cigarettes | Rare | Present | Increase |
| Juniper-berry skewers | Present | Present | Decrease |
| Wooden tablitas | | Rare | Present |
| Miniature bows and arrows | | | Introduced |

(Continued on next page)

Table 15 (Continued)

| ARTIFACT TYPE | MOGOLLON PERIOD | | |
|---|---|---|---|
| | 1, Early | 1, Late | 3 |
| Ceremonial bows | | | Introduced |
| Medicine man's bag | | | Present |
| Pahos | | | |
|   Corncob on stick | Introduced | | Present |
|   Feather on stick | | Present | Present |
|   Deer hoof charm | Present | Present | Present |
|   Reed stalk on stem | Introduced | Present | Present |
|   Painted stick | | Rare | Present |
|   Stick with pattern | | | |
|     incised on bark | Present | Present | Present |
| Sticks with fiber, hair, | | | |
|   or sinew binding | Present | Present | Decrease |
| Wood with fiber tied | | | |
|   around it | Present | | |
| Stick with knotted | | | |
|   yucca binding | | | Introduced |
| Bundle of sticks | Present | | |
| Split sticks | | Present | Present |
| Tooth-marked sticks | | | Present |
| Wooden cylinders | Present | | Decrease |
| Reed tubes | Present | Present | Present |
| Twigs tied in loops | Present | Present | |
| Hoop-like object | Present | Present | |
| Netted hoop | Present | | Present |
| Worked gourd rind | Present | Present | Present |

Table 15. Mogollon perishable artifacts from Tularosa and Cordova caves, by period.

Table 15 represents an abstraction of data from the study of Martin and his associates (1952:485-495), somewhat modified to accord with the chronological framework used in this study. I have, however, retained the Pine Lawn - Georgetown sequence, but have substituted the terms Mogollon 1, Early, and Mogollon 1, Late. San Francisco Phase is Mogollon 3. For details of artifact technology and variations in typology, the reader is referred to the original study.

Martin has noted certain trends in perishable materials (1952:497). In general, these are as follows.

1. Wickerwork sandals are early, beginning in preceramic time, whereas plaited sandals are late.

2. Multiple warp sandals, resembling Basketmaker III sandals, are most common in Georgetown period (late Mogollon 1) of Tularosa Cave.

3. Cotton cloth first appears at the beginning of San Francisco Phase (Mogollon 3).

4. Coiled basketry was predominant from preceramic times to San Francisco Phase, when it declined as a major type in favor of twilled basketry.

5. "At or about the advent of the San Francisco Phase, we find that hunting bows (and arrows) and ceremonial and miniature bows and arrows appeared. The atlatl was gradually displaced by the bow." But see trait list (ibid.:488) where hunting bows and arrows are indicated for preceramic horizons and all later phases, based on evidence of proximal fragments of arrow shafts recovered from those horizons (ibid.:385 and figs. 130, 131, 132).

6. Popularity of juniper-berry skewers declines as miniature bows and arrows appear.

7. Frequency of reed cigarettes increased in San Francisco Phase.

8. Tablitas, parts of ceremonial headdresses (?), increased in popularity during San Francisco Phase.

Nothing can be added to these observations of general trends in Mogollon dry materials, but a few additional examples from other sites, preserved by charring, may be noted even though they add little information. There are several specimens from Crooked Ridge Village, including a charred wooden fragment that may be part of a tablita. Its occurrence would correspond generally with the early occurrence in Tularosa Cave. Fragments of a twined woven sash or belt also belong in Mogollon 1, thus placing it somewhat earlier than similar fabrics from Tularosa Cave. From the Mogollon 2 horizon at Crooked Ridge Village are a square knot tied in yucca fiber, unwoven roof matting, and a second piece of fabric woven over-one-under-one of bast fiber, again somewhat earlier than its Tularosa Cave counterparts. Two charred examples of two-rod-and-bundle foundation basketry were recovered from Bear Ruin in a Mogollon 3 horizon. From Harris Village are fragments of a two-rod-and-bundle basket with interlocking stitches, a heavily matted woven fabric, and several hundred hackberry seed beads, all dating from Mogollon 4 period.

Of the basic elements of the Mogollon subsistence pattern
there can be little doubt.  Hunting, gathering, and agriculture each played its part.  However, the question of relative
importance of each in the total pattern has never been satis-
factorily answered.  There is ample evidence that each was
practised; but only for one small area do we have the quantitative data necessary to assess their status.

A rich fauna recovered at Harris and Mogollon villages
led Haury to postulate heavy reliance on hunting as well as
on agriculture (Haury 1936b:92-93).  A similar situation prevailed at Forestdale Ruin during Mogollon 3, where the number
of deer bones recovered makes it seem likely that as much reliance was placed on hunting as on agriculture (Haury 1941).
The evidence for earlier times, however, led Haury and Sayles
(1947:82-83) to conclude that hunting was of slight importance
as compared to food gathering and agriculture.  Sayles (1945:
58) states that animal bones of several species were common in
the trash, and that their frequency (quantity, or species?)
varied from phase to phase.  Since he does not mention the
nature of the differences, it does not elucidate the relative
importance of hunting to agriculture and gathering, which are
indicated by grinding tools.

In Crooked Ridge Village the meager evidence indicated
that hunting, gathering, and agriculture each played its part,
but it was not possible to say in what proportion.  In Pine
Lawn Valley the nature of stone tools, and relative quantities

155

of food remains, caused Martin and Rinaldo (1947:290-291) to postulate a primary dependence on seed gathering, both hunting and agriculture being secondary. By Reserve Phase (Mogollon 5) they (Martin and Rinaldo 1950b:453-454) see a shift from seed gathering toward hunting, but with agriculture being the most important single subsistence activity. Data from Cibola and Jornada branches are inconclusive, but it seems clear that both agriculture and hunting were practised.

With the above deductions based on the scanty evidence of open sites, it is interesting to turn to the remains from Tularosa and Cordova caves and to compare their evidence with that of open sites. There are, of course, certain necessary reservations to remember in doing this. First, the question of whether these caves are typical or not must await excavation of caves in other parts of the Mogollon area; and second, whether these abundant data may not, themselves, be biased, although inherently less so than those of open sites.

With no data of comparative nature, it is necessary only to outline the trends noted by Cutler, Martin, and Rinaldo (Martin et al. 1952:461-479, 486, 498-500). The list of vegetal products recovered from the prepottery horizon is interesting, especially if it can be checked against materials from other Mogollon caves. It includes maize, beans, squash, yucca pods, gourd, cacti, black walnuts, acorns, grass seeds, desert primrose leaves, and sunflower seeds. The same plants are reported for Pine Lawn Phase (Mogollon 1, Early). Following this phase there was a notable increase in frequency of wild plants over cultivated plants, with much less corn present (actual, or percentagewise?). The corn was improved, the greatest change (in average number of rows per cob) coming between Georgetown (Mogollon 1, Late) and San Francisco (Mogollon 3) phases. Tobacco was used in reed cigarettes around A. D. 500 (estimated). A study of animal bones also indicated certain trends. Frequency of animal bones was greater in Georgetown and pre-Georgetown phases than later, probably indicating greater dependence on hunting in the earlier periods. Deer was the favorite game animal, while bison is not reported before San Francisco Phase. Bear were rarely hunted, and no mountain lion bones were recovered. Turkey appeared in the earliest ceramic levels, and muskrats only in the early, suggesting either a climatic change or a cultural one, or perhaps only accident of inclusion.

There is no evidence to indicate whether these trends were consistent throughout the Mogollon area or reflect entirely local conditions. In any event, they contradict the hypotheses based on stone remains from equivalent periods in Pine Lawn Valley, for they indicate that, beginning in pre-ceramic times, agriculture was the primary means of subsistence, temporarily changed during Georgetown Phase, and then reinforced in San Francisco Phase by the addition of a new type of corn.

In the final determination of the role that gathering, hunting, and agriculture played at any particular time period, it must not be forgotten that to a large extent these activities are seasonal in nature, are complementary rather than mutually exclusive, and that the local environment must have had a considerable effect during all periods.

Martin and his associates (1950b:556-569) have essayed a most interesting reconstruction of the social organization of the Mogollon Indians of Pine Lawn Valley. It is not my purpose here to criticize this attempt in toto, for I consider it valuable and stimulating, if not proven or provable; nor to offer an alternative reconstruction. However, from the point of view of the total Mogollon cultural pattern, I should like to point out certain discrepancies in the Martin hypothesis and to indicate another approach to the matter that has recently received some attention.

Martin et al. postulated bilateral nuclear family units during late Cochise times, changing into matrilinear extended family units during Pine Lawn Phase (Mogollon 1), and then returning to the simpler nuclear family in later times, but continuing matrilineal descent. This reconstruction was founded on the basis of comparative house size during the various periods as represented in Pine Lawn Valley. But, as I have indicated above, this great house size is clearly a local and atypical development, and might logically be correlated with the specialization of interior storage pits rather than with expanded family units. If this correlation is correct, Pine Lawn Valley accords with the remainder of the Mogollon area. The emerging pattern of social organization would thus be simplified, and could be supported for the entire Mogollon area. The matrilineal assumption of Martin and his associates may perhaps be supported by more substantial evidence than

158

mere percentile correlation of agricultural and matrilineal
societies, for recent historical reconstructions of Southwestern prehistory by Reed, Hawley, and others, have shown
the likelihood that Western Pueblo, with its thoroughly
ingrained matrilineal complex, may well represent the ultimate
development of Mogollon. It is this ethnohistorical avenue of
approach that may in time lead to a more convincing and fruit-
ful reconstruction of earlier Mogollon social organization.

The reconstruction proposed by Martin and his associates
was possible at all only because of their carefully controlled
excavations in Pine Lawn Valley. The completeness and ade-
quateness of their data are perhaps not equalled anywhere else
in the Southwest. Certainly there is insufficient evidence
concerning culture trends in most of the Mogollon areas to
allow any such reconstruction. Thus, I feel that, while the
Chicago reconstruction should be held as a goal for Southwestern archeologists to shoot at, the time is not yet here
for such an attempt on a culture-wide scale.

Having surveyed the cultural content of the sites called Mogollon by their excavators, and those obviously belonging to the same cultural expression, we may now ask whether there is, or was at any period, a pattern which may be recognized as a functioning cultural entity. This, of course, leaves aside the question of relationships with other cultural patterns, which does not affect the problem at hand. Table 16 brings together the culture elements which characterize the Mogollon Culture Pattern.

Table 16

| CULTURE ELEMENT | MOGOLLON PERIOD | | | |
|---|---|---|---|---|
| | 1 | 2 | 3 | 4 |
| Branch | | | | |
| San Simon | x | x | x | x |
| Mimbres | x | | x | x |
| Pine Lawn Valley | x | | x | x |
| Cibola | | | | x . |
| Forestdale | x | x | x | |
| Black River | x | x | x | x |
| Jornada | | | | x |
| Time Period | | | | |
| 200 B. C. - A. D. 400 | x | | | |
| A. D. 400 - A. D. 600 | | x | | |
| A. D. 600 - A. D. 900 | | | x | |
| A. D. 900 - A. D. 1000 | | | | x |
| Phases | | | | |
| Penasco | x | | | |
| Pine Lawn | x | | | |
| Hilltop | x | | | |
| Georgetown | x | | | |
| Circle Prairie (Early) | x | | | |
| Dos Cabezas | | x | | |
| San Lorenzo (postulated) | | x | | |
| Cottonwood | | x | | |
| Circle Prairie (Late) | | x | | |
| Pinaleno | | | x | |
| Galiuro | | | x | |
| San Francisco | | | x | |
| Forestdale | | | x | |

(Continued on next page)

160

Table 16 (Continued)

| CULTURE ELEMENT | MOGOLLON PERIOD | | | |
|---|---|---|---|---|
| | 1 | 2 | 3 | 4 |
| Cerros | | | | x |
| Three Circle | | | | x |
| **Village Pattern** | | | | |
| Scattered houses with ceremonial structure | x | x | x | x |
| Random trash disposal | x | x | x | x |
| **Domestic Architecture** | | | | |
| Irregular, no lateral entry | x | | | |
| Roundish, no lateral entry | x | | x | x |
| One or more sides flat, no lateral entry | x | | x | |
| Quadrangular, no lateral entry | x | | x | x |
| Irregular, short lateral entry | x | | | |
| Roundish, short lateral entry | x | | x | |
| One or more sides flat, short lateral entry | | x | | x |
| Quadrangular, short lateral entry | | | x | x |
| Roundish, large broad entry | x | | x | |
| Roundish, long lateral entry | x | | x | x |
| Quadrangular, long lateral entry | x | x | x | x |
| Ovoid, entry at end | x | x | x | |
| Ovoid, entry at side | x | x | | |
| D-shape, short lateral entry | x | x | | |
| D-shape, long lateral entry | x | | | x |
| Bean-shape, short entry | x | | | |
| Bean-shape, long entry | x | | | |
| Roundish, vestibule (antechamber) entry | x | | x | x |
| Quadrangular, vestibule (antechamber) entry | x | | | |
| Quadrangular, southern annex | x | x | x | x |
| **Ceremonial Architecture** | | | | |
| Roundish, no lateral entry | x | | x | x |
| Quadrangular, no lateral entry | | | x | x |
| Roundish, short lateral entry | x | | x | |
| Bean-shape, short entry | x | | | |
| Bean-shape, long entry | | | x | |
| Quadrangular, short entry | | x | | |
| Ovoid, long entry | | | x | |
| D-shape, long entry | x | | x | |
| Quadrangular, long entry | | | | x |
| Entry oriented to east | x | x | x | x |
| Inclined entry | x | x | x | x |
| Hearth near entry | x | x | x | x |
| Hearth near center | x | x | x | x |
| Large intramural floor pits | x | x | x | x |
| Small intramural floor pits | x | x | x | x |
| Central post hole plan | x | x | x | x |
| Marginal post hole plan | x | x | x | x |
| Quadrilateral post hole plan | x | x | x | x |
| Gable roof plan | x | x | x | x |
| Extramural storage pits | x | x | x | x |
| Extramural hearths | x | x | x | x |
| Flexed burials, reclining in pit | x | x | x | x |
| Flexed burials, on side | x | x | x | x |

(Continued on next page)

Table 16 (Continued)

| CULTURE ELEMENT | MOGOLLON PERIOD | | | |
|---|---|---|---|---|
| | 1 | 2 | 3 | 4 |
| Subfloor burials | x | | | x |
| | | | | |
| Pottery | x | x | x | x |
| Plain brown ware | x | x | x | x |
| Red slipped ware | x | x | x | x |
| Broad-line red-on-brown | | x | x | |
| Narrow-line red-on-brown | | | x | x |
| Red-on-white | | | | x |
| Black-on-white | | | | x |
| Smudged ware | x | x | x | x |
| Textured and neck-banded ware | x | x | x | x |
| Deep hemispherical bowls | x | x | x | x |
| Shallow hemispherical bowls | x | x | x | x |
| Globular jars with outcurved rim | x | x | x | x |
| Globular jars with vertical neck | x | x | x | x |
| Neckless barrel-shaped jars | x | x | x | x |
| Neckless "seed" jars | x | x | x | x |
| Bottles | x | | | x |
| Use of handles and lugs | | | x | x |
| Miniature vessels | x | x | x | x |
| Miniature ladles | x | x | x | x |
| Pottery pipes | x | x | x | x |
| Human figurines | x | | x | x |
| Animal figurines | x | x | x | |
| Sherd discs | x | x | x | x |
| | | | | |
| Stone Artifacts | | | | |
| Basin metates | x | x | x | x |
| One-end-closed trough metates | x | x | x | |
| Full-trough metates | | | x | x |
| Ovoid uniface manos | x | x | x | x |
| Ovoid biface manos | x | x | x | x |
| Rectangular manos | | | x | x |
| Wedge manos | x | x | x | |
| Hand stones | x | x | x | x |
| Metate mortars | x | x | x | |
| Boulder mortars | x | x | x | x |
| Pebble mortars | x | x | x | x |
| Multiface pestles | x | x | x | x |
| Elongate angular pestles | x | x | x | x |
| Elongate digging tools | x | | | x |
| Stone bowls | x | x | x | x |
| Pitted pebbles | x | x | x | x |
| Polishing and abrading stones | x | x | x | x |
| Hammer stones | x | x | x | x |
| Grooved mauls | x | x | x | x |
| Stone hoes | x | | x | x |
| Tubular stone pipes | x | x | x | x |
| Stone balls | x | | x | x |
| Leaf-shaped projectile points | x | x | x | |
| Diagonally notched projectile points | x | x | x | x |
| Shallow side-notched projectile points | x | x | x | x |
| Deep side-notched projectile points | x | x | x | x |
| Straight-stemmed points | x | | x | |

(Continued on next page)

Table 16 (Continued)

| CULTURE ELEMENT | MOGOLLON PERIOD 1 | 2 | 3 | 4 |
|---|---|---|---|---|
| Flake knives | x | x | x | x |
| Leaf-shaped knives | x | x | x | |
| Expanded-base drills | x | x | x | x |
| Flake side-scrapers | x | x | x | x |
| Flake end-scrapers | x | x | x | x |
| Concave-edged scrapers | x | x | x | x |
| Large gravers | x | x | x | |
| Scraper planes | x | x | x | x |
| Choppers | x | x | x | x |
| | | | | |
| Bone and Antler Artifacts | | | | |
| Splinter bone awls | x | x | x | x |
| Deer ulna awls | x | | x | x |
| Split metapodial plain awls | x | x | x | x |
| Split metapodial side-notched awls | x | x | x | x |
| Long flat "needles" | x | | x | x |
| Large bone tubes | x | x | x | x |
| Antler flakers | x | | x | x |
| | | | | |
| Ornaments | | | | |
| Olivella shell beads | x | x | x | x |
| Shell disc beads | x | x | x | x |
| Stone disc beads | x | x | x | x |
| Shell pendants | x | x | x | x |
| Stone pendants | x | x | x | x |
| Thin shell bracelets | x | x | x | x |
| Bone dice | x | x | x | x |
| | | | | |
| Perishable Materials | | | | |
| Wickerwork sandals | x | | x | |
| Concentric warp sandals | x | | x | |
| Fur cord blankets | x | | x | |
| Digging sticks | x | | x | |
| Netted carrying bags | x | | x | |
| Wooden fire drills | x | | x | |
| Atlatls and darts | x | | x | |
| Hunting bows and arrows | x | | x | |
| Two-rod-and-bundle coiled baskets | x | | x | |
| Bundle-with-rod-core coiled baskets | x | | x | |
| Twilled matting | x | | x | |
| Unfired pottery | x | | x | |
| Wooden dice | x | | x | |
| Reed cigarettes | x | | x | |
| Juniper-berry skewers | x | | x | |
| Feather-on-stick pahos | x | | x | |
| Deer-hoof charms | x | | x | |
| | | | | |
| Subsistence | | | | |
| Corn | x | x | x | x |
| Beans | x | x | x | x |
| Squash | x | x | x | x |
| Bottle gourd | x | | x | |
| Hunting | x | x | x | x |
| Gathering | x | x | x | x |

Table 16. Characteristic Mogollon culture elements.

Analysis of Table 16 shows that choice of site location and characteristic village layout clearly indicate a basically similar pattern of living and of trash disposal. The presence of a ceremonial house in nearly every large village shows the importance of communal effort. In architecture, at each of the defined technological levels, all branches share certain basic house types and features; and while type frequency varies from branch to branch, it follows the same general trends toward quadrilateral houses with long lateral entries. The burial custom varies little from one area to another and follows the same general trends through time. In pottery, consistencies of technology, form, and clearly related typology leave little doubt that a single basic cultural pattern is being observed. In lithic tools there are also definite trait constellations: in metates and manos, mortars and pestles, grooved mauls and the exclusion of grooved axes, and in tubular stone pipes, there are uniformities of pattern that must be attributed to general intrarelationships. Uniformities are to be observed, also, in chipped stone artifacts, projectile point types, and especially in scraper planes, hand axes, and choppers. Bone tools are limited in number and simple in character; but the spatial and temporal distribution of the notched bone awl clearly marks it as a characteristic form. Ornaments are generally few in number and simple in nature; but the consistencies of basic types indicate, if not a pattern of manufacture, definite trade relationships which can be traced. Finally, in the matter of subsistence, insofar as it can be traced, basic uniformities certainly outweigh any variation caused by local environment.

It would appear, after a study of uniformities as well

as divergencies, that there is to be recognized a number of
regional expressions of culture which, while differing in
some details, nevertheless constitute a definite and definable
pattern in which the resemblances between areas are greater
than the differences.  Such differences as do appear are in
many cases due to influences of environment, others to some
degree of isolation from the main stream of culture, or
proximity to other cultural patterns.  It may be observed
that, in general, as one moves outward in any direction from
the central part of the Mogollon area, there is no sharp
cultural boundary.  It is this problem, and the related
historical problems, that shall concern us in the concluding
part of this study.

## Frames of Reference

In the preceding part of this study I have tried to
determine the functional trait constellation and cultural
orientation of the Mogollon people.  In the following pages
I shall attempt to trace the relationships of this group to
other Southwestern groups, both prior and contemporaneous.
In this paper I am not concerned with the relative taxonomic
status of the various groups.  Haury, Colton, Reed, Martin,
Rinaldo, Nesbitt, Brew, and others have discussed various
aspects of this problem at some length.  Much of the Mogollon
controversy has been philosophical and semantic in orientation
and it does not seem necessary to review the various arguments
here.  Clearly there were temporal and cultural differences,
as well as similarities, between these groups, and it is the
examination of the nature and extent of these aspects that I
propose.

Because many traits were shared by two or more of the
Southwestern culture patterns, however, it seems necessary to
define my position in using traits or trait complexes in comparing various groups.  First, I have assumed that the number
of traits, as such, possessed by a group has no bearing on
the integrity of that group as a cultural unit, but only with
its complexity.  Second, I have assumed that any trait normally

166

occurring among a group of people belongs to their culture,
regardless of its ultimate origin, which is in reality a
historical problem.  Third, I have assumed that the cultural
orientation of peoples sharing many traits makes it possible
to distinguish between those groups.

Thus, it would appear useful to distinguish clearly between different frames of reference in dealing with archeological problems involving trait-culture correlations.

1. Functional level: The fact that a trait was in customary use by a particular group makes it a part of the trait
constellation of that group, regardless of its historical
origin.  Thus, tobacco smoking is an English trait regardless
of the fact that it did not appear first among the English.

2. Orientation level: This is closely related to the
first.  It is obvious that similar or identical traits can be
at home in different cultures and yet play an entirely different role in each.  Thus, hunting is for modern Americans a
sport, for many primitive tribes a means of livelihood.

3. Historical level: Here the point of origin, or more
often the point of diffusion of traits, becomes the primary
problem.

4. Comparative level: The differences in form or use of
similar or identical traits; for example, variations in the
shapes of Anasazi and Mogollon pipes.  It may be argued that
the minor but consistent variations in styles and techniques
represent only adaptations to local environment, or idiosyncratic characteristics that have become incorporated into
regional styles.  But if this be true, then there is no way
to distinguish between cultures of any sort---pithouses are
pithouses, basketry is basketry, and pottery is just pottery.

Ultimately the taxonomic status of the Mogollon groups may be established. For the present they will be considered as one of the (perhaps many) different Southwestern groups of various backgrounds. The Mogollon groups conformed, to some extent, to traditions of their own progenitors, but even though sometimes isolated, they did not live in a vacuum. Ideas and discrete objects passed to and fro, usually along well established trade routes. Undoubtedly there was a time when there were wide gaps of area between peoples, but even then some things, such as agriculture and perhaps the idea of pottery, were transmitted from one group to another. Cultural frontiers must have existed in one form or another, yet these were crossed, and indeed, fluctuated, from time to time. It is the nature of the interrelations of the Mogollon group to other Southwestern groups that will concern us here.

### Relative Chronology of the Mogollon

Of fundamental importance in the study of cultural interrelations is the control of relative chronology. Yet, for large portions of the Southwest, time factors are only imperfectly known. Especially true of the Hohokam area, this is but slightly less true of the Mogollon area. Nevertheless, it is necessary to determine, as closely as possible, the relative dates of the various cultures, branches, and phases. Five lines of evidence may be adduced toward this end.

1. Dendrochronology: This is by far the most accurate, and under ideal conditions results in absolute dendrodates. (The term, dendrodate, which I shall use here, has been proposed by Kidder (Kidder and Cosgrove 1949) to replace the term, tree-ring date.)

2. Radioactive Carbon-14: Less accurate than dendrodates, but absolute in the sense that it produces dates in terms of the Christian calendar.

3. Cross-dating: Primarily, this is a process of relative dating, but when dealing with intrusive material which has been dendrodated elsewhere, it indicates a general time horizon in terms of actual years.

4. Stratigraphy: Under normal conditions this is absolutely accurate in establishing sequence, but unless combined with one of the methods listed above, it does not produce relative dating except for the contained sequence.

5. Geological dating: Various geological techniques have been used in the dating of archeological sites, but these require additional evidence in order to approach absolute dating. Otherwise, it is like stratigraphy in affording relative dating only for the immediate site.

Typological seriation might also be used, but inasmuch as it may be highly unreliable, and because wherever employed it has usually been accompanied by stratigraphic evidence, it will not be considered here as a primary means of dating.

These methods, as they apply to Mogollon dating, will now be considered in order, except that stratigraphy, or culture units isolated by stratigraphy, will be used throughout.

Dendrochronology

In applying dendrochronology for dating the Mogollon Culture, I have used only those dendrodates reported by Smiley (1952) and arrived at by the Douglass method. Certain of the dates announced by Gladwin (1948) are probably correct, but since some appear invalid, it does not seem logical to use any of them.

It is not my purpose to criticize Gladwin's method of dating tree-rings. The methodology, as such, has been appraised by investigators more capable than I, and both its strengths and weaknesses have been pointed out. Of more concern at the moment is the manipulation of data by Gladwin, whose chief test for the accuracy of a dendrodate is whether or not it fits the archeology. This test has certain points in its favor; where it fails is in that a dendrodate is simply that. It is a unit of data, and as such, it must be explained by the archeologist. If there is a discrepancy between the date and the rest of the evidence, it often leads to important discoveries which otherwise might not be made. Gladwin's use of this test, however, is somewhat different. To begin with, if the date does not agree with the archeology, Gladwin's technique, a percentage correlation, permits him to adjust the date to another position in the calendar. Since most of our ideas concerning cultural progression in the Southwest are based on dendrodates, changing a date to fit the archeology may result only in obscuring any changes which might actually have occurred. It hardly needs to be added that many of Mr. Gladwin's ideas as to the correct archeology are at considerable variance with known archeological data apart from dendrodates. Therefore, while it has been pointed out that many dates yielded by the Gladwin method coincide with, or closely approach, those determined by the Douglass method, it does not seem, to the writer, at least, that these dates can be used with any degree of certainty that they are correct. For this reason I have not used any of the dates published by Gladwin for Mogollon sites.

The following dates have been published for Mogollon

sites (Smiley 1952), together with their rating, and phase
and period assignments.

Table 17

| BRANCH<br>Site<br>Pithouse | RANGE<br>OF<br>DATES<br>A. D. | NUMBER OF<br>SPECIMENS | SITE<br>DATING | PHASE | PERIOD |
|---|---|---|---|---|---|
| FORESTDALE | | | | | |
| Bluff Site | | | | | |
| Pithouse 1 | -287 | 1 | Poor | Hilltop | 1 |
| 2 | -306 | 1 | Poor | Hilltop | 1 |
| 3 | -292 | 1 | Poor | Hilltop | 1 |
| 5 | 280 -320 | 31 | Good | Hilltop | 1 |
| 6 | -296 | 1 | Poor | Hilltop | 1 |
| Bear Ruin | | | | | |
| Pithouse 1 | 636+-667+ | 2 | Poor | Forestdale | 3 |
| Kiva | -667+ | 1 | Poor | Forestdale | 3 |
| PINE LAWN VALLEY | | | | | |
| Turkey Foot Ridge | | | | | |
| Pithouse B | 777, 778 | 2 | Poor | Three Circle | 4 |
| E | 772, 776 | 2 | Poor | San Francisco | 3 |
| F | 748 -778 | 6 | Good | San Francisco | 3 |
| H | 758 -786 | 9 | Good | San Francisco | 3 |
| K | 767 -773 | 3 | Poor | San Francisco | 3 |
| O | 738+-746+ | 3 | Poor | San Francisco | 3 |
| Twin Bridges | | | | | |
| Pithouse D | 744 -784 | 17 | Good | Three Circle | 4 |
| MIMBRES | | | | | |
| Mogollon Village | | | | | |
| Pithouse 2 | -898 | 24 | C* | San Francisco | 3 |
| 4 | -896 | 3 | Good | San Francisco | 3 |
| 5b | -897 | 1 | Poor | San Francisco | 3 |
| 8 | -908 | 1 | Poor | San Francisco | 3 |
| Starkweather Ruin | | | | | |
| Pithouse I | -927 | 2 | Poor | San Francisco | 3 |

Table 17. Mogollon dendrodates.  C* = conclusive date.

The list is not impressive, yet it clearly fixes several
points in time for part of the Mogollon area.  Three seeming
discrepancies appear, which, however, little affect the major
outline.  These dates are for Pithouse B at Turkey Foot Ridge,

Pithouse D at Twin Bridges, and Pithouse I at Starkweather Ruin. In the first two instances it seems clear that construction of the houses must have taken place during San Francisco Phase, even though occupation continued into Three Circle Phase. This condition was noted by Martin and Rinaldo (1950a) for several houses at Turkey Foot Ridge and unquestionably accounts for the early dates of the Turkey Foot Ridge and Twin Bridges houses assigned to Three Circle Phase. It has been indicated previously that, on the basis of contained pottery, Pithouse I at Starkweather Ruin should be considered Three Circle Phase. Martin and Rinaldo (1949:197-198) have also reclassified this and other Starkweather houses. Possibly House 2 at Mogollon Village should also be considered Three Circle Phase on the basis of the contained Mimbres Bold Face Black-on-white; but in either case, it seems clear that the transition from San Francisco Phase to Three Circle occurred some time about A. D. 900. There are no bottom dates for San Francisco Phase, but dates in the middle 700's from Pine Lawn Valley indicate that it was in full swing at that time. Bear Ruin (Forestdale Branch), into which Mogollon Red-on-brown is intrusive, has dates somewhat later than A. D. 667, which constitutes a limiting date.

There are no dendrodates for Mogollon 2, but the series of Mogollon 1 dates for Hilltop Phase of Forestdale Branch provides an anchor point in time for a critical area so far as cultural interrelations are concerned. One point should be noted, however. In relation to the central Mogollon area, these sites are clearly marginal, a fact which increases (but does not prove) the possibility that they are also relatively late. That this is true, however, is suggested also by the

Carbon-14 dates for Pine Lawn Phase to the southeast.

Radioactive Carbon-14

While inherently not so accurate as dendrodates, Carbon-14 dates nevertheless indicate the order of magnitude of time intervals.  There are several Carbon-14 dates which bear on the dating of the Mogollon culture pattern.  As listed in Johnson (1951), these are as follows.

| SITE | DATE | PHASE |
|------|------|-------|
| Benson:5:10 (Sayles 1941) | A. D. 189 ± 430 | San Pedro Stage |
| Benson:5:10 (Sayles 1941) | B. C. 512 ± 310 | San Pedro Stage |
| Tularosa Cave (Martin et al. 1952) | B. C. 272 ± 200 | Chiricahua Stage |
| Tularosa Cave (Martin et al. 1952) | B. C. 349 ± 200 | Chiricahua Stage |
| Tularosa Cave (Martin et al. 1952) | B. C. 161 ± 230 B. C. 226 ± 225 | Pine Lawn Phase Pine Lawn Phase |
| Average | B. C. 194 ± 160 | Pine Lawn Phase |

The dates for Bat Cave (Dick, in preparation) are not listed here, for although ultimately they will prove of significance for archeological sequence dating, up to this time they have been used only for dating the evolution of maize in that site.

Without reviewing all the potential pitfalls of Carbon-14 dating, one factor may be mentioned.  Any contamination of specimens is likely to raise the computed date rather than lower it.

The two dates for the last Cochise Stage in the southern Mogollon area are important chiefly in placing a bottom limiting date on the appearance of the Mogollon Culture in that area.  There is some discrepancy between the two available dates, however, and it is not possible to determine whether

both are accurate, and if not, which one is.  Based purely on
archeological evidence, the A. D. 189 date seems somewhat too
late, but there is no proof that it is incorrect.  The lower
limit of its probable error overlaps the upper limit of the
earlier (512 B. C.) date, while the upper limit would place
the end of the San Pedro Stage at A. D. 619, which seems much
too late.  However, until more Carbon-14 dates are secured,
or until dendrodates become available, the matter must rest
unsolved, but with the probability that a B. C. date is
correct.

The situation in Tularosa Cave appears much more secure,
for both sequence and the clustering of dates indicate their
probable correctness within the probable error.  These dates
indicate that the transition from Cochise to Mogollon (that
is, addition of pottery to the Cochise complex) occurred between 300 and 200 B. C.  This date seems satisfactory, based
as it is on two samples each of dry material.

Cross-dating

This method is less satisfactory than dendrodating and
Carbon-14, but nevertheless seems to outline, in general
terms, the relative chronology of sites where it can be used.
Unfortunately, evidence is scarcest for the early periods
where we most need enlightenment.  Moreover, except for rare
occurrences of whole vessels on house floors, or of intrusives
into single-phase sites, it is not always possible to determine precise relationships of foreign pottery.  Only when
associations have recurred a number of times is there sure
proof of contemporaneity.

There are several cases of association of central Mogollon pottery types with other Mogollon types, with Anasazi

types, and with Hohokam types.  These data have been brought
together in Table 18, an analysis of which brings out a number
of interesting facts regarding the relative chronology of the
Mogollon, Hohokam, and Anasazi culture patterns.

Since temporal placement of Hohokam phases rests on
cross-dating, intrusives moving in either direction can do no
more than establish contemporaneity, and thus have very little
dating value as such.  On the other hand, intrusives into
dated Anasazi sites, and dated Anasazi types intrusive into
Mogollon sites (some of which are also dated by tree-rings),
can provide fairly secure datings.

Unfortunately, the most widespread identifiable Mogollon
intrusive has been San Francisco Red, an exceptionally long-
lived type which has almost no dating connotation other than
as a limiting date.  San Francisco Red, Mimbres variety, intrusive into every phase at Snaketown, proves that, whatever
date may be assigned to Vahki Phase at Snaketown, the Mogollon
ceramic complex was already in existence.  It was also intrusive into every San Simon phase except perhaps Penasco.  It
occurred in Forestdale Phase in Forestdale Branch, and in
Circle Prairie Phase in Black River Branch, but did not occur
in Bluff Site during Hilltop and Cottonwood phases.  In the
Anasazi area it occurred at Site 1, Cahone Canyon; and at
White Mound.  The Pueblo II horizon at Tseh So in the Chaco
produced some trade sherds identified as San Francisco Red.
Red wares that may be San Francisco Red are occasionally
reported from Basketmaker III sites, and even less often for
what appears to be Basketmaker II associations, but the associational data have yet to be validated.  The possibility
that these red wares are not San Francisco Red variants or

derivatives must not be overlooked.

Like San Francisco Red, Alma Plain pottery and its several local variants had too long a life span to be of much value in dating. Furthermore, it did not have so wide a distribution. It did not occur at Snaketown until Santa Cruz Phase. The Bluff variety of Alma Plain occurred in Circle Prairie Phase in Black River Branch. Alma Plain, Mimbres variety, is reported for White Mound and for Site 4 of the Akmen-Lowry Sites. Other Alma variations were the textured forms which may have been intrusive into Kiatuthlanna and La Plata Site 41. These might be local experimentations or copies, but their rarity certainly suggests Mogollon influence. The time range is from Basketmaker III to Pueblo III.

---

Table 18. Pottery Cross-dating for Mogollon Phases.
U - resident type, V - minor type for that phase. Other letters indicate references to publications giving the particular associations. Lower case letters indicate that the association is in question. The lettered references follow:

A - Roberts 1929:117, 118; Morris 1927:186
B - Martin et al. 1952:67
C - Wheat 1954
D - Gladwin et al. 1937:214
E - Morris 1927:186; Milton Wetherill (in conversation)
F - Gladwin 1945:25; Rinaldo 1941:7, 9
G - Brand et al. 1937:167, 170
H - Roberts 1931:122
I - Morris 1939: pl. 293
J - Sayles 1945:47
K - Martin and Rinaldo 1950b:510
L - Roberts 1930:79; 1931:117, 118; Brand et al. 1937:167, 170
M - Haury 1936b:26, 66
N - Haury 1936b:26, 66; Martin et al. 1952:67
O - Haury 1936b:26, 66; Martin and Rinaldo 1950b:510
P - Haury 1941:78, 79
Q - Roberts 1930:79; 1931:117, 118
R - Martin 1949:187, 190
S - Hough 1919
T - Haury and Sayles 1947:56

Table 18

PHASE

| POTTERY TYPE | Basketmaker II | Basketmaker III | Pueblo I | Pueblo II | Pueblo III | Georgetown | Hilltop | Circle Prairie (Early) | Cottonwood | Circle Prairie (Late) | Pinaleno | Galluro | San Francisco | Forestdale | Cerros | Three Circle | Luna | Encinas | Pioneer | Colonial | Sedentary |
|---|---|---|---|---|---|---|---|---|---|---|---|---|---|---|---|---|---|---|---|---|---|
| San Francisco Red | e | F | F | G |  | U |  | U |  | U | U | U | U | P | U | U | U | U | D | D | D |
| Alma Plain |  | F | F |  |  | U | U | U | U | U | U | U | U | U | U | U | U | U | U | D | D |
| Alma Textured |  | h | i |  |  | V | T |  |  |  |  |  | U |  |  | U |  |  |  |  |  |
| Reserve Smudged |  | a | l |  |  | V |  |  |  |  |  |  | U |  |  | U |  |  |  |  |  |
| Forestdale Smudged |  | a | l |  |  |  |  |  | U |  |  |  |  | U |  |  |  |  |  | D | D |
| Woodruff Smudged |  | a | l |  |  | T |  |  |  |  |  |  |  | P |  |  |  |  |  |  |  |
| Forestdale Red |  | a | Q |  |  |  |  |  |  |  |  |  |  | U |  |  |  |  |  |  |  |
| Woodruff Red |  |  |  |  |  |  |  |  |  |  |  |  |  | P |  |  |  |  |  |  |  |
| Unnamed Red |  |  |  |  |  | T | C | T | C |  |  |  |  |  |  |  |  |  |  |  |  |
| San Lorenzo R/B |  |  |  |  |  |  |  |  | C | J |  | V |  |  |  |  |  |  |  |  |  |
| Mogollon R/B |  |  |  |  |  | b |  |  |  | J | J | U | P | J |  |  |  |  |  | D |  |
| Three Circle R/W |  |  |  |  |  |  |  |  |  |  |  | V |  | J |  | V | S |  |  | D | D |
| Bold Face B/W |  |  |  |  |  |  |  |  |  |  |  |  |  |  |  | U | S | J |  |  | D |
| Mimbres B/W |  |  |  |  |  | b |  |  |  |  |  |  |  |  |  |  |  | J |  |  |  |
| Reserve B/W |  |  |  |  |  | B |  |  |  |  |  |  |  |  |  | M |  |  |  |  |  |
| Adamana Brown |  |  |  |  |  | T |  |  | T |  |  |  |  | P |  |  |  |  |  |  |  |
| Aquarius Brown |  |  |  |  |  |  |  |  |  |  |  |  |  | P |  |  |  |  |  |  |  |
| Vahki Plain |  |  |  |  |  |  |  | c | C |  |  |  | c |  |  |  |  |  | U |  |  |
| Gila Plain |  |  |  |  |  |  | T |  | C |  |  |  |  |  |  |  |  |  | U | U | U |
| Sweetwater R/G |  |  |  |  |  |  | t |  | C | J |  |  |  |  |  |  |  |  | V |  |  |
| Snaketown R/Bu |  |  |  |  |  |  | t |  | C | J | J |  |  |  |  |  |  |  | V |  |  |
| Gila Butte R/Bu |  |  |  |  |  |  |  |  |  | J | C | P |  |  |  |  |  |  | V |  |  |
| Santa Cruz R/Bu |  |  |  |  |  |  |  |  |  |  |  | B |  |  |  |  |  |  |  |  |  |
| Dragoon R/Br |  |  |  |  |  |  |  |  |  |  |  |  |  |  |  |  |  |  |  | D | D |
| Lino Gray | U | V |  |  |  | b |  | T | c |  |  |  | N | m |  |  |  |  |  |  |  |
| Kana-a Gray |  | U |  |  |  |  |  |  |  |  |  |  |  | m | m |  |  |  |  |  |  |
| Lino Smudged | V |  |  |  |  |  |  |  |  |  |  |  |  | P |  |  |  |  |  |  |  |
| Lino & LaPlata B/G | U |  |  |  |  |  |  |  |  |  |  |  |  | P | m |  |  |  |  |  |  |
| Kana-a B/W |  |  | U |  |  |  |  |  |  |  |  |  |  |  |  |  |  |  |  | D | D |
| Kiatuthlanna B/W |  | U |  |  |  | b |  |  |  |  |  |  | m | N | s |  |  |  |  |  |  |
| White Mound B/W | V | V |  |  |  |  |  |  |  |  |  |  | m | N |  |  |  |  |  |  |  |
| Abajo R/O | V | V |  |  |  |  |  |  |  |  |  |  |  | r |  |  |  |  |  |  |  |
| Deadmans B/R |  | U |  |  |  |  |  |  |  |  |  |  |  |  |  |  |  |  |  | D | D |
| Red Mesa B/W |  |  | U |  |  |  |  |  |  |  |  |  |  |  |  | O |  |  |  |  |  |
| Black Mesa B/W |  |  | U |  |  |  |  |  |  |  |  |  |  |  |  |  |  |  |  |  | D |
| Puerco B/W |  |  | U |  |  |  |  |  |  |  |  |  |  | K |  |  |  |  |  |  |  |

Table 18. See legend on opposite page.

Alma Neck-banded and Three Circle Neck-corrugated wares are of little value in correlation because the technologically similar forms in the Anasazi area either prevented their spread as intrusives, or, by similarity, rendered their identification difficult when found in the north.

Smudged wares of Mogollon origin or derivation were widely traded over the Southwest. Alma Smudged (Wheat 1954) and its later variant, Reserve Smudged (Martin et al. 1949: 187) have been established too recently for distribution data to come to hand, but it seems possible that the gray-exterior smudged wares from Shabik'eshchee Village, Kiatuthlanna, Piedra, and Northeastern Arizona may belong to Reserve or Alma Smudged, while those with reddish-brown exteriors are probably referable to Forestdale Smudged or Woodruff Smudged. All these associations are Basketmaker III and Pueblo I. Mogollon smudged ware also was intrusive into Pueblo I associations at Tseh So.

Forestdale Red appears identical to Forestdale Smudged except for lack of smudging. Unslipped, its color derives from pigment inherent in the paste. It appears as an intrusive in a number of Anasazi sites, such as Northeastern Arizona and Shabik'eshchee Village, in White Mound Phase contexts on the Puerco River, and in Gila Butte Phase associations of the Hohokam from a site near Globe. This is primarily a Basketmaker III temporal distribution, but it carries over into Pueblo I.

Painted wares are inherently better time markers than plain wares. However, no San Simon Branch painted type has yet been reported as intrusive into any other site. San Lorenzo Red-on-brown was intrusive in Pinaleno Phase in San

Simon Village, and in Circle Prairie (Late) Phase in Crooked
Ridge Village, showing at least partial contemporaneity of
these phases. Stratigraphically associated with this ware at
San Simon were small percentages of Mogollon Red-on-brown,
Sweetwater Red-on-gray, Snaketown Red-on-buff, and larger
amounts of Mimbres variety San Francisco Red and Alma Plain.
At Crooked Ridge Village San Lorenzo Red-on-brown was stratigraphically associated with Vahki Plain, Sweetwater Red-on-
gray, and Snaketown Red-on-buff, thus substantiating the San
Simon occurrences. It has not been reported in association
with Anasazi pottery in an unmixed occurrence.

Mogollon Red-on-brown was the most common traded Mogollon
type except for the later Mimbres black-on-white types. It
was intrusive into Pinaleno, Galiuro, and Cerros phases in
San Simon Branch, reaching its peak in Galiuro, indicating
the general contemporaneity of San Francisco Phase with late
Pinaleno and Galiuro phases. Occurring in Galiuro Phase, and
presumably temporally equivalent, are Snaketown Red-on-buff,
Gila Butte Red-on-buff, and San Francisco Red, Mimbres variety. At Mogollon Village one Kiatuthlanna and four White
Mound Black-on-white sherds occurred in room fill of abandoned
San Francisco Phase houses, while at Harris Village one sherd
each of Lino and Kana-a Gray was intrusive in room fill of
San Francisco Phase houses. At Tularosa Cave "...it was
found that La Plata Black-on-white sherds had their greatest
frequency in the more pure San Francisco Phase levels, and
White Mound Black-on-white and Kiatuthlanna Black-on-white...
a greater frequency in the levels above." At Bear Ruin
Mogollon Red-on-brown was intrusive in a pure-phase site.
Intrusive pottery types associated with it in this phase are

Woodruff Red, Woodruff Smudged, Adamana Brown, Aquarius Brown, Gila Plain, Gila Butte Red-on-buff, Lino Black-on-gray, White Mound Black-on-white, Lino Gray, and Lino Smudged. One house at Crooked Ridge Village may be of San Francisco Phase. Here, associated in the floor fill with Mogollon Red-on-brown, were Vahki Plain and Gila Butte Red-on-buff.

Turning now to sites outside the Mogollon area, Mogollon Red-on-brown was intrusive into Snaketown in Santa Cruz Phase, during which time Kana-a Black-on-white, Deadmans Black-on-red, Dragoon Red-on-brown, San Francisco Red, Forestdale Smudged, Alma Plain, Alma Neck-banded, and one sherd of Three Circle Red-on-white also were intrusive.

Three Circle Red-on-white and Mimbres Bold Face Black-on-white may well be considered together inasmuch as they are usually associated, although Three Circle Red-on-white came into being somewhat earlier and died out earlier. At San Simon, Three Circle Red-on-white is intrusive into Cerros Phase, but Mimbres Bold Face Black-on-white does not appear until the following Encinas Phase, during which phase Mimbres Classic also appears. These associations, together with the ceramic complex at San Simon Village, as such, make a one-to-one correlation of Cerros and Three Circle phases impossible. In San Simon Branch, Cerros Phase begins with the introduction of red-on-white pottery. If this occurred at the same time as in the Mimbres, then Cerros Phase is partly or wholly contemporaneous with late San Francisco Phase, and Encinas Phase began some time during Three Circle and continued on into Mangus or Mimbres Phase.

At Harris Village one sherd of Lino Black-on-gray and two of Red Mesa Black-on-white were found in floor fill of Three

Circle Phase houses, while ten sherds of Reserve Black-on-white occurred in the room fill of an abandoned house of the same phase. The decorated Lino sherd seems out of context in this association. At Mogollon Village no houses were assigned to Three Circle Phase, but the occurrence of Mimbres Bold Face Black-on-white in definite floor association shows that the house, built toward the end of San Francisco Phase, continued in use into Three Circle Phase, or else that San Francisco Phase held on at Mogollon Village while Three Circle was already under way elsewhere.

Martin and his associates found no evidence of Three Circle Phase occupation in Tularosa Cave and, while Cordova Cave apparently was occupied during this time, the associational evidence is not clear. Turkey Foot Ridge, occupied in part during Three Circle Phase, produced no trade sherds in floor association during the second season of excavation, but the recovery of Red Mesa and Puerco black-on-white types in the room fill indicates abandonment of those houses during or before the Anasazi Red Mesa Phase. However, during the first season small amounts of San Lorenzo Red-on-brown; Red Mesa, Reserve, and Tularosa black-on-white types; and Abajo Red-on-orange were found in what is obviously a mixed association. Twin Bridges Site produced one Abajo Red-on-orange and one indeterminate black-on-red sherd in the room fill of Three Circle Phase houses.

It has been pointed out above that Three Circle Phase at Luna Village had, either as an intrusive type or as a part of the complex, Kiatuthlanna Black-on-white or what may be an early form of Reserve Black-on-white (Danson 1952), as well as Three Circle Red-on-white and Mimbres Bold Face Black-on-

white (Survey collection in Arizona State Museum).  No equivalent Mogollon period was found in Forestdale Branch, and only
one of the houses at Crooked Ridge Village may be provisionally
assigned to Three Circle Phase.  Here, in a mixed association,
both Three Circle Red-on-white and Mimbres Bold Face Black-on-
white were found with Vahki Plain, neck-corrugated, corrugated,
Kiatuthlanna Black-on-white, Four Mile Polychrome, Point of
Pines Polychrome, and Gila Polychrome.  Therefore, it is felt
that no usable data can be derived from this house.

At Snaketown one sherd of Three Circle Red-on-white was
reported in Santa Cruz association, but the type increases
during Sacaton Phase, at which time Mimbres Bold Face Black-
on-white is also introduced.  This would indicate a general
contemporaneity of Three Circle and Sacaton phases.  Also in
stratigraphic association with Sacaton Phase were Kana-a and
Black Mesa black-on-white types, Deadmans Black-on-red,
Dragoon Red-on-brown, Forestdale Smudged, San Francisco Red,
and Alma Plain.

Late in Three Circle Phase, judging by the Bold Face -
Classic transitional type of Mimbres Black-on-white, a
Mogollon ceramic complex was being established in Jornada
Branch.  Associated types were El Paso Polychrome, Chupadero
Black-on-white, and Three Rivers Red-on-terracotta.

Turning now to pottery cross-dating of Mogollon 1, we
find little evidence of trade with the Anasazi.  There is no
evidence of trade of any kind in Pine Lawn, nor in Penasco
Phase.  During Hilltop Phase at Bluff Site, with dendrodates
at about A. D. 300, only Mogollon and Hohokam types were
intrusive.  These types are Alma Scored, Woodruff Smudged, an
unnamed red ware, Adamana Brown, Gila Plain, and a Hohokam

red-on-buff from room fill, the latter judged to be neither very early nor very late in the Hohokam red-on-buff sequence.

Two reported associations of Anasazi pottery with Georgetown Phase now need to be examined. Martin et al. (1952:67) report that "Lino Gray was recovered from Georgetown Phase levels and all later levels, but had its greatest frequency in the mixed San Francisco - Tularosa Phase levels." None of the sherd counts listed shows Lino Gray for levels assigned by them to Georgetown Phase, but sherd counts are not given for all squares. However, 24 sherds of Mogollon Red-on-brown were reported from Georgetown Phase levels (ibid.:56) and an examination of published sherd tables shows that one sherd each of Kiatuthlanna, Reserve, and Mimbres Classic black-on-white types, and six sherds of corrugated ware are also reported from levels assigned to Georgetown Phase. Therefore, while Lino Gray may actually be associated with Georgetown Phase, it appears likely that the levels are incorrectly assigned. Certainly, the quantity of Mogollon Red-on-brown in some levels points to the doubtfulness of this assignment. A second instance is reported for Starkweather Ruin by Nesbitt (1938:89), who states that five sherds with Basket-maker III - Pueblo I affiliations were found in Georgetown Phase houses. However, he does not identify the types, the houses where they occurred, nor state whether they derived from floor fill or room fill. Therefore, the undocumented statement cannot stand as conclusive evidence of such association.

The first secure evidence for pottery cross-dating occurs in Cottonwood Phase (Mogollon 2) at Bluff Site, where Haury and Sayles (1947:56) note three sherds of Lino Gray.

Stratigraphically associated with these were Adamana Brown, an unnamed red ware, and Forestdale Smudged.

## Geological Dating

This technique bears on the dating of Mogollon Culture in but one instance, and here only indirectly. This is in the attempt to assign terminal dates to Cochise Culture sites. On the basis of geological and climatological history of the Southwest, Antevs (Sayles and Antevs 1941:55) estimated the end of San Pedro Stage at circa 500 B. C.

### Summary of Mogollon Chronology

The evidence that has been presented may now be brought together in a correlation chart (Fig. 12). There are many uncertainties present, especially for the southern Mogollon and the Hohokam. Neither Cibola nor Jornada branch has been given because we do not control sufficient data for Cibola, and the time horizon of Jornada is generally beyond the scope of this study.

The best Mogollon dating is for Forestdale and Mimbres branches and Pine Lawn Valley. The bases on which the correlation has been made are as follows.

1. Anasazi divisions are based on dendrodates falling in the various periods (see Smiley 1952) and on cross-dating of pottery. The earliest actual dendrodate for Basketmaker II is A. D. 46.

2. Forestdale Branch is placed by dendrodates (Haury 1941:120-121; Haury and Sayles 1947:80-82).

3. Three Circle Phase, beginning dates, in Pine Lawn Valley, Mimbres and Black River branches, are based on dendrodates for the end of San Francisco Phase at Mogollon Village (Haury 1936b:116) and an early Three Circle Phase date at

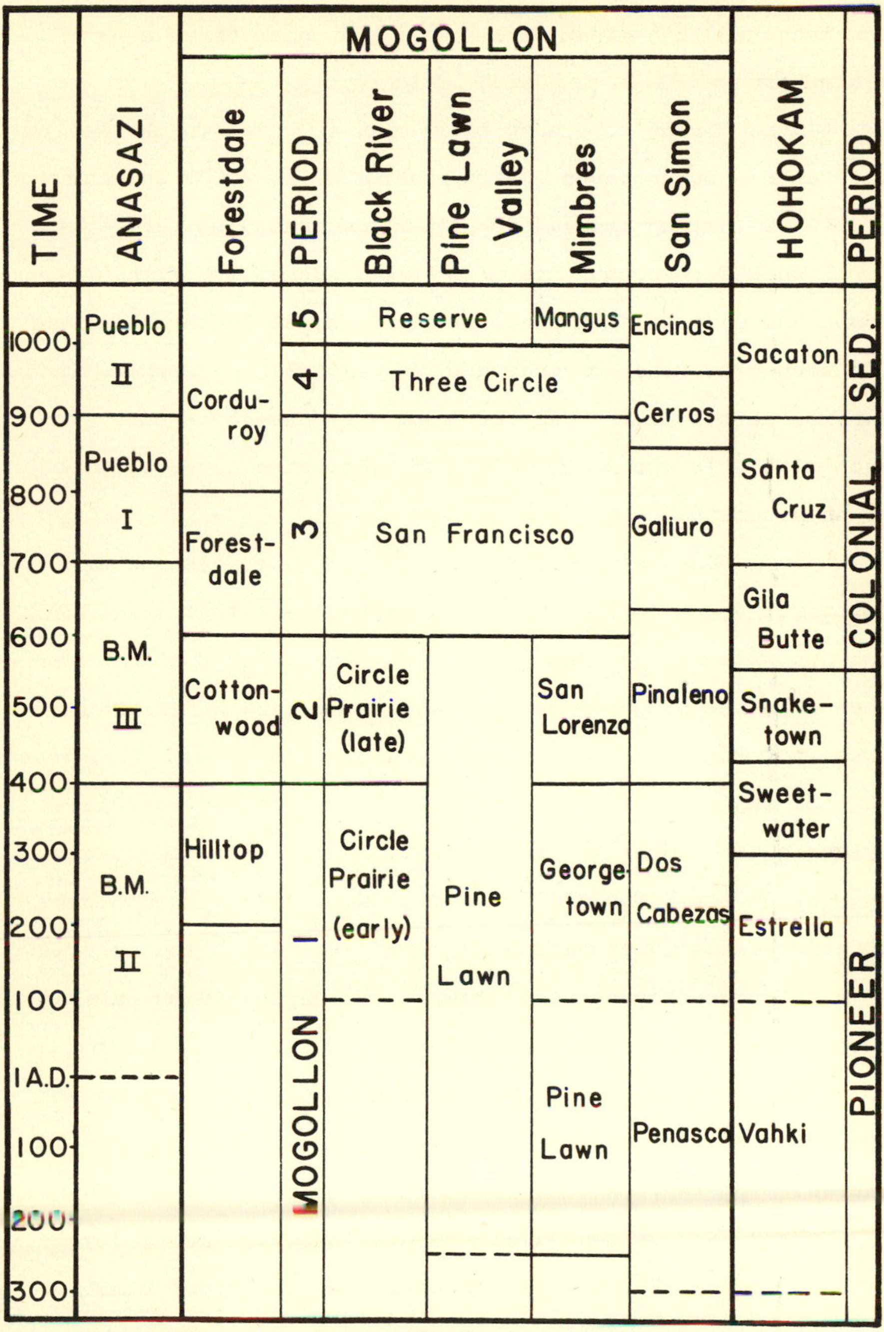

Figure 12 — Correlation of Mogollon-Hohokam-Anasazi Cultures

| TIME | ANASAZI | MOGOLLON | | | | | | HOHOKAM | PERIOD |
|---|---|---|---|---|---|---|---|---|---|
| | | Forestdale | PERIOD | Black River | Pine Lawn Valley | Mimbres | San Simon | | |
| 1000 | Pueblo II | | 5 | Reserve | | Mangus | Encinas | Sacaton | SED. |
| 900 | | Cordu-roy | 4 | Three Circle | | | Cerros | | |
| 800 | Pueblo I | | 3 | San Francisco | | | Galiuro | Santa Cruz | COLONIAL |
| 700 | | Forest-dale | | | | | | Gila Butte | |
| 600 | B.M. III | | | | | | | | |
| 500 | | Cotton-wood | 2 | Circle Prairie (late) | | San Lorenzo | Pinaleno | Snake-town | |
| 400 | | | | | | | | Sweet-water | |
| 300 | B.M. II | Hilltop | | Circle Prairie (early) | Pine Lawn | George-town | Dos Cabezas | | |
| 200 | | | 1 | | | | | Estrella | |
| 100 | | | | | | | | | PIONEER |
| 1 A.D. | | MOGOLLON | | | Pine Lawn | Pine Lawn | Penasca | Vahki | |
| 100 | | | | | | | | | |
| 200 | | | | | | | | | |
| 300 | | | | | | | | | |

Figure 12. Correlation of Mogollon-Hohokam-Anasazi Cultures.

Starkweather Ruin (Nesbitt 1938). The upper dates are estimates.

4. San Francisco Phase placement is based on the following facts. Dendrodates in the middle A. D. 700's and circa A. D. 900 (Smiley 1952). The chief decorated pottery type, Mogollon Red-on-brown, has been found associated with White Mound and Kiatuthlanna black-on-white types in the later part, and with Lino Black-on-gray and La Plata Black-on-white in the earlier part. Therefore, the type must have come into use some time prior to A. D. 700. The suggested date, A. D. 600, is an estimate.

5. In Pine Lawn Valley, Pine Lawn Phase is shown as lasting until about A. D. 600, based on the fact that, excepting one possible Georgetown Phase house, there is no evidence of change in the isolated valley until some time during San Francisco Phase.

6. San Lorenzo Phase in the Mimbres area is postulated. Evidence to support it is intrusive San Lorenzo Red-on-brown pottery in San Simon and Crooked Ridge Village, in horizons stratigraphically preceding San Francisco Phase and associated with early Hohokam pottery types. Its dating is in part a guess.

7. Georgetown Phase dating is an estimate based on the fact that no good evidence is available, as yet, to show by intrusive pottery that it should be placed later. If the Lino Gray - Georgetown Phase correlation in Tularosa Cave (Martin et al. 1952:67) is correct, then the upper limit of Georgetown Phase should approximate A. D. 500. In any event, if San Lorenzo Phase is valid, as seems likely, then some time must be allowed for it.

8. Pine Lawn Phase in Mimbres Branch is based on Tularosa Cave (Martin et al. 1952), and the bottom date on Carbon-14 dates, both from the end of the Cochise and the beginning of Mogollon Culture. The transition date to Georgetown is purely an estimate.

9. Placement of Circle Prairie Phase (Late) (Wheat 1954) is based on intrusive San Lorenzo Red-on-brown and on Pioneer Period Hohokam intrusives which duplicate the association found in Pinaleno Phase by Sayles (1945:47). No Anasazi intrusives were found.

10. Early Circle Prairie Phase (Wheat 1954) is typologically equivalent to Georgetown. No evidence was recovered to indicate a phase equivalent to Pine Lawn Phase.

11. All dates in San Simon Branch are estimates based on cross-finds of pottery. Mimbres Bold Face Black-on-white is first found in Encinas Phase. Cerros Phase is to be equated in part with late San Francisco Phase of the Mimbres Branch and in part with Three Circle Phase, on the basis of correspondence in pottery complex and on trade sherds. Galiuro appears to correspond to the major part of San Francisco Phase. Pinaleno, as indicated above, corresponds mainly with late Circle Prairie Phase, and probably with San Lorenzo. Dos Cabezas, on the basis of the broad-line red-on-brown pottery, is to be equated with early Circle Prairie of Black River Branch. The lower date of Penasco Phase is based in part on Antevs' geological dating (Sayles and Antevs 1941:55); in part on the overlap of probable errors of Carbon-14 dates for the end of San Pedro Stage; and finally, in line with current archeological theory, on assumption that pottery was introduced from the south, making it likely that it was

somewhat earlier in the southern part of the area.

12. Dating of the Hohokam is least secure, especially for early phases. Sacaton, Santa Cruz, and at least part of Gila Butte, seem fairly well dated by intrusives into Snaketown (Gladwin et al. 1937:241), Roosevelt:9:6 (Haury 1932:128), Forestdale (Haury 1941:79), and Sinagua (Colton 1946:245). The earlier phases are more difficult to correlate. Galiuro Phase contained both Gila Butte and Snaketown red-on-buff intrusives; Pinaleno contained Snaketown and Sweetwater red-on-buff intrusives. Therefore, it seems either that Snaketown and Sweetwater phases should be compressed, or what is more likely, that while phase designating types reached a peak in their respective periods, they nevertheless continued to be produced in adjacent phases. The beginning date of Sweetwater Phase has been placed at A. D. 300, on the basis of Hohokam painted pottery (not of the earliest type) intrusive into Hilltop Phase at Bluff Site dendrodated at circa A. D. 300. Estrella Phase is generally equated with Dos Cabezas and early Circle Prairie on the basis of pottery typology. The beginning date for Vahki Phase is an estimation based on general equivalence of Vahki, Penasco, and Pine Lawn phases.

None of the earlier dates outside of Forestdale, Pine Lawn Valley, and the northern part of Mimbres Branch can be considered as more than approximations. However, since most contact with the Anasazi occurred during the period of time for which our dates are reasonably accurate, and the contacts with the Hohokam can be compared on the basis of mutual cross-dating, we are now in a position to examine the cultural interrelations of the Mogollon.

# XII / THE RELATION OF MOGOLLON TO PREPOTTERY HORIZONS

It has been stated that with the addition of pottery the
Cochise Culture became the Mogollon.  The idea is not new.
Although the first reports on the Mogollon (Gladwin 1934,
1935, 1936; Haury 1936b) visualized them as intruders into
the Southwest from an eastern source, by 1941 the idea was
being expressed that there was a genetic connection between
the prepottery Cochise and the later Mogollon.  Haury (1941:
130) suggested that pottery, house building, earth burial,
agriculture, and a few minor traits added to San Pedro Stage
was the beginning of the Mogollon.  Sayles (Sayles and Antevs
1941:61) suggested that the introduction of pottery terminated
the last stage of Cochise.  McGregor (1941:189) also proposed
this sequence.  The excavation of Ventana Cave led Haury (1943)
to suggest that Hohokam, as well as Mogollon, had its source
in Cochise.  In Ventana Cave Haury (1950) detailed the transition for the Hohokam.  The discovery of what appeared to be a
late variation of Chiricahua Stage of the Cochise Culture in
Pine Lawn Valley, and a study of the lithic complex of the
same area, led Martin and his associates (1949) to believe
that here, too, there had been a direct transition.  This was
confirmed by excavation of Tularosa and Cordova caves (Martin
et al. 1952), and of Bat Cave (Dick, in preparation).  Finally, Lehmer (1948) proposed that the Hueco Cave Dwellers be
considered a variant of Cochise into which was introduced a
developed Mogollon ceramic complex.  I have criticized this
thesis above and there is no need to consider it further here.

Excavation of Bat Cave (Manglesdorf and Smith 1949) and the confirming evidence of Tularosa and Cordova caves (Martin et al. 1952) made it clear that agriculture had been practised in late Cochise times. Sayles (1945:1-3) demonstrated a late Cochise architecture, as did Martin and his associates (1950b: 430). This leaves pottery the major distinguishing feature between the last Cochise and the first Mogollon.

We may now examine these relationships more closely. Evidence for preceramic agriculture has come only from the area centering about Reserve, New Mexico. That it was present, to some degree, in the rest of the Mogollon area is argued by the development of grinding tools suitable for processing corn and by the presence of houses suggesting a stable economy. This is not conclusive as such, but further evidence is available for the southern Mimbres Branch, where Cosgrove (1947) shows agriculture apparently preceding pottery. The earliest maize is a quite primitive pod-pop corn. Subsequent changes have been noted (Manglesdorf and Smith 1949; Cutler in Martin et al. 1952). The prepottery cultivated plants at Tularosa Cave (Martin et al. 1952:486) included squash and beans, as well as maize. Thus, there is an established agricultural pattern continuing from late Cochise, in this case a hold-over Chiricahua Stage, into early Mogollon.

Architecturally, the San Pedro houses excavated by Sayles (1945:1-3) differ very little from the earliest Penasco houses. The interior storage pit has been moved outside, and a longer lateral entry was sometimes used; but size, shape, depth, and fire pit remain much the same. In the Pine Lawn area the continuing relationships are not so clearly evidenced (Martin et al. 1950:430). Undercut storage pits of the preceramic stage

(Haury 1936b:22; Sayles and Antevs 1941:23; and Sayles 1945:3)
continued into the Mogollon pattern, as did various sorts of
outside hearths.

Sayles (1945:4, Fig. 3) shows continuation of the following similar or identical artifact types from San Pedro Stage
to Penasco Phase: Basin metates, flat grinding slabs, hand
stones or manos, mortars, pestles, projectile points, flake
axes or choppers, flake knives, keeled end scrapers, hammer
stones, stone and shell ornaments, simple bone awls.

Martin and Rinaldo (1949:211, Fig. 78) show essentially
the same carry-over. The most complete evidence thus far published showing the direct continuity from Cochise into Mogollon has come from Tularosa and Cordova caves (Martin et al.
1952:485-495), for it includes perishable as well as non-
perishable artifacts. Artifact types which continue are as
follows:

Wickerwork, concentric warp, and leather winter sandals;
shell bracelets; bone tube beads; basin and slab metates, and
small metate-like grinding stones; ovoid one-hand manos; digging sticks; grass beds; storage pits; plant fiber scouring
pads; flexible cradles; netted carrying bags; fire drill
hearths; corner-notched, expanding-stem, thinned-base projectile points; small laterally notched projectile points; slender laterally notched, expanding-base projectile points;
diagonally notched expanding convex-base projectile points;
large laterally notched spear points; atlatls and darts;
atlatl dart bunts; hunting bows and arrows; narrow straight-
edged blades; ovoid convex-base blades; asymmetric blades;
leaf-shaped blades with basal edge straight; random flake
knives; blade-like knives; random flake side-scrapers;

nodular, serrate side-scrapers; end-scrapers; thin flake side-scrapers; concave scrapers; discoidal blades; uniface choppers; hammer stones; rubbing and abrading stones; plain shafted drills; small, abruptly widened, flange-base drills; broad-base drills; sharpened flake drills; gravers; stubby bone awls; notched ribs; bone fleshers; antler rubbers or hammers; wooden knife handles; wooden scoops; wood and bark trowels; feather carders; two-rod-and-bundle basketry; bundle-with-rod-core basketry; leather bags; unfired pottery; reed flutes; wooden and bone dice; stone balls; paint grinding stone and pigments; use of crystals; juniper-berry skewers; stick with incised bark patterns; sticks with binding of fiber, sinew, or hair; wooden cylinders; twig hoops.

When the Bat Cave excavations are published, further artifact continuities may become apparent. Upon analysis, it seems that many of the above traits are of such generic character that their occurrence means little in determining specific cultural continuity; but others have such detailed resemblances that there can remain little doubt that the late Cochise people of the eastern part of their area became the Mogollon.

In the present state of knowledge it would appear useless to speculate upon the specific source of some of the traits that modified the Cochise. Agriculture, beyond much question, came from Middle America, but by what route is not yet clear. The ultimate source of pottery was probably to the south, also, perhaps in the Archaic or Middle Culture horizons of Mexico; but we know so little of the archeology of the intervening areas that it would not be possible to demonstrate the route by which it was introduced. Although the idea of

Mogollon - Eastern connections has generally fallen into disrepute, no one has yet otherwise explained the introduction of texturing and scoring of pottery into the easternmost part of the Mogollon area some time during Mogollon 1 period. Use of pithouses is so widespread that until specific data can be brought to bear on the problem, there seems little reason to speculate on their source.

Haury (1943, 1950) has demonstrated that Hohokam was an outgrowth of a western and slightly differentiated branch of San Pedro Stage, as Mogollon developed out of the eastern branch.  Certain similarities in ceramic and lithic complexes of Mogollon and Hohokam in the earliest phases of each leave little doubt that there were close relationships at that time. Nevertheless, there existed technological differences in the pottery, and other differences, which require explanations before we can judge the nature of the relationships and whether or not more than a single source for pottery is indicated.

There is little evidence to show whether or not agriculture was introduced into Hohokam before pottery.  There are no data for the Gila Basin, and the desert environment about Ventana Cave prevented agriculture from being more than a minor trait at any time.  Due to moistness of prepottery deposits at Ventana, the presence of agriculture at that stage could be determined only by stone grinding tools; so it cannot be stated, as of now, whether the Hohokam, like the Mogollon, received agriculture before pottery.  Nor is there any evidence concerning prepottery architecture.

Haury (1936b:121) states that, while both Mogollon and Hohokam built their houses in pits, the succession of forms in each area was reversed.  Since that time, however, it has become clear that early houses in the Mogollon were more diversified in form, and that, rather than a sharp boundary,

194

there was a gradual blending in house types from east to west, the eastern forms tending more to roundness, the western to rectangularity. However, certain differences are to be noted in these early houses. Gladwin (1948:112-123) undertook a reanalysis of the architectural sequence at Snaketown, and while certain of his conclusions are distorted by the theoretical bias of his paper, those concerned with house types, size, and use appear to explain the data better than those of the original report (Gladwin et al. 1937:59-84).

Leaving aside Gladwin's dating, which is unacceptable, and his idea that there must be a house type for each period, his consideration of the architectural sequence in an early, intermediate, and late group is adequate for our purpose here. His conclusion that the very large Vahki Phase houses were ceremonial rather than domestic appears sound. Whether the largest houses of later phases also were ceremonial, as Gladwin suggests, remains to be seen; but there is a good possibility that they may have been. If the remaining houses are considered domestic, there is a general and gradual increase in size from Sweetwater times on, rather than a decrease in size as originally postulated (Gladwin et al. 1937: 79). This trend would agree with the gradual increase in house size among the Mogollon (except in Pine Lawn Valley), although the actual size of Hohokam houses was somewhat larger than Mogollon houses. The succession of forms remains as originally suggested, from squarish early houses, through rectanguloid intermediate houses, to elliptical late houses. This sequence differs from eastern Mogollon in general, but is partly paralleled in western Mogollon, as at San Simon (Sayles 1945:6-12, 19-30) and at Crooked Ridge Village (Wheat

1954).

Differences in early houses of the Mogollon and Hohokam appear in the basic structural plan, however. Except for their earliest houses, it is clear the Hohokam built houses in pits, not pithouses like those of the Mogollon. This is an arbitrary distinction, but it is so consistent that it must be recognized. Ordinarily, Mogollon houses utilized the sides of the pits as the lower walls. The later Hohokam houses had walls set inside the excavation, frequently in an encircling groove. In general, Mogollon house excavations were deeper, although this varied somewhat, becoming more shallow in the average from east to west.

Entryways also differed in general. Mogollon houses which had lateral entries usually had ramps, while all but one of the Hohokam houses of the period had lateral entries, some of which were very slightly inclined but more of which terminated in a step to the old ground level.

A considerable variety of roofing plans was used by the Mogollon, while the Hohokam generally used a quadrangular form, in common with the western Mogollon, or a peripheral support plan supplemented by interior posts as required. Placement of the fire pit near the entry was perhaps more consistent among the Hohokam than the Mogollon, although that was the common situation when the Mogollon house had a lateral entry. Hohokam hearths usually were somewhat more formalized than those of the Mogollon, frequently having plastered or clay-coped basins. Interior storage pits are not mentioned for the Hohokam at any period, whereas they occur sporadically among the Mogollon and have a localized specialization in Pine Lawn Valley.

During Santa Cruz Phase most Hohokam houses were rectangular, as were many of the Mogollon 3 period. However, this general statement is misleading, for most Hohokam houses were relatively long and narrow, while those of the Mogollon approached being square; and while some Mogollon houses had rounded corners, the ends of Hohokam houses began to be rounded, producing the elliptical form which became more prevalent during Sacaton Phase. Entries continued much the same, those of Mogollon usually being inclined, those of Hohokam generally ending with a step. In the Mogollon there was a growing uniformity in use of quadrangular roof plans, while the peripheral wall posts and random interior roof support plan continued in Hohokam. Floor details remained much the same as in earlier periods in the Hohokam, but there was an increasing trend toward uniformity among the Mogollon.

By Mogollon 4 the architectural similarities to Hohokam are largely passed, for Hohokam houses of Sacaton Phase are mostly elliptical with bulbous stepped entries, but with roofs much the same except for a trend toward single ridge gable roofs. Clay curbs built around the floor perimeter to prevent water seepage through the walls have no counterpart among the Mogollon. There remains to be noted, however, a gradual change in San Simon Branch architecture, which, during Encinas Phase, shows increasing similarity to contemporary Hohokam architecture as a result of influence exemplified in other traits, as well.

As previously mentioned, outside pits occur in Hohokam sites, as among the Mogollon, but usually have sloping rather than straight or undercut sides. Another parallel here is that most pits in both areas are early rather than late.

Earth ovens also were used by both groups.

Perhaps in no other trait do the Hohokam and Mogollon differ more than in disposal of the dead. The basic Hohokam pattern was, with few exceptions, cremation, although in the Desert Branch (Haury 1950) burials were more common. On the other hand, flexed inhumation was the standard Mogollon pattern, with only an occasional cremation. It is important to note that in the rare Mogollon cremations, the same type sequence occurred as in the Gila Basin (Gladwin et al. 1937:94).

In any discussion of the similarities of Mogollon and Hohokam pottery complexes, and of their influences on each other, it must be realized that we control too little evidence to do more than suggest certain affinities until late in the sequence when the increasing complexity of Hohokam ceramics leaves little doubt as to the direction the influences were moving. We have at our disposal, however, two anchor points; one at the later end of the scale when cross-dating makes close relative dating possible, and the other at the early end where typological relationships of plain wares and of the first painted wares serve as points of reference.

One basic fact should be remembered when comparing these two ceramic complexes; namely, that from the earliest times, Hohokam pottery was produced by the coil and paddle-and-anvil method, while Mogollon pottery was made by the coil-and-scrape technique. The significance of this extends beyond the central Hohokam - Mogollon problem, for it enters into the question of origin and relationship of such pottery types as Adamana Brown, and the taxonomic position of such culture patterns as the Patayan and Sinagua. There is no need at present to speculate on the ultimate significance of this

technological dichotomy, but that it bears on the question of
single or multiple origin for Southwestern ceramic complexes
cannot be denied.

Regardless of this, Mogollon and Hohokam pottery had much
in common in the earliest defined phases.  Both had plain
brown, and slipped and polished red wares.  There were differences in relative popularity of the types, however, for among
the Hohokam only about four percent of the pottery produced
was red ware, while among the Mogollon of San Simon Branch it
reached about seven percent, and further east in the Mimbres
and Pine Lawn Valley, it amounted to 20 percent or more.
Certain similarities of form in the simple bowl and jars with
outcurved rims also are apparent, although it is clear that a
much greater variety of shapes was produced by the early Mogollon potters than by the Hohokam.  One further point of difference is that while the Mogollon made polished wares from
the earliest known phases, they were also producing cruder,
unpolished types which were technologically more simple.
There is no known counterpart in the Hohokam Culture, whose
earliest pottery was all polished.  Whether this indicates a
time difference cannot be answered at present.

The earliest painted types are so similar in concept and
execution that often it is only with difficulty that they can
be distinguished.  This is especially true of the polished-
over-the-decoration variety of Estrella Red-on-gray, believed
to be earlier than the unpolished variety, and Dos Cabezas
Red-on-brown.  Designs in these types consisted of broad lines
forming chevrons, triangles pendant from the rim, or combinations of these, to produce sectioned layouts.  With the unpolished variety of Estrella Red-on-gray, however, use of

curvilinear lines and small unit figures begins, and from that point on the Hohokam decorative repertory diverges from the Mogollon. Whatever the source of subsequent Hohokam pottery development, whether indigenous or extraneous, it is plain that Mogollon was not its inspiration, for the majority of vessel forms, design layouts, and decorative elements do not occur there.

A certain amount of cultural interchange is evidenced, though the direction of its movement can only be surmised, through the intermediate phases leading up to Gila Butte and Santa Cruz phases of the Hohokam, and Pinaleno, Galiuro, and San Francisco phases of the Mogollon. These relationships lie in the continuing development of basic layout and designs of Dos Cabezas Red-on-brown and Estrella Red-on-gray, which, through refinement and increasing complexity, culminated in the quartered, offset-quartered, and sectioned layout of Gila Butte and Santa Cruz Red-on-buff, and Pinaleno, Galiuro, and Mogollon red-on-brown types. These particular designs are so similar that some direct relationship cannot be doubted. Rim solids and opposed solids with intervening lines were used by both, but characteristically were more complex among the Hohokam, as were the checkerboard, zig-zag, ticked lines, and cross-hatching. These layouts and design elements comprised almost the total of Mogollon painted decoration of the time, while among the Hohokam they were less common than several other styles of decoration. One pattern, concentric geometric panels, seems to have been a Mogollon development, for it does not occur in Hohokam pottery.

Beginning with the introduction of Three Circle and Cerros Red-on-white, for which there is no Hohokam typological

equivalent, and increasing in Bold Face Black-on-white, the
use of curvilinear elements such as simple and interlocking
scrolls, and the introduction of life forms are probably to
be credited to Hohokam influence.  Finally, the pottery of
Encinas Phase, and to a somewhat less extent, of Mimbres
Phase, shows heavy use of Hohokam design vocabulary and
all-over layout.

    In the stone work of Mogollon and Hohokam there are some
similarities, mostly in simple flaked tools that carried over
from preceramic times, and some notable differences, primarily
in ground stone tools and in the high degree of elaboration
reached in some categories by the Hohokam.  The full-trough
metate and its associated mano form, which characterized
Hohokam from the earliest phase, did not enter the Mogollon
area until very late in Mogollon 4, when three-quarter-grooved
axes and carved stone palettes were introduced, along with an
elaboration of carving in shell.  Stone bowls were made by
both groups, but were never common among the Mogollon, and
when decorated at all, had only simple incised designs.
Flaked stone tools were generally more abundant among the
Mogollon, and only in the Desert Branch of the Hohokam, where
agriculture could not be exploited to the extent that it was
in the Gila Basin, were they common.  Projectile points were
not numerous during early Hohokam, and the elaborate forms of
late Hohokam phases did not occur among the Mogollon.

    In bone and shell, as with stone, the Hohokam were far
apart from the Mogollon.  Neither material was widely used for
utilitarian objects by the Hohokam who, instead, directed
their attention to decorative use.  Bone and antler were
carved, incised, and painted, as was shell, which was further

embellished in late phases by etching.  Only a few bone awls
were found; one of these, from Sacaton Phase context, was
notched, suggesting influence or intrusion from the Mogollon
area (Gladwin et al. 1937:154).  It is interesting that the
evolution of bone tubes, from early carved forms to late plain
tubes, was the same in the Hohokam area and the adjacent
Mogollon San Simon Branch.

Certain trade relationships appear definite, inasmuch as
there was some interchange of pottery; and rare intrusives,
such as a three-quarter-grooved stone axe into Crooked Ridge
Village, indicate trade.  Furthermore, the evidence suggests
that most, if not all, shell bracelets occurring in Mogollon
and Anasazi sites were produced by the Hohokam, for only in
Hohokam sites do shell wastage and the specialized abraders
occur to imply the manufacture of shell artifacts.  Such may
also be the case of the rare turquoise ornaments found in
early Mogollon sites.

It has already been pointed out that in architecture,
and in some other traits, there was no sharp boundary dividing
Mogollon and Hohokam.  Between the Santa Cruz and San Pedro
rivers, and to some distance east of the latter, there is an
area where the culture is a distinct blend of traits.  The
work of Fulton (1934a, 1934b, 1938, 1941), Fulton and Tuthill
(1940), Tuthill (1947), Di Peso (1951, 1953), and Trishka
(1933) have delineated a culture area that is neither specifically Mogollon nor Hohokam, but rather a blend of the two,
with certain traits of its own which either were not shared
or were elaborations of basically simple traits shared with
one or both of its neighbors.  Architecturally, there does
not seem to have been a blend so much as the application of

two traditions side by side.  There is in the area a specialized development of the cooking pits common to both Mogollon
and Hohokam.  Method of disposal of the dead shows a shift
from early inhumation to later cremation.  The pottery is a
blend of Mogollon and Hohokam techniques with vessel forms
and design vocabulary showing increasing Hohokam flavor from
early to late.  Stone objects are most like Hohokam, with a
specialized form of stone paddle that is rare outside of the
area.

It seems clear that Hohokam elements are strong, even in
the earliest defined phases, but they appear to have increased,
especially during the time they were beginning to spread
farther east into Mogollon territory.  The question remains
as to whether the basic group was Mogollon or Hohokam, or was
from the first a blended group.  This can be settled only by
further work in early sites in the area.  At present it is
one of the clearest examples of a cultural blend in
Southwestern archeology.

Another area which appears to involve a blend of Mogollon
and Hohokam traditions is the Sinagua area.  Colton (1939)
tentatively aligned the Sinagua with the Mogollon root, but
has since not considered the matter as settled.  Gladwin (1943)
criticized the concept of the Sinagua Branch, but there can
be little doubt that it is sufficiently distinct to merit
separate taxonomic status as detailed by Colton (1946).  The
basic point at issue is whether it should be regarded as
belonging to the Mogollon root or to some other.  Schroeder
(in preparation) has reanalyzed the data and now proposes to
align it with the earliest Hohokam.  As previously suggested
by Colton (1946:310), it is intermediate in many respects

between Mogollon, Hohokam, and Anasazi, and it would perhaps
be better to regard it simply as a culture blend. Architecturally it lies somewhat closer to Mogollon, but there are
numerous Hohokam features, and a few that do not occur in
either. Disposal of the dead follows a mixture of traits
perhaps attributable to early Mogollon influence, with later
Anasazi influence. Pottery is clearly a blend of Hohokam
paddle-and-anvil technology with a Mogollon-like emphasis on
polishing and smudging. Later influence in design points to
both Hohokam and Anasazi. For the rest of the material culture we do not control sufficient data even to suggest the
focus of affiliation. Therefore, until further excavation
can establish more definite relationships, it would seem
useful to regard this as another example of cultural blend,
albeit one of which we do not know the proportions of the
mixture.

One of the chief problems confronting Southwestern archeologists today is the definition of relationships between the
Anasazi and the Mogollon, for regardless of the position taken
as to their taxonomic status, the fact that differences did
exist in some degree demands investigation. Such investigation is by no means easy, because there are many similarities
between the two groups. To understand these, it is necessary
to control the relative chronology; and for this our evidence
is poorest for the period most critical in the relationships,
that is, prior to A. D. 600. Nevertheless, recent advances
in our knowledge make such an attempt necessary.

First, perhaps the bare outline of the cultural history
of the two groups should be stated so far as it concerns this
study. We do not know the origin of the Anasazi, although it
is not unlikely that they represent an eastern extension of
early Great Basin hunters and gatherers. Since the Cochise
appear also to have moved out of the Great Basin at a somewhat earlier date, certain generalized trait resemblances may
reflect a very early relationship between these groups. This
separation appears to have taken place at a fairly remote
time and to have been almost, if not entirely, complete.

Evidence connecting Mogollon with Cochise seems clear.
In both areas agriculture and architecture preceded pottery-
making; but present evidence indicates that agriculture was
earlier, by some 2,000 years, and richer among the late Cochise
forerunners of the Mogollon than among the Basketmakers. The

advent of pottery-making also occurred about 500 years earlier among the Mogollon. To some extent, Mogollon or Cochise architecture was earlier and more diversified than was that of the Basketmakers.

Following this initiatory period was one of development, seemingly more rapid among the Anasazi than among the Mogollon, for after about A. D. 700 a number of elements which had their Southwestern development among the Basketmakers began to diffuse southward. Judging from the continuing southern tradition underlying and reorienting these northern elements, this was primarily a movement of ideas and techniques rather than of people. During this period the Mogollon appear to have been peripheral to the Anasazi development, continuing, however, to maintain their integrity as a group even though they had partially adopted masonry pueblos, black-on-white pottery, and other traits. The ultimate fate of the Mogollon Pueblos and the Anasazi Pueblos is partly known, but details of cultural identity still remain obscure.

Proceeding to a more detailed analysis, agricultural patterns may first be examined. The first Cochise (preceramic Mogollon) corn from Bat Cave has been dated at about 2000 B. C. (Johnson 1951; Dick, in preparation). This, the most primitive corn yet found, was a small-cobbed pod-pop corn without any trace of teosinte in its composition. Associated with this early maize was squash. About 1000 B. C. another variety of maize appeared showing contamination with teosinte, which apparently improved its vigor. At the same time, beans were added to the agricultural complex. Abundant evidence of prepottery maize occurred also at Tularosa and Cordova caves (Martin et al. 1952), dating to circa 300 B. C. With the

prepottery corn were beans (_Phaseolus_ _vulgaris_), squash
(_Cucurbita_ _pepo_), and Lagenaria, or bottle gourd. This agricultural complex continued into the earliest ceramic horizon,
Pine Lawn Phase, without any major change. Slightly later, so
far as present knowledge goes, agriculture was introduced to
the Basketmakers. Only corn and squash were known. According
to Carter (1945), the types of corn and squash differed from
southern varieties, specifically Hohokam, and represented a
different source. However, these contentions are in controversy (Jones, Willey, and Roberts 1946), and it is not necessary to review here the arguments involved. For our purposes
it is necessary only to note (1) the relative lateness of the
introduction of agriculture to the Basketmakers, (2) that all
early northern squash yet reported is apparently _Cucurbita_
_moschata_ or _C_. _mixta_ rather than _C_. _pepo_, and (3) that beans
are lacking from the complex.

It should be pointed out, also, that more recent data,
including Carbon-14 dates, for the Southeast add plausibility
to some of Carter's hypotheses. Beans were not introduced
into the Anasazi area until after A. D. 400, and did not
become common until about A. D. 700. Later changes in Anasazi
corn are attributed to introduction of new types from the
north and east.

We may sum up the situation, as presently known, by
saying that agriculture was considerably earlier among the
Mogollon than among the Anasazi, and that it was more varied.
However, knowledge of prehistoric Southwestern agriculture is
in a state of flux, and the time and amount of influence
moving in either direction during early phases cannot be
estimated on the basis of present knowledge.

In the architectural development of Mogollon and Anasazi there are early differences and late similarities. San Pedro houses (preceramic Mogollon) were true pithouses with upper walls presumably made of uprights covered with brush or twigs and plastered (Sayles 1945:1-4). A very large storage or sleeping pit occupied nearly half of the small floor area. A simple fire pit was near the center. Entry was by a step at the side. Morris's Basketmaker II houses (Anonymous 1941:28) were not pithouses, but rather, were shallow, saucer-shaped floors ranging from 9 to 30 feet in diameter (hence much larger than the Cochise houses), with roofs supported by the walls of log and mud masonry. The absence of uprights marks a fundamental difference between known Basketmaker II houses and those of Basketmaker III. Pits filled with sand and ash, but relatively unburned, were located in the center. Slab-lined storage pits with domed mud roofs were characteristic floor features. These floors were built on terraces made by excavating part of the hillside and piling the removed earth in front. As many as nine floors were superimposed.

Thus it can be seen that the basic patterns differed, both in conception and in detail. There is a difference in time, as well, the Basketmaker houses dating to the early centuries after Christ, those of the San Pedro perhaps as early as 500 B. C.

Storage pits are common features of both areas, those of San Pedro being straight-sided or undercut, unlined pits, those of the Basketmaker occasionally undercut or jug-shaped, but characteristically lined with slabs and covered with a fiber-tempered, mud domed roof supported by sticks or built of wood and mud masonry (Kidder and Guernsey 1919:74-90, 27-32;

Guernsey and Kidder 1921:19-22, 30-33, 38-40; Nusbaum 1922;
Haury 1945:12). While these are commonly held to be storage
units only, diameters up to 20 feet (Haury 1945:12) and the
nature of the construction of some at Cave II, Kimboko Canyon
(Kidder and Guernsey 1919:84-90) make this an open question.
One example of slab-lined and -floored sleeping and storage
cists has been reported from Steamboat Cave in the Mogollon
area (Cosgrove 1947:10-12) which may belong to the San Pedro
Stage, but the evidence is not clear. One difference between
the two patterns is in the use of caves. The Basketmakers
used them primarily for storage and burial of the dead, the
Cochise frequently used them as dwelling areas.

While the above comparison has been made on the basis of
technological equivalence, differences are even more striking
when the analysis is made in terms of contemporaneous patterns, for at the time the Basketmakers were building domed,
log masonry structures, as noted above, the Mogollon of Pine
Lawn and Hilltop phases, and probably Penasco, Georgetown,
and early Circle Prairie phases, were living in villages of
pithouses generally clustered around a great ceremonial house.
Both domestic and ceremonial pithouses showed a considerable
variety of types, roundish to quadrangular, with or without
long lateral entries. One type of pithouse found at Crooked
Ridge Village, and probably contemporaneous with late Basketmaker II, consists of a rectangular or roundish pithouse in
which the entry was expanded to form an antechamber.

True pithouses appear in the Anasazi area about the
beginning of Basketmaker III. Regional architectural styles
are apparent in Basketmaker III, or more correctly, the
eastern part contains a wider variety of houses. Occurring

in western Basketmaker territory are roundish pithouses with walls of plastered earth, or of upright stone slabs (Kidder and Guernsey 1919:41-45, 71-72; Guernsey 1931:2-13, 18, 22-27, 32-36; Baldwin 1939:48-49). Conical roofs were sometimes made by driving poles into the upper wall at an angle so that they met over the center of the room at about six feet. Walls of shallow structures were sometimes built up by courses of small stones, or hand-molded "turtle-back" adobes, set in much clay. For the most part, hearths were simple depressions or fire areas, although clay-rimmed hearth and floor ridges appeared some time during Basketmaker III.

This type of house is found in the eastern San Juan, also (Roberts 1929:24-26, 37-41, 55-61, 68-70; Morris 1925; 1936: 34-36; Haury 1936; Adams 1951), where some are also rectanguloid. These houses lack lateral entries, so must have been entered by ladder or, in the shallow houses, by a step from the old ground level. Many, perhaps most, of these houses had a quadrangular roof, central fire pit, and clay floor ridges, and although the latter are not mentioned for the early houses in Mummy Cave (Morris 1925) nor for Obelisk Cave (Morris 1936), they occurred in the Basketmaker III pithouses in Broken Flute Cave (Morris, personal communication) and in some of the Canyon del Muerto caves. Houses with narrow lateral entryways have a sparse distribution in Anasazi territory over a considerable time range. They are reported from the Red Rock country (Morris 1936), Cahone Canyon, Site 2 (Martin and Rinaldo 1939), Awatovi area (Brew 1946:80). These would seem to reflect Mogollon influence.

Houses with antechambers occur at Shabik'eshchee as a typical form (Roberts 1929:10-16, 22-24, 26-37, 41-46) but have not been dated. At Mesa Verde (Lancaster and Watson 1943:193; Smiley 1949:171; O'Bryan 1950:104) and in the La Plata Valley (Morris 1939:63, 64) antechamber houses were constructed from about A. D. 600 to about A. D. 700 and perhaps later. In southeastern Utah (Brew 1946:248), and southwestern Colorado (Martin and Rinaldo 1939) this type of house continued in use after the middle 700's. Most of these are rectanguloid and have floor ridges.

I have entered this consideration of the dates of antechamber houses to demonstrate that, so far as we know now, this type of structure was diffusing northward. This is also suggested by the fact that before the end of Basketmaker III the antechamber had been modified into a ventilator in the Chaco area (Roberts 1929:17-22, 62-68). The ventilator type house was the only kind found at White Mound (Gladwin 1945) at a time when antechamber houses were still being made in the northern area. Important, too, is the fact that antechamber houses occur as part of the standard architectural complex in a Mogollon site probably at least 200 years prior to their first appearance among the Basketmakers (Wheat 1954).

Late in Basketmaker III, during a phase transitional to Pueblo I, the storage cists, which had been clustered around pithouses in such sites as Obelisk Cave (Morris 1936), had been developed into contiguous surface rooms, some used for storage and others as living rooms (Brew 1946; Roberts 1939). One or more pithouses, or proto-kivas, in which slab and mud partitions had replaced the clay floor ridges, and with ventilator complex instead of antechamber, were constructed in the sheltered side of the arc of surface rooms. Some villages of this type were very large (Brew 1946; Morris 1919; 1939).

With the shift to contiguous surface units there was also a shift to stone masonry, which became the most characteristic feature of subsequent Anasazi horizons. While stone masonry is usually considered a local development, Kroeber (1939:46) has suggested that it is only one of several traits radiated from the Mexican area. During Pueblo I another innovation appeared. This was the jacal type of structure characteristic of the northeastern Pueblo extension well exemplified by those in the Piedra district of Colorado (Roberts 1930). It would be interesting to know the temporal relationships of the distribution, for on available evidence it seems to have moved west and south from an earlier appearance in the upper San Juan.

In the western San Juan area, especially around Kayenta, the circular pithouse continued in favor (Kidder and Guernsey 1919:41-45, 54-55; Guernsey 1931:17, 28-32, 57-60; Beals, Brainerd, and Smith 1945:24-42; Judd 1926:90-123). Most of these houses had ventilators, apparently introduced from the east, for there is no evidence of their local evolution.

Stratigraphic placement and cross-dating indicate that Mogollon 2 is generally contemporaneous with early Basketmaker III. The equivalence of Mogollon 3 with late Basketmaker and all of Pueblo I is more firmly established. Mogollon architecture of these periods has been described in detail in Chapter IV and therefore need not be discussed here. It is necessary only to point out that roundish and rectanguloid pithouses, with and without lateral entries, continued to be made. Houses with antechambers are reported, and houses with a southern annex developed probably out of the antechamber houses. Architecture of Mogollon 4 is marked by the advent

of stone masonry pueblos, presumably introduced from the
Anasazi.

One other architectural form needs to be considered.
Great houses, apparently ceremonial in nature, occur in every
Mogollon branch but San Simon, and in every period. The early
ceremonial houses are bean-shaped with short entries, D-shaped
with long lateral entries, rectanguloid or circular with short
stepped entries, or with no lateral entry. Early northern
Mogollon great houses are roundish, most like the early great
kivas of the Anasazi. Dendrodates for the Bluff Site ceremonial house at about A. D. 320, and the probable pre-400
dates of those at SU, Promontory, and Crooked Ridge Village
sites, leave little doubt that the idea of the great house
was earlier among the Mogollon than among the Anasazi. Their
early distribution in Anasazi sites is also interesting.
Great kivas occur at Shabik'eshchee (Roberts 1929:73-81) and
in southwestern Colorado (Martin and Rinaldo 1939:350-359;
Morris 1939:82-84) at dates ranging from a probable A. D. 600
or later at Shabik'eshchee to A. D. 831± in the La Plata,
suggesting that they were moving north. Another Basketmaker
III great kiva is reported at Juniper Cove near Marsh Pass
(Baldwin 1939:49), but because of lack of data its significance cannot be assessed at this time. Present evidence,
then, points to the Mogollon as the source of the great kiva.

Village layouts of early Basketmaker III and early Mogollon sites were generally similar, but two points of difference
may be noted. Mogollon villages, as previously stated, were
commonly clustered around a great house, a feature that does
not become common among the Anasazi until a much later date.
The second difference, the inception of surface structures

among the Anasazi, comes about the beginning of Pueblo I, at which time there is a notable shift toward a village plan with houses in rows opening to the southeast. Still another general difference was the method of trash disposal. The Anasazi usually placed trash in definite rubbish heaps (Roberts 1929: 105; 1939:20; 1931:43; 1930:36; Morris 1939:28, 33), while the Mogollon scattered it on the ground around the houses or in abandoned houses. Contrasting with both, the Hohokam deliberately built mounds of considerable proportions.

Flexed burial was the usual method of disposal of the dead among both Anasazi and early Mogollon. Because of this, it has sometimes been asserted that the patterns were the same. There were, however, several differences. Basketmaker II burials were usually, if not always, made in abandoned storage cists or specially dug pits, and so far as our evidence goes, usually in caves. Most graves contained several bodies, tightly flexed; one pit contained 19 (Kidder and Guernsey 1919:27-32). A few burials were placed in a reclining position, others were encased in adobe. Burial offerings were often elaborate.

Burials of the contemporaneous Mogollon were most often in special pits dug at random through the village, but occasionally in abandoned storage pits or on the floors of abandoned houses. Rarely was more than one body placed in a grave. Bodies were usually flexed or semiflexed, often were placed in a half-sitting position, and were sometimes covered with rocks. This pattern continued through most of Mogollon history until late in Mogollon 4, when subfloor burial became common. Early Mogollon burials usually had little of an imperishable nature with them, but offerings of pottery became very common in Mogollon 4 and 5.

Burials of Basketmaker III generally continued the Basketmaker II pattern. However, multiple burials declined somewhat in frequency, and bodies were as often buried in the open, in rock crevices, talus slopes, or in refuse heaps, as in caves. Numerous burial offerings were customary. By Pueblo I, single flexed burials placed in pits in the refuse heaps had become characteristic and were marked by a high frequency of burial goods.

Thus it can be seen that the Anasazi burial pattern differs markedly from that of the contemporaneous Mogollon.

At this point it would be logical to introduce a discussion of differences in physical types between Mogollon and Anasazi, but there does not exist any usable collection of data with the necessary detailed comparison by a physical anthropologist. Until an adequate overall comparative study is made, it appears worse than useless to the writer to attempt to compare these cultural groups in terms of physical types. Certainly, Seltzer's (1944) study seems inadequately based for the broadness of the generalizations derived.

One of the most distinctive features of the Mogollon culture pattern is the ceramic complex. Since there are developmental pottery sequences in both Mogollon and Anasazi, and inasmuch as there are certain technological and decorative parallels, pottery offers a number of problems of interrelation. Carbon-14 dates for the introduction of pottery in Tularosa Cave (Martin et al. 1952), and dendrodates for the established ceramic complex at Bluff Site (Haury and Sayles 1947) clearly demonstrate the precedence of Mogollon pottery over Anasazi.

The mere fact that the Mogollon had pottery several
centuries before the Basketmakers, however, cannot be taken
as proof that pottery-making was introduced from south to
north. Rather, we must rely on specific evidence of detailed
similarities in techniques, shapes, and other factors such as
associated traits which were introduced at the same time.
There is, as yet, at least, very little evidence of this sort.
It seems clear that there were Mogollon groups northwest of
the White Mountains by A. D. 300, at or shortly before the
time the Basketmakers first began to make pottery. It is not
quite so certain that Mogollon villages were also northeast
of the White Mountains, although the evidence of Danson's
survey (1952) makes this seem likely. However, proximity and
opportunity no more prove the transmission of the trait than
does prior possession. It may have provided a stimulus, if
it did not directly inspire. Certain specific differences,
however, require explanation. Some of these, such as the
matter of temper, are more apparent than real. It now seems
clear that northern Mogollon potters utilized sand as well as
crushed rock and potsherds for temper, and equally certain
that some Basketmakers used crushed rock rather than sand.
Whatever difference remains in this respect seems to be partly
determined by environment, partly by preference, and in any
event, is one of predominance rather than of exclusion.

Perhaps the most important difference is the matter of
firing atmosphere. This remains the only indication that the
Basketmakers may have developed their own ceramic processes
with only the stimulus coming from an outside source. It is
distinct not only from all other Southwestern techniques, but
generally from all primitive pottery manufactures. Here,

again, we need more evidence.  However, selected sherds of
Black River variety of Alma Plain, which apparently increase
in number as one goes northeast from Black River and Crooked
Ridge Village (Gila Pueblo Surveys), can be distinguished from
Lino Gray only by the specific minerals used as aplastics.
These sherds are gray-tan, gray, or white, and the temper
particles protrude through the surface, causing tiny thermal
fracture marks radiating away from them.  Nevertheless, it
cannot be asserted that this complex gave rise to Lino Gray
and later wares, at least until excavation of sites where
Black River variety of Alma Plain is at home.  Furthermore,
the matter of materials needs to be considered in some detail.
Shepard (1939) has pointed out that no really controlled
reducing or oxidizing atmosphere existed under primitive conditions.  It is therefore clear that the distinctiveness of
gray or brown pottery depends largely on the mineral composition, particularly the iron content, of the local clays used.
That some cultural distinction did exist seems clear, but
future research may well reduce its significance.

The problem of fiber-tempered, unfired vessels, which
frequently show evidence of having been partly molded in
baskets, can no longer be considered in the simple evolution-
istic sense that Morris presented (1927, 1939).  Such vessels
were not limited to Basketmaker; they occurred among the Mogollon along with fired pottery and increased in late times.
Furthermore, in the western San Juan they are more characteristic of Basketmaker III (Guernsey and Kidder 1931:84-85) than
of the earlier period (Guernsey and Kidder 1921:98), and
continue into Pueblo I.  Rinaldo (Martin et al. 1952:70-73)
has suggested that they have a specialized function, as well

they might have.  They certainly are not purely developmental.

The techniques of coiling and scraping pottery are held
in common by Mogollon and Basketmaker, in contrast to coil
and paddle-and-anvil of the Hohokam, but this cannot be taken
as proof that the San Juan inhabitants learned the process
from the Mogollon.  Certainly, other pottery makers may have
maintained contact not yet delineated in our research.  That
the Mogollon were not the only possible tutors is indicated
in the range of vessel forms which occur in Basketmaker.
This is aside from Morris's argument (1927) that many of the
forms are locally inspired by gourds and such, for there is
little evidence that the gourd-like vessels appeared until
very late Basketmaker III or Pueblo I---not early.  There are
several vessel forms in late Basketmaker ceramics that appear
neither in Mogollon nor in Hohokam.  Such forms are the duck
pots, boot-shaped pots, stirrup-spout, double spout, and
slender-necked bottles; pots with trilobed base, vessels with
lateral spouts, "submarine" bottles, and perhaps others.
Most, if not all, of these are standard ceramic components of
the archaic complexes of Middle America and Peru, and are of
such a nature that it appears beyond the realm of logic to
suggest that they represent independent inventions by the
Basketmaker potters.  Whatever source Basketmaker pottery may
prove to have, these traits must be accounted for before the
whole story can be known.

I have suggested elsewhere (Wheat 1953) that, based on
the mutual interchange or possession of ceramic forms, full-
grooved and notched stone axes, celts, contracting-stemmed
projectile points, races of maize, and perhaps jacal architecture, late Basketmaker III was undergoing heavy influence from

the "Middle Mississippi" culture horizon centering about the
St. Francis and White rivers in eastern Arkansas. Recent
Carbon-14 dates for this horizon add weight to the hypothesis.

Regardless of the ultimate source of Basketmaker pottery,
certain specific ceramic traits appear to have had their
Southwestern development in Mogollon territory and to have
been passed northward to the Anasazi potters. This series of
traits began to move northward about the middle of Basketmaker
III, probably about A. D. 600, and in certain cases became the
hallmark of later Pueblo periods. Some of these traits remain
in contention, but evidence is constantly accumulating to show
that the movement was from south to north, not in the reverse
direction.

To begin with culinary wares, neck-banding may first be
considered. Haury (1941:80-83) discussed this problem in some
detail, but new evidence may now be adduced. The fact that
Alma Neck-banded constitutes a minor but consistent element
of Georgetown Phase ceramics indicates a date not later than
A. D. 700, and as suggested above, probably pre-A. D. 500 in
the south. Furthermore, evidence from Danson's survey tends
to show that Three Circle Neck-banded was already supplanting
Alma Neck-banded when Kana-a Gray was coming into use. This
would accord also with the somewhat earlier dates suggested
for San Francisco Phase in the south. In the eastern peripheral area described by Mera (1935:29) brown ware coiling is
always finer than that on contemporary white ware. Therefore,
it seems most probable that neck-banding spread from south to
north in the Southwest.

Smudging also has been reviewed by Haury (1941:87-90).
Here, again, new evidence from Crooked Ridge Village (Wheat

1954), where it occurs in early Circle Prairie Phase, supports
the view that the technique had long been employed by the
Mogollon.  In the northern Mogollon area it became a dominant
ware and was traded extensively with the southern and eastern
Anasazi.  Apparently it also inspired a rare local Anasazi
smudged type with typical Lino paste features but possessing
a well polished and smudged interior.

One factor usually held to separate early Anasazi from
Mogollon pottery is the degree of smoothness of the Mogollon
types.  This was based on the idea that wherever polished
brown ware was found in early Anasazi sites it represented
intrusion from Mogollon sites, and that the only local types
were unpolished Lino Gray and its painted versions.  The work
of O'Bryan (1950:91, 105) at Mesa Verde, however, would seem
to demonstrate conclusively that the Basketmakers were producing a polished brown ware, Twin Trees Plain.  This, or a
similar type, had been recognized by Morris (1936:35-36) in
caves of Red Rock Valley.  While this undoubtedly makes it
more difficult to determine from published descriptions
whether a potsherd is local Twin Trees Plain or intrusive
Alma Plain, it also shows a closer resemblance, technologically, between early Anasazi and Mogollon pottery.  The exact
relationship of these types remains to be worked out.

Slipping is evidently much older in Mogollon than in
Anasazi; the latter did not practise it extensively prior to
A. D. 700.  The predominant slipped Mogollon ware was San
Francisco Red.  It has been suggested that fugitive red ware
of Basketmaker III and Pueblo I might be an attempt to duplicate the Mogollon red wares, as it might well be.  However,
the possibility must not be overlooked that it was not

generically associated with San Francisco Red, or that it was diffused from another source. Nevertheless, the evidence as it now stands suggests Mogollon influence.

Late in the Basketmaker period or early in Pueblo I, two pottery innovations suggest the possibility of Mogollon influence on Anasazi pottery. The first of these is La Plata Black-on-red ware (Brew 1946:253). In the western San Juan is found another similar type, Bluff Black-on-red (Colton and Hargrave 1937:69-70). The origin of these types is obscure. Neither is slipped, but depends for its color on oxidized firing, in which respect it is markedly similar to Forestdale Red of the Mogollon series. Decoration of these types is occasionally like that of the companion black-on-white types, but more often differs completely in style. Regardless of pattern, the lines are heavy and broad, and vessels are frequently polished over the decoration, a typical Mogollon technique but distinctly uncommon among the Anasazi. Design and layout will be discussed below. The second of these types is Abajo Red-on-orange (Brew 1946:254, 259-270). Like the black-on-red types, its base color is due to firing, not to a slip. Like the black-on-reds, the decoration is in general much heavier in style than on the black-on-whites, but apparently polishing over the decoration was not carried out.

Turning now to a comparison of layout and design of early Anasazi and Mogollon pottery, marked differences are to be noted. Among the Mogollon, a period during which no painted ware was made was followed by a broad-line period when the chief design elements were concentric chevrons or rim triangles banded by chevrons. Subsequent periods saw increasing complexity of this type of design, usually in a quartered, offset-quartered, or sectioned layout. Rim solids with fringing lines are common. These devices continued into Mogollon 5. It is not clear if there was ever a plain ware horizon among the Anasazi. The first painted types continued the designs with which the people were most familiar. These were copied from baskets or occasionally from pictographs.

In late Basketmaker III and early Pueblo I, several new design elements and layout schemes appear. Although temporal data are not well controlled, these seem to appear first in the southern part of the eastern San Juan at Shabik'eshchee (Roberts 1929:121, pl. 17), White Mound (Gladwin 1945: pls. XI, XII), and Kiatuthlanna (Roberts 1931: pls. 13, 15, 19-22), and have their most intense local development in that area. These decorative devices are: use of rim solids such as tri-angles; fringing lines; chevrons; checkerboards; concentric rectangles; and quartered, offset-quartered, and sectioned layouts. There are others, as well, but these are the ones which concern us here. Martin and his associates (1949:202) have discussed some of these devices in comparing Abajo Red-on-orange and Mogollon Red-on-brown. They conclude that 8 out of 36 design elements on Abajo Red-on-orange resemble those of Mogollon Red-on-brown. Brew (1946:292) has pointed out that many Abajo designs have their origin in the decorated basketry that preceded this pottery type. However, in considering the similarities rather than the dissimilarities, it is important to note that those designs and layout elements held in common during the late Basketmaker III - Pueblo I, and San Francisco Phase are preceded by a long period of development in the Mogollon, whereas they appear full-blown among the Anasazi. Taking these points into consideration, there can remain little doubt that these decorative techniques were diffused from south to north.

That this is true, however, does not prove that either black-on-red or red-on-orange ware owes its origin to Mogollon influence, although there is a possibility, perhaps a probability, that they do. However, in view of other culture elements which apparently were diffusing into Basketmaker country at about the same time, it is possible that both red-on-orange and red wares had their source in the Middle Mississippi culture horizon to the east, where similar types were also native (Wheat 1953). If this were proved to be the case, the roughly simultaneous innovations of red and red-on-orange wares, and the decorative devices mentioned above from the Mogollon, would have been coincidental.

Miscellaneous objects of clay are common in both Anasazi and Mogollon. Miniature vessels occur in every pottery horizon in both areas and, in general, reflect the pottery styles in vogue at that time and place. One form, however, appears to be typically Mogollon. This is the miniature ladle. Although full-size ladles are much more typical of Anasazi than of Mogollon, where they do not occur until late, the miniature form is rare among the Anasazi.

Pottery pipes occur in both areas, but shape differences can be noted. Most Anasazi clay pipes are elongate-conical or tubular, while those of the Mogollon are shaped like a cigar-holder. Cornucopia- or funnel-shaped clay objects, sometimes identified as model carrying-baskets, are typical of Basketmaker III and Pueblo I, but have occurred, possibly as intrusives, in Mogollon sites of San Francisco Phase.

Human figurines of clay among the Anasazi and Mogollon

are not so well modeled as those of the Hohokam, and resemble each other in general. Bodies are flat, features indicated rather than modeled, and both occasionally have punctate designs. They appear more commonly among the Basketmakers, but occur earlier in Mogollon; therefore, it remains an open question as to whether the Mogollon introduced these into Basketmaker, or both received them from other sources.

Animal figurines are rare to absent in both areas, but do occur in the later phases. Unfired pot covers are reported from both areas, and there is no essential difference, although Anasazi specimens are sometimes fitted with finger-grips.

Use of potsherds for artifacts occurs in both Anasazi and Mogollon, but there are interesting differences in the classes of objects made. Both groups made scrapers from sherds. Large sherds, smoothed and used as trays or scoops, occur sporadically among the Mogollon but are quite common among the Anasazi. By contrast, sherd discs, both perforate and plain, were common among the Mogollon but rare or absent among the Anasazi except at sites in contact with the Mogollon, such as Kiatuthlanna (Roberts 1931:149) and Allentown (Roberts 1940:109).

In the remaining classes of artifacts, differences between Mogollon and Anasazi are often typological only. They consist in slightly but consistently differing ways of making the same tools. Because of this fact, it is possible to stress either the similarities in general terms, as Nesbitt (1938) did, or the differences in specific terms, as Haury (1936b, 1941), Haury and Sayles (1947), and Martin and his associates (1943, and others) have done. Thus, differences

of opinion as to the separateness of Mogollon and Anasazi have
been partly based on whether the observer was a "lumper" or a
"splitter".

Typological differences are also to be observed in the
artifacts of ground or pecked stone. So far as grinding tools
are concerned, it is clear that the Mogollon carried over a
tradition of long standing into later periods. Metate types
shared by early Mogollon and Anasazi are slab or basin, and
one-end-closed trough metates. It is very difficult to get
data on Basketmaker grinding stones, and it is certain that
they constituted a very minor culture element in strong contrast to the Mogollon. The few known from publications are
casual stone slabs, although Morris (in conversation) has
stated that closed-end trough metates occur rarely in the
Durango district. By Basketmaker III, and continuing until
Pueblo III, Anasazi metates are closed-end troughs. So are
those of the Mogollon, but they differ in being generally
concave on both grinding axes and unshaped, whereas those of
the Anasazi are more often shaped, and the grinding surfaces
flatter and squarish.

Anasazi manos are generally more rectangular, longer, and
flatter. Stone mortars are quite typical of the Mogollon, and
occur sporadically among Basketmaker III, but are more common
in the southern Anasazi territory (Morris 1939:132-133).
Stone bowls follow the same distribution. The most common
pestles in both areas are selected cobbles. Pitted pebbles
do not occur, so far as I can ascertain, among the Anasazi.

Grooved stone mauls occur in both areas. In the Mogollon
area they occur as early as Chiricahua Stage of the Cochise
Culture, and continue through all periods of the Mogollon

culture.  In the Anasazi area they do not occur until Basketmaker III and never become a dominant tool form, although they
continue in use until historic times.  Morris (1939:137) states
that the small, late, grooved stones were used as club-heads,
a use that probably did not pertain to the Mogollon mauls.
Grooved stone axes are typical of Anasazi from late Basketmaker III on.  They do not occur in Mogollon sites until late,
their place being taken by hand-axes and choppers, which
appear correspondingly rare among the Anasazi except in the
Durango Basketmaker II sites (Morris, in press).

Tubular stone pipes are present in both areas, but they
show certain differences.  Basketmaker II pipes are usually
made of stone, in conical form, for use both with and without
bone or wooden stems.  After Basketmaker II, pottery pipes
gradually replace pipes of stone.  Among the Mogollon the
usual pipe is tubular and is biconically drilled, requiring
use of a mouthpiece.  Clay pipes occur from the earliest
Mogollon period.  Whether these were introduced along with
pottery techniques cannot be said, but in any event, they are
earlier in the south than in the north.

Flaked stone artifacts vary in some ways.  Early Anasazi
projectile points were generally side-notched, in contrast to
the diagonally notched points of the Mogollon, although, as at
Durango where diagonally notched points occur with some frequency (Morris, in press), there is some overlapping of types.
Drills, knives, and scrapers are quite similar.  The chief
difference lies in the quantity of heavy flaked scrapers,
pulping planes, choppers, and hand-axes typical of the Mogollon but rare or absent in most Anasazi sites.

Such bone tools as were shared show little difference

except in the notched bone awl characteristic of the central Mogollon area. They rarely occur in Anasazi sites, but are reported from Shabik'eshchee (Roberts 1929: pl. 21) and Kiatuthlanna (Roberts 1931: pls. 25, 29), and as far north as southwestern Colorado (Martin 1939:426). There can be little doubt that this southern form was moving north at the same time as a number of other traits. A much greater variety of bone tools was made by the Anasazi than by the Mogollon.

Until the excavation of Tularosa and Cordova caves (Martin et al. 1952) it was impossible to compare the perishable material culture of the two areas. It is possible now only to repeat the conclusions derived from Tularosa Cave. Some of the perishable artifacts that distinguish Mogollon from Anasazi are ceremonial items such as wooden tablitas, juniper-berry skewers, bark-incised sticks, reed cigarettes, and the early appearance of miniature bows and arrows. The hunting bow was also used from preceramic times, but did not displace the atlatl until about the same time that the bow was introduced to the Anasazi, perhaps by the Mogollon.

Grooved clubs or fending sticks were rare among the Mogollon. There are differences in sandals of the two areas. Wickerwork sandals are southern and early, but may have diffused northward where they appear during Basketmaker III. Plaited sandals from San Francisco Phase also appear to be a Mogollon development; although these occur as early as Basket- maker III, they do not become common in the north until Pueblo III. Coiled basketry was common to both areas, but there appear to be frequency differences in subtypes. Twined and twilled basketry appear earlier in Mogollon than in Anasazi.

Throughout the discussion above, certain traits have

been suggested as intrusive into Anasazi culture from the
Mogollon during Basketmaker III and early Pueblo I times.
That these traits appeared at about the same time and were
generally earlier in the southern Anasazi area suggests that
they had a Mogollon origin.  This argument is strengthened by
two factors.  First, most or all of the traits had undergone
a long period of development among the Mogollon; and second,
the fact that a whole complex of traits apparently moved together, strengthens the argument that each component trait
actually did diffuse northward.  The traits composing this
constellation are as follows:

Pithouses with narrow lateral entries

Antechamber type of dwelling and probably the idea of
rectangular pit rooms

Ceremonial houses of the great kiva type

Smudging of pottery

Slipping and polishing (?) of pottery

Neck-banding of pottery

Quartered, offset-quartered, and sectioned layout of
pottery decorative designs

Use of rim solids, chevrons, checkerboard, fringing lines,
and concentric rectangles in pottery decoration

Broad-line painting, and polishing over the decoration
on pottery vessels

Possibly red and red-on-orange pottery wares

Stone mortars and bowls

Grooved stone mauls

Clay pipes of "cigar-holder" type

Notched bone awls (may be only intrusive)

Bow and arrow (?)

Beans (?)

Cotton (?)

Some of these traits may well have come from another source into the Anasazi pattern, but the fact of prior Mogollon possession and the temporal pattern of their distribution in Anasazi territory lend weight to the hypothesis that they were diffused from the Mogollon. Another argument lies in the nature of spatial distribution of these traits, for most of them are limited to the eastern San Juan, although some have a wider spread.

After A. D. 700, and increasingly so after A. D. 900, a number of traits began to move south into Mogollon territory and to modify the culture pattern there. Most important of these traits was the use of stone masonry, but black-on-white pottery and elaboration of bone tools, as well as other traits, mark the transition.

In discussing relationships of Hohokam and Mogollon, I have pointed out that there was no sharp boundary between the two, but rather, an area in which certain culture elements show blending. It was also suggested that the Sinagua Branch of the Flagstaff area was a blend of Anasazi and Mogollon on a Hohokam base. In some respects it is possible to assert that an area of cultural blend existed between Anasazi and Mogollon. This is certainly to be expected. The chief difficulty in examining this phenomenon is the lack of excavated sites in the area in question during the time period when such a blend would be most noticeable. Even so, certain sites showing a mixture of traits can be pointed out. Kiatuthlanna and Allentown (Roberts 1931, 1939, 1940), and to a lesser extent, Shabik'eshchee (Roberts 1929) clearly have an Anasazi base, yet share a few traits which have their center of distribution to the south in Mogollon territory. Earlier sites

in the area of Kiatuthlanna, and those closer to the northern
Mogollon boundary, might be expected to show culture blending
even more clearly.

There remains one site to be considered, Wendorf's Flattop Site in the Petrified Forest (1950a:43-50). The site
appears to be early and should satisfy some of the conditions
noted above for blend sites. However, details are not yet
available on which to base an estimate of its position. The
few data at hand suggest an architectural blending of Mogollon
pithouse and slab-lined Basketmaker house, but specific details differ from both. Pottery resembles neither Anasazi nor
Mogollon except in that it is oxidized like that of the latter.
In being constructed and finished by the paddle-and-anvil
technique, it more closely resembles Hohokam. Stone tools,
as briefly reported, share typological relationship with both
Anasazi and Mogollon. It may be, therefore, that this is
another example of a blend involving three, rather than two,
culture patterns. As such, it might be considered an eastern
or northeastern extension of the Sinagua or Hohokam pattern
with influence from other sources. However, the possibility
must not be overlooked that it represents still another
pattern than any yet delineated in the Southwest.

Having considered in detail the internal growth and the functional culture pattern of the Mogollon, and the relationships of the Mogollon to Cochise, Hohokam, and Anasazi, we may now ask, and attempt to answer, some questions concerning the taxonomic status of the various groups.

1. Should Mogollon and Hohokam be considered as variants of the same culture pattern?

It seems clear that both cultures grew out of late Cochise horizons by the addition of pottery to a continuing lithic complex. We do not know the relative time of this innovation in Hohokam, but two separate sources are suggested by the ceramic complexes as well as other divergent traits. There is an obvious interrelationship between the first decorative pottery styles, but subsequent modification in Hohokam leads to divergent patterns. Architectural features show gradual shift in styles from west to east, with distinct patterns at each extreme. Considering these factors, it would seem that, while Hohokam and Mogollon were related in pre-ceramic times and mutually influenced each other in early pottery times, they pursued differing courses throughout most of their history and thus represent separate cultural patterns.

2. Should Mogollon and Anasazi be considered as variants of the same culture pattern?

Until dates were firmly established for the early Mogollon periods, this question could not be answered with any certainty. Agriculture, architecture, and pottery are

all from 2,000 to 500 years earlier in the Mogollon than in
Anasazi.  This would mean little, as such, but the cultural
content and orientation of the earliest horizons of both are
somewhat divergent.  The agricultural patterns differ in content and probably in the degree to which they were practised.
Architectural patterns are markedly different in the earliest
period.  There is no clear indication of contact or influence
between the two groups until some time between A. D. 300 and
A. D. 400.  Introduction of pottery, true pithouses, bow and
arrow, and perhaps beans, to the Basketmakers occurred at
about this time; and it seems likely that certain house types,
such as antechamber houses and great kivas, which reached
their highest development among the Anasazi, had a Mogollon
origin.

The ceramic complexes have a few basic shapes in common,
but otherwise show little resemblance until, toward the end
of Basketmaker III, there was a northward diffusion of neck-
banding and smudging, design and layout elements, and perhaps
of oxidized red ware pottery types.  Although the evidence
has not been given here, it would seem that many ceramic
elements, as well as some others, reached the Anasazi through
heavy influence of the "Middle Mississippi" horizon of the
Southeastern archeological area (Wheat 1953).  Beginning in
the A. D. 700's and continuing, there was heavy Anasazi influence in the Mogollon area, leading to the cultural blend recognized as the Western Pueblo Complex (Reed 1948b).  Thus, it
can be asserted with considerable support for such a position,
that Anasazi and Mogollon followed separate cultural developments, but with the Mogollon early influencing the Anasazi
to bring about similarities deriving from somewhat different

cultural bases.   Later Anasazi influence on Mogollon again
produced related cultural expressions, but throughout their
histories each group maintained its own cultural integrity.

It is to be noted that this is just the reverse of the
Mogollon - Hohokam situation, where close relationships
existed early, but through time the cultures continued to
diverge except for the late influence of Hohokam on southern
Mogollon.

3. If the suggested reconstructions above prove valid,
should Anasazi, Mogollon, Hohokam, and Patayan be considered
as separate basic cultures?

It seems to me that to argue this point is peculiarly
useless.   Its answer depends almost entirely on philosophical
and semantic argument.   Furthermore, the fact that, on a
broader plane, all these culture patterns are peripheral to
higher culture centers of Middle America which, presumably,
were the ultimate source of agriculture and pottery for the
Southwest, if not, indeed, architecture, makes the concept of
a "basic" culture barren and futile.   The answer, if there is
one, lies in recognizing that each of these groups, and perhaps other groups not yet defined, underlying their mutual
relationships, maintained a more or less functional unity
apart from each of the others.   To this extent, and no
farther, they are basic cultures.   More important are the
questions growing out of historical relationships between
these groups, and between these and other culture patterns
lying beyond the Southwestern cultural frontiers.

Adams, R. N.
  1951      Half house: a pithouse in Chaco Canyon, New
            Mexico.  Papers of the Michigan Academy of
            Science, Arts, and Letters, Vol. 35, 1949.

Anonymous
  1939      Notes and news.  American Antiquity, 5:2:163.

  1940      Notes and news.  American Antiquity, 5:4:342.

  1941      Notes and news.  American Antiquity, 6:3:282.

Antevs, Ernst
  1941      See Sayles, E. B. and Ernst Antevs.

Atwood, W. W.
  1940      The physiographic provinces of North America.
            Boston, Mass.

Baldwin, Gordon
  1939      A Basket Maker III sandal tablet.  Southwestern
            Lore, 5:3:48-52.

Beals, R. L., G. W. Brainerd, and Watson Smith
  1945      Archeological studies in northeast Arizona.
            University of California Publications in
            American Archeology and Ethnology, 44:1.
            Berkeley, Cal.

Bradfield, Wesley
  1931      Cameron Creek Village.  El Palacio Press,
            Santa Fe, N. M.

Brand, D. D., F. M. Hawley, F. C. Hibben, et al.
  1937      Tseh So, a small house ruin, Chaco Canyon, New
            Mexico.  Preliminary report.  University of New
            Mexico Bull. 308, Anthropological Ser. 2:2.
            Albuquerque, N. M.

Brew, J. O.
  1946      Archeology of Alkali Ridge, southeastern Utah.
            Papers, Peabody Museum of American Archeology
            and Ethnology, Harvard University, Vol. 21.
            Cambridge, Mass.

Bryan, Bruce
  1931      Excavation of the Galaz Ruin, Mimbres Valley,
            New Mexico.  Art and Archeology, 32:1, 2.
            Washington, D. C.

Carter, G. F.
    1945     Plant geography and culture history in the
             American Southwest.  Viking Fund Publications
             in Anthropology, No. 5.  New York, N. Y.

Colton, H. S.
    1939     Prehistoric culture units and their relationships
             in northern Arizona.  Museum of Northern Arizona,
             Bull. 17.  Flagstaff, Ariz.

    1946     The Sinagua.  Museum of Northern Arizona, Bull.
             22.  Flagstaff, Ariz.

Colton, H. S. and L. L. Hargrave
    1937     Handbook of northern Arizona pottery wares.
             Museum of Northern Arizona, Bull. 11.  Flagstaff,
             Ariz.

Cosgrove, C. B.
    1947     Caves of the upper Gila and Hueco areas in New
             Mexico and Texas.  Papers, Peabody Museum of
             American Archeology and Ethnology, Harvard
             University, 24:2.  Cambridge, Mass.

Cosgrove, H. S. and C. B.
    1932     The Swarts Ruin, a typical Mimbres site of
             southwestern New Mexico.  Papers, Peabody Museum
             of American Archeology and Ethnology, Harvard
             University, 15:1.  Cambridge, Mass.

Cutler, H. C.
    1952     See Martin, P. S., J. B. Rinaldo, Elaine Bluhm,
             H. C. Cutler, and Roger Grange, Jr.

Daifuku, Hiroshi
    1952     A new conceptual scheme for prehistoric cultures
             in the southwestern United States.  American
             Anthropologist, 54:2.

Danson, E. B.
    1952     An archeological survey of west-central New
             Mexico and east-central Arizona.  Ph. D. thesis,
             Harvard University.  Cambridge, Mass.

Darton, N. H.
    1925     A resume of Arizona geology.  University of
             Arizona College of Mines and Engineering, Bull.
             119, Geological Ser. No. 5.  Tucson, Ariz.

Dick, Herbert
    n. d.    Bat Cave.  (In preparation)

Di Peso, C. C.
    1951     The Babocomari Village site on the Babocomari
             River, southeastern Arizona.  The Amerind
             Foundation, No. 5.  Dragoon, Ariz.

    1953     The Sobaipuri Indians of the upper San Pedro
             River Valley, southeastern Arizona.  The Amerind
             Foundation, No. 6.  Dragoon, Ariz.

Fenneman, N. M.
    1931       Physiography of Western United States.
                McGraw-Hill, New York, N. Y.

Fulton, W. S.
    1934a      Archeological notes on Texas Canyon, Arizona.
    1934b      Museum of the American Indian. Heye Foundation,
    1938       Contributions, 12:1, 2, 3. New York, N. Y.

    1941       Winchester Cave: a ceremonial cave in the
                Winchester Mountains. The Amerind Foundation,
                No. 2. Dragoon, Ariz.

Fulton, W. S. and Carr Tuthill
    1940       An archeological site near Gleeson, Arizona.
                The Amerind Foundation, No. 1. Dragoon, Ariz.

Gladwin, H. S. in E. B. Sayles
    1936       An archeological survey of Chihuahua, Mexico.
                Medallion Papers, No. 22. Gila Pueblo, Globe,
                Ariz.

Gladwin, H. S.
    1943       A review and analysis of the Flagstaff Culture.
                Medallion Papers, No. 31. Gila Pueblo, Globe,
                Ariz.

    1945       The Chaco Branch. Excavations at White Mound
                and in the Red Mesa Valley. Medallion Papers,
                No. 33. Gila Pueblo, Globe, Ariz.

    1948       Excavations at Snaketown, IV: review and
                conclusions. Medallion Papers, No. 38. Gila
                Pueblo, Globe, Ariz.

Gladwin, H. S., E. W. Haury, E. B. Sayles, and Nora Gladwin
    1937       Excavations at Snaketown, I: material culture.
                Medallion Papers, No. 25. Gila Pueblo, Globe,
                Ariz.

Gladwin, W. and H. S.
    1934       A method for the designation of cultures and
                their variations. Medallion Papers, No. 15.
                Gila Pueblo, Globe, Ariz.

    1935       The eastern range of the Red-on-buff Culture.
                Medallion Papers, No. 16. Gila Pueblo, Globe,
                Ariz.

Guernsey, S. J.
    1931       Explorations in northeastern Arizona. Papers,
                Peabody Museum of American Archeology and
                Ethnology, Harvard University, 12:1. Cambridge,
                Mass.

Guernsey, S. J. and A. V. Kidder
    1921       Basket-maker caves of northeastern Arizona.
                Papers, Peabody Museum of American Archeology
                and Ethnology, Harvard University, 8:2.
                Cambridge, Mass.

Haury, E. W.
1932      Roosevelt:9:6, a Hohokam site of the Colonial
Period. Medallion Papers, No. 11. Gila Pueblo,
Globe, Ariz.

1936      Vandal Cave. Kiva, 1:6.

1936a     Some Southwestern pottery types, Ser. IV.
Medallion Papers, No. 19. Gila Pueblo, Globe,
Ariz.

1936b     The Mogollon Culture of southwestern New Mexico.
Medallion Papers, No. 20. Gila Pueblo, Globe,
Ariz.

1941      Excavations in the Forestdale Valley, east-
central Arizona. University of Arizona Bull.
11:4 (Social Science Bull. No. 12). Tucson,
Ariz.

1943      A possible Cochise-Mogollon-Hohokam sequence.
Proc., American Philosophical Society, 86:2.

1945      Painted Cave, northeastern Arizona. The Amerind
Foundation, No. 3. Dragoon, Ariz.

1950      The stratigraphy and archeology of Ventana Cave,
Arizona. The University of New Mexico Press:
The University of Arizona Press.

Haury, E. W. and E. B. Sayles
1947      An early pit house village of the Mogollon
Culture, Forestdale Valley, Arizona. University
of Arizona Bull. 18:4 (Social Science Bull.
No. 16). Tucson, Ariz.

Holden, Jane
1952      The Bonnell Site. Bulletin of the Texas Archeological and Paleontological Society, Vol. 23.
Lubbock, Tex.

Hough, Walter
1903      Archeological field work in north-eastern Arizona.
The Museum-Gates Expedition of 1901. Report of
the United States National Museum for 1901.
Washington, D. C.

1919      Exploration of a pithouse village at Luna, New
Mexico. Proc., United States National Museum,
55:2280. Washington, D. C.

Jennings, J. D. and George Neumann
1940      A variation of Southwestern Pueblo Culture.
Laboratory of Anthropology, Technical Series,
Bull. 10. Santa Fe, N. M.

Johnson, Frederick, ed.
1951      Radiocarbon dating. Society for American
Archeology, Memoir No. 8.

Jones, V. H., G. R. Willey, and F. H. H. Roberts, Jr.
　　1946　　Review, Plant geography and culture history in
　　　　　　the American Southwest by George F. Carter.
　　　　　　American Antiquity, 11:4.

Judd, N. M.
　　1926　　Archeological observations north of the Rio
　　　　　　Colorado.　Bureau of American Ethnology,
　　　　　　Bull. 82.　Washington, D. C.

Kidder, A. V. and S. J. Guernsey
　　1919　　Archeological explorations in northeastern
　　　　　　Arizona.　Bureau of American Ethnology, Bull.
　　　　　　65.　Washington, D. C.

Kidder, A. V., H. S. and C. B. Cosgrove
　　1949　　The Pendleton Ruin, Hidalgo County, New Mexico.
　　　　　　Contributions to American Anthropology and
　　　　　　History, No. 50.　Carnegie Institution of
　　　　　　Washington, Publication 585.　Washington, D. C.

Kroeber, A. L.
　　1939　　Cultural and natural areas of native North
　　　　　　America.　University of California Publications
　　　　　　in American Archeology and Ethnology, Vol. 38.
　　　　　　Berkeley, Cal.

Lancaster, J. A. and D. W. Watson
　　1943　　Excavation of Mesa Verde pithouses.　American
　　　　　　Antiquity, 9:2.

Lehmer, D. J.
　　1948　　The Jornada Branch of the Mogollon.　University
　　　　　　of Arizona Bull. 19:2 (Social Science Bull.
　　　　　　No. 17).　Tucson, Ariz.

McGregor, J. C.
　　1941　　Southwestern archeology.　Wiley, New York, N. Y.

Manglesdorf, P. C. and C. E. Smith, Jr.
　　1949　　New archeological evidence on evolution in maize.
　　　　　　Botanical Museum Leaflets, Harvard University,
　　　　　　13:8.　Cambridge, Mass.

Martin, P. S.
　　1940　　The SU Site, excavations at a Mogollon village,
　　　　　　western New Mexico, 1939.　Field Museum of
　　　　　　Natural History, Anthropological Series 32:1.
　　　　　　Chicago, Ill.

　　1943　　The SU Site, excavations at a Mogollon village,
　　　　　　western New Mexico, second season, 1941.　Field
　　　　　　Museum of Natural History, Anthropological
　　　　　　Series 32:2.　Chicago, Ill.

Martin, P. S. and J. B. Rinaldo
　　1939　　Modified Basket Maker sites, Akmen-Lowry area,
　　　　　　southwestern Colorado, 1937.　Field Museum of
　　　　　　Natural History, Anthropological Series 23:3.
　　　　　　Chicago, Ill.

1947    The SU Site, excavations at a Mogollon village, western New Mexico, third season, 1946. Field Museum of Natural History, Anthropological Series 32:3. Chicago, Ill.

1950a    Turkey Foot Ridge Site. A Mogollon village, Pine Lawn Valley, western New Mexico. Fieldiana: Anthropology, 38:2. Chicago, Ill.

1950b    Sites of the Reserve Phase, Pine Lawn Valley, western New Mexico. Fieldiana: Anthropology, 38:3. Chicago, Ill.

1951    The Southwestern co-tradition. Southwestern Journal of Anthropology, 7:3.

Martin, P. S., J. B. Rinaldo, and Ernst Antevs
1949    Cochise and Mogollon sites, Pine Lawn Valley, western New Mexico. Fieldiana: Anthropology, 38:1. Chicago, Ill.

Martin, P. S., J. B. Rinaldo, Elaine Bluhm, H. C. Cutler, and Roger Grange, Jr.
1952    Mogollon cultural continuity and change. The stratigraphic analysis of Tularosa and Cordova caves. Fieldiana: Anthropology, Vol. 40. Chicago, Ill.

Mera, H. P.
1934    Observations on the archeology of the Petrified Forest National Monument. Laboratory of Anthropology, Technical Series, Bull. 7. Santa Fe, N. M.

1935    Ceramic clues to the prehistory of north-central New Mexico. Laboratory of Anthropology, Technical Series, Bull. 8. Santa Fe, N. M.

1943    An outline of ceramic developments in southern and southeastern New Mexico. Laboratory of Anthropology, Technical Series, Bull. 11. Santa Fe, N. M.

Moore, Mrs. G. E.
1947    Twelve Room House Ruin. Bulletin of the Texas Archeological and Paleontological Society, Vol. 18. Lubbock, Tex.

Morris, E. H.
1919    Preliminary account of the antiquities of the region between the Mancos and La Plata rivers in southwestern Colorado. Bureau of American Ethnology, Annual Report No. 33. Washington, D. C.

1925    Exploring the Canyon of Death. National Geographic Magazine, 48:3.

1927       The beginnings of pottery making in the San Juan area. American Museum of Natural History, Anthropological Papers, 28: Part 2.

1936       Archeological background of dates in early Arizona chronology. Tree-Ring Bulletin, 2:4.

1939       Archeological studies in the La Plata District, southwestern Colorado and northwestern New Mexico. Carnegie Institution of Washington, Publication 519. Washington, D. C.

Morris, E. H. and R. F. Burgh
1954       Basket Maker II sites near Durango, Colorado. Carnegie Institution of Washington, Publication 604. Washington, D. C. (In press)

Nesbitt, P. H.
1931       The ancient Mimbreños. Logan Museum Bull. No. 4. Beloit College, Beloit, Wis.

1938       Starkweather Ruin. Logan Museum Publications in Anthropology, Bull. No. 6. Beloit College, Beloit, Wis.

Nichol, A. A.
1943       The natural vegetation of Arizona. Technical Bull. No. 68 (reprint). University of Arizona, Tucson, Ariz.

Nusbaum, J. L.
1922       A Basket-Maker cave in Kane County, Utah. Museum of the American Indian, Heye Foundation, Indian Notes and Monographs, No. 29. New York, N. Y.

O'Bryan, Deric
1950       Excavations in Mesa Verde National Park, 1947-1948. Medallion Papers, No. 39. Gila Pueblo, Globe, Ariz.

Reed, E. K.
1948a      The dating of early Mogollon horizons. El Palacio, 55:12.

1948b      Western Pueblo archeological complex. El Palacio, 55:1.

Rinaldo, J. B.
1941       Conjectures on the independent development of the Mogollon Culture. American Antiquity, 7:1.

Roberts, F. H. H., Jr.
1929       Shabik'eshchee Village. Bureau of American Ethnology, Bull. 92. Washington, D. C.

1930       Early Pueblo ruins in the Piedra District, southwestern Colorado. Bureau of American Ethnology, Bull. 96. Washington, D. C.

1931    The ruins at Kiatuthlanna, eastern Arizona.
Bureau of American Ethnology, Bull. 100.
Washington, D. C.

1935    A survey of Southwestern archeology.  American
Anthropologist, 37:1 n. s.

1939    Archeological remains in the White Water
District, eastern Arizona.  Part I.  Bureau of
American Ethnology, Bull. 121.  Washington, D. C.

1940    Archeological remains in the White Water
District, eastern Arizona.  Part II.  Bureau of
American Ethnology, Bull. 126.  Washington, D. C.

Ruppé, R. J., Jr. and A. E. Dittert, Jr.
1950    The archeology of Cebolleta Mesa: a preliminary
report, season of 1950 (mimeographed).  Peabody
Museum, Harvard University.  Cambridge, Mass.

1951    The archeology of Cebolleta Mesa and Acoma
Pueblo: a preliminary report based on further
investigation, season of 1951 (mimeographed).
Peabody Museum, Harvard University.  Cambridge,
Mass.

Sayles, E. B.
1945    The San Simon Branch, excavations at Cave Creek
and in the San Simon Valley.  I: material
culture.  Medallion Papers, No. 34.  Gila
Pueblo, Globe, Ariz.

Sayles, E. B. and Ernst Antevs
1941    The Cochise Culture.  Medallion Papers, No. 29.
Gila Pueblo, Globe, Ariz.

Schroeder, A. H.
1953    The problem of Hohokam, Sinagua, and Salado
relations in southern Arizona.  (In preparation)

Seltzer, C. C.
1944    Racial prehistory in the Southwest and the
Hawikuh Zunis.  Papers, Peabody Museum of
American Archeology and Ethnology, Harvard
University, 23:1.  Cambridge, Mass.

Shepard, Anna O.
1939    See Morris, E. H., 1939.

Smiley, T. L.
1949    Pithouse Number 1, Mesa Verde National Park.
American Antiquity, 14:3.

1952    A summary of tree-ring dates from some
Southwestern archeological sites.  University
of Arizona Bull. 22:4 (Laboratory Bull. of
Tree-Ring Research, No. 5).  Tucson, Ariz.

Trishka, Carl
1933  Hohokam: a chapter in the history of Red-on-buff Culture of Arizona. Scientific Monthly, Vol. 37.

Tuthill, Carr
1947  The Tres Alamos Site on the San Pedro River, southeastern Arizona. The Amerind Foundation, No. 4. Dragoon, Ariz.

Wendorf, Fred
1950a  The Flattop Site in the Petrified Forest National Monument. Plateau, 22:3:43-50.

1950b  A report on the excavation of a small ruin near Point of Pines, east-central Arizona. University of Arizona Bull. 21:3 (Social Science Bull. No. 19). Tucson, Ariz.

Wheat, J. B.
1953  Some conjectures on Southwestern culture history. Paper read at the 1953 session, American Association for the Advancement of Science, Southwestern Division.

1954  Crooked Ridge Village (Arizona W:10:15). University of Arizona Bull. 25:3 (Social Science Bull. No. 24). Tucson, Ariz.

| | Harris | | Crooked Ridge | | Cave Creek | | | | San Simon | | | | | | sub | | Starkweather | | Bluff | Crooked | | | | | |
|---|---|---|---|---|---|---|---|---|---|---|---|---|---|---|---|---|---|---|---|---|---|---|---|---|---|
| | 29 | 32 | 1 | 4 | 1 | 2 | 3 | 6 | 39 | 41 | 56 | 59 | 55 | 60 | 28 | 52 | C | Q | 4a | 2 | 6 | 8 | 10 | 11 | 12 |
| | | | | | | | | | | | | | | | | | | | | | | | | | |
| | | | | | | | | | | | | | | | | | | | | | | | | | |
| | | | | | | | | | | | | | | | | | | | | | | | | | |
| | | | | | | | | | | | | | | | | | | | | | | | | | |
| | X | X | X | X | | | | | | | | | | | | | | | | | | | | | |
| | | | | | X | X | X | X | X | X | X | X | X | X | | | | | | | | | | | |
| | | | | | | | | | | | | | | X | X | X | | | | | | | | | |
| | | | | | | | | | | | | | | | | | X | X | X | X | X | X | X | X | X |
| | 11 | 8 | 36 | 13 | 10 | 11 | 15 | 10 | 6 | 6 | 9 | - | - | - | - | - | 19 | 23 | 7 | 17 | 20 | 26 | 15 | 25 | 15 |
| | 90 | 90 | 120 | 70 | 35 | 55 | 50 | 35 | 20 | 25 | 20 | - | - | - | - | - | 107 | 81 | 160 | 100 | 75 | 115 | 60 | 75 | 80 |
| | X | X | X | X | | | | | | | | | | | | | X | X | X | X | X | X | X | X | X |
| | | | | | | | | | | | | | | | | | | X | | | | | | | |
| | | | | X | | | | | | | | | | | | | | | X | | X | | X | | |
| | NE | NE | E | E | | | | | | | | | | | | | E | E | N | E | N | E | E | E | E |
| | | X | X | X | X | X | X | X | X | X | | | | | | | | | | X | ? | 2 | X | X | X |
| | | | | | | | | | | | X | | | | | | | | | | | | X | | |
| | | X | X | X | X | X | X | X | X | X | | | | | | | | | | X | | X | | X | |
| | | Y | | X | | | | | | | | | | | | | | | | | | X | | | |
| | | | | | | | | | | | | | | | | | | | | | | X | | | |
| | | | 1 | 2 | | | | | | | | | | | | | ? | | | | | | | | |
| | | | 1 | | | | | | | | | | | | | | ? | | | | | | | | |
| | X | ? | | | | | | | | | X | | | | | | | | | | | | | | |
| | X | ? | | | | | | | | | | | | | | | | | | | | | | | |
| | | | X | | | | | | | | | | | | | | X | X | | X | X | X | X | X | X |
| | | ? | | X | | | | | | | | | | | | | | | X | | | | | | |

| | Harris | | | | | Mogollon Village | | | | | | | Starkweather | Turkey Foot | Turkey Foot | | | | Bear Ruin | | | Crooked Ridge | Starkweather |
|---|---|---|---|---|---|---|---|---|---|---|---|---|---|---|---|---|---|---|---|---|---|---|---|
| | 1 | 11 | 18 | 22 | 28 | 1 | 2 | 4 | 5b | 7 | 8 | 9 | D | C | E | F | H | I | 9 | 12 | Stor. | 23 | O-P |
| | | | | | | | | | | | | | | | | | | | | | | | |
| | | | | | | | | | | | | | | | | | | | | | | | |
| | X | X | X | X | X | X | X | X | X | X | X | X | X | X | X | X | X | X | X | X | X | X | X |
| | 2 | 21 | 42 | 10 | 12 | 17 | 26 | 16 | 21 | 16 | 13 | 9 | 10 | 13 | 35 | 26 | 22 | 18 | 19 | 24 | 6 | 27 | 12 |
| | 5 | - | 140 | 120 | 130 | - | 145 | 100 | 125 | - | 110 | - | 81 | 130 | 82 | 95 | 120 | 120 | 90 | 170 | 40 | 100 | 91 |
| | X | X | X | X | X | X | X | X | X | X | X | X | X | X X X | X | X X | X ? | X ? | X | X | X ? | X | |
| | W | S | E | NE | NE | E | E | NE | E | SW | E | SE | SE | SE | SE | SE | E | NW | E | SE | SW | E | S |
| | X | X | | X | X | X | X | X | X | X | X | X | | X | | | X | X | | X | | X | X |
| | | | | | | | | | | | | | | | | X | | | X | | | | X |
| | X | | | X | X | X | X | X | X | X | X | X | | X | | | X | X | | X | | X | X |
| | | | | | | | | | | | | | | | | | X | | | | | | |
| | | | | | | | | 1 | | | | 1 | | | | 1 | | 1 | 1 | 2 4 | | 1 | |
| | | | | | | | | X X | X X | ? ? | | ? | | | | | | | | | | | |
| | X | | | X | X | X | X | ? | ? | ? ? | ? ? | ? | X | X | X | X | X | X | X X X | X | X | X | X |

# Table 4

| Turkey Foot | Turkey Foot | Mogollon Village | Harris | Harris | Cameron Creek | Cameron Creek | Cameron Creek | Cameron Creek | Cameron Creek | Cameron Creek | Cameron Creek | Cameron Creek | Cameron Creek | Turkey Foot | Turkey Foot | Bear Ruin | Bear Ruin | Bear Ruin | Bear Ruin | San Simon | San Simon | San Simon | San Simon | Harris | Bear Ruin | San Simon |
|---|---|---|---|---|---|---|---|---|---|---|---|---|---|---|---|---|---|---|---|---|---|---|---|---|---|---|
| N | 128 | 142 | 6 | 12 | 113a | 133 | 123B | 137N | 140 | Sub 71 | 106 | 113 | 135w | K | N | L | 1 | 5 | Stor. 2 | 11 | 2 | 10 | 20 | 13 | 44 | 14 |
|  |  |  |  |  |  |  |  |  |  |  |  |  |  |  |  |  |  |  |  |  |  |  |  |  |  |  |
|  | X | X | ? |  |  |  |  |  |  |  |  |  |  |  |  |  |  |  |  |  |  |  |  |  |  |  |
|  |  |  |  | X | X | X | X | X | X | X | X | X | X | X | X | X | X | X | X |  |  |  |  |  |  |  |
|  |  |  |  |  |  |  |  |  |  |  |  |  |  |  |  |  |  |  |  | X | X | X | X | X |  |  |
|  |  |  |  |  |  |  |  |  |  |  |  |  |  |  |  |  |  |  |  |  |  |  |  |  | X | X |
| 6 | 21 | 13 | 24 | 9 | 13 | 20 | 16 | 16 | 12 | 11 | 10 | 16 | 22 | 9 | 7 | 26 | 18 | 18 | 8 | 15 | 17 | 9 | 8 | 11 | 11 | 15 |
| 0 | - | - | - | - | - | - | - | - | - | - | 52 | 52 | 52 | 127 | 162 | 120 | 35 | 120 | 60 | 70 | 80 | 70 | - | 50 | 50 | 70 |
|  |  |  |  |  |  |  |  |  |  |  |  |  |  |  |  |  |  |  |  | X | X | X | X | X | X | X |
|  |  |  |  |  |  |  |  |  |  |  |  |  |  |  |  |  |  |  |  | X | X | X |  |  | X |  |
|  |  |  |  |  |  |  |  |  |  |  |  |  |  |  |  |  |  |  |  | X | X | X |  |  | X | X |
|  |  |  |  |  |  |  |  |  |  |  |  |  |  |  |  |  |  |  |  | W | N | E | SW | E | E | SE |
|  |  |  |  |  |  |  |  |  |  |  |  |  |  |  |  |  |  |  |  | ? | X | X | X |  | X | X |
|  | X | X |  |  | X | X |  |  | X | X |  |  | X |  |  | ? | X | X |  |  |  |  |  | X |  |  |
|  | X |  |  | X |  | X |  |  |  |  |  |  |  |  | X |  |  |  |  |  |  |  |  |  | X |  |
|  | X | X |  |  | X |  |  |  | X | X |  |  | X |  |  |  | X |  |  |  | X | X | X | X | X | X |
|  |  |  |  |  |  |  |  |  |  |  |  |  |  |  |  |  | X |  |  |  |  |  |  |  |  |  |
|  |  |  |  |  |  |  |  |  |  |  |  |  |  |  |  | 4 | 1 | 1 |  |  |  |  |  |  |  |  |
|  |  |  |  |  |  |  |  |  |  |  |  |  |  |  |  | 1 | 1 | 1 |  |  |  |  |  |  |  |  |
|  | ? |  |  | X |  | ? |  |  | ? | X |  |  |  |  | ? |  | x |  | x |  | X |  |  |  | X | X |
|  |  | X |  |  | X | X |  |  |  |  |  |  |  |  | X | X | x | X | x | ? | ? | X |  |  | X | X |
|  |  |  |  |  |  |  |  |  | ? |  |  |  |  |  | ? |  |  |  |  |  |  |  |  |  |  |  |

Table 4.  Domestic architecture of Mogollon 3

| SITE | | | Cameron Creek | Bear Ruin | | Turkey Foot | | | Bear Ruin | | | | | | |
|---|---|---|---|---|---|---|---|---|---|---|---|---|---|---|---|
| **HOUSE NO.** | | | 141 | 136 | 2 | 10 | J | M | O | 7 | 8 | 11 | 14 | 3 | 4 | 6 |
| Roundish | no lateral entry | | X | X | X | X | | | | | | | | | | |
| | short entry | | | | | | X | X | | | | | | | | |
| | large broad entry | | | | | | | | X | | | | | | | |
| | long entry | | | | | | | | | X | X | X | X | | | |
| | vestibule | | | | | | | | | | | | | X | X | |
| Ovoid | side entry | | | | | | | | | | | | | | | X |
| | end entry | | | | | | | | | | | | | | | |
| One or more sides flat | no entry | | | | | | | | | | | | | | | |
| Quadrangular | no lateral entry | | | | | | | | | | | | | | | |
| | short entry | | | | | | | | | | | | | | | |
| | long entry | | | | | | | | | | | | | | | |
| | southern annex | | | | | | | | | | | | | | | |
| Floor area in square meters | | | 7 | 19 | 28 | 15 | 23 | 31 | 12 | 14 | 22 | 28 | 15 | 38 | 36 | 11 |
| Depth in centimeters | | | - | 52 | 55 | 110 | 100 | 120 | 135 | 155 | 180 | 115 | 125 | 110 | 215 | 70 |
| Entry | inclined | | | | | | X | X | X | X | X | X | X | | | ? |
| | starting with step | | | | | | X | X | X | X | X | | X | | X | |
| | ending with step | | | | | | ? | X | ? | X | X | X | X | | | |
| | orientation | | | | | | E | E | W | SE | E | E | E | E | E | SE |
| Hearth | near entry | | | | | | X | X | X | | | | | | | |
| | near center | | X | | X | X | X | | | | | X | X | X | X | X |
| | elsewhere | | | X | | | | | | | X | | | | | |
| | fire area | | | | | | | | | | | | | | | |
| | depression | | X | X | X | X | X | X | X | X | X | X | X | X | | |
| | stone lined | | | | | | | | | | | | | | | X |
| | clay lined | | | | | | | | | | | | | | | |
| Floor pits | large | | | | | | | 3 | | 1 | | | | 1 | 5 | |
| | small | | | | | | | | | 3 | | 1 | 1 | | | |
| Posthole and Roof plan | central | | | | | | | | | | | | | | | |
| | marginal | | ? | | | | | | | | | ? | x | | x | |
| | quadrilateral | | | X | X | ? | ? | | | X | X | ? | X | | x | X |
| | Gable | | | | | | | ? | X | | | | | | X | |

Cameron Creek

| | 3 | 17 | 100 | 144 | 120 | 148 | 124 | 112 | 114 | 117 | 122 | 134 | 130 | 116 | 125 | 110 | 107 |
|---|---|---|---|---|---|---|---|---|---|---|---|---|---|---|---|---|---|
| Round | | | | | | | | | | | | | | | | | |
| "D"-sh | | | | | | | | | | | | | | | | | |
| One o | | | | | | | | | | | | | | | | | |
| Quadr | X | X | X | X | X | X | X | X | X | X | X | X | X | X | X | X | |
| Floor | 1 | 13 | 18 | 22 | 24 | 31 | 23 | 22 | 25 | 25 | 22 | 21 | 18 | 17 | 16 | 19 | 25 |
| Depth | 0 | 150 | 150 | 150 | 150 | 150 | 150 | 150 | 150 | 150 | 150 | 150 | 150 | 150 | 150 | 150 | 150 |
| Entry | 1 | 2 | X<br>X<br>X | X | X<br>X | 2 | X | ? | 2 | X | X | 2 | X<br>X | X | X | X | X |
| | W | N/S | S | E | SE | N/E | S | SE | E/W | N | SE | E/W | E | S | SE | S | SE |
| Heart | | X | X | X | | | | ? | | X | ? | X | X | X | X | X | X |
| | | X | | | | | X | X | ? | | | | | | | | |
| | | | | | X | | | | | | | | | | | | |
| | X | X | X | | X | X | X | | X | | X | X | X | X | X | X | |
| Floor | | | | | | | | | | | | | | ? | ? | ? | ? |
| | | | | | | | | | | | | | ? | ? | | | |
| Posth<br>Roof | ? | X | X | ?<br>? | X<br>? | | | ? | | | X | X | X | X | ?<br>? | X | X |